AN
EVENTFUL LIFE

MAURICE ODLE

First published in Great Britain by Hansib Publications in 2024

Hansib Publications Limited
76 High Street, Hertford, SG14 3TA, United Kingdom

info@hansibpublications.com
www.hansibpublications.com

Copyright © Maurice Odle, 2024

Maurice Odle has asserted his right under the Copyright, Designs and Patents Act 1988 to be identified as the author of this work.

ISBN 978-1-7395636-3-9
ISBN 978-1-7395636-4-6 (Kindle)
ISBN 978-1-7395636-5-3 (ePub)

A CIP catalogue record for this book
is available from the British Library

All rights reserved.
Without limiting the rights under copyright reserved above, no part of this publication may be reproduced, stored in or introduced into a retrieval system, or transmitted, in any form or by any means (electronic, mechanical, photocopying, recording or otherwise), without the prior written permission of both the copyright owner and the publisher of this book.

Production by Hansib Publications
Printed in Great Britain

www.hansibpublications.com

To all those struggling for a better life and a better world

Contents

Preface 7

CHAPTER ONE: Early Awakening (1937-1960)

Family and Society 9
Primary School Pressures 12
Secondary School Challenges 17
Aspiring Civil Servant: Guyana 25

CHAPTER TWO: Inspiring London School of Economics (1961-1966)

First Impressions of European Society 32
Civil Servant of Convenience: Britain 35
Socio-Economic and Political Enlightenment 39
Off-Campus Social Spill-Overs 45

CHAPTER THREE: Academia and Activism (1966-1980)

Uneventful Lectureship at Middlesex University 49
Guyana University – A Cauldron of Activity 53
Nexus with Caribbean Political Economy 61
University/Guyana Government Denies Walter Rodney Professorship
and Consequences 63
Research as Refuge 73

CHAPTER FOUR: Enlightening United Nations (1980-1997)

Physical and Emotional Dislocation 79
Policy Research on the Operations of Transnational Corporations 84

Technical Assistance to Host Countries 90
Contentious Code of Conduct 108
Assessing the Experience 110

CHAPTER FIVE: CARICOM External Negotiations (1997-2008)

Returning Home (Once Again) 114
Free Trade Area of the Americas 115
Economic Partnership Agreement (with the EU) 124

CHAPTER SIX: CARICOM Integration Challenges (2000-2011)

Required Research 147
Intra-CARICOM Negotiation Dynamics 160
Inadequate Marketing 175
Critical Analysis of Integration Experience 185

CHAPTER SEVEN: Coalition Blues: Guyana (2015-2020)

Re-Entry into Political Activism 200
An Intellectual Interlude 203
Tax Reform Disappoints 204
NICIL in Turmoil 206
Emerging Land Policy 212
Environmental Tax Ruling 224
Unfinished Business 228

CHAPTER EIGHT: Reflections

At the National Level 236
At the Regional Level 246
At the International Level 251

Index 275

Preface

The idea of writing about my experiences was mentioned to me from time to time, especially in recent years, by my wife, Valerie, when, in bouts of retirement boredom, I would relate some interesting incidents that occurred during my childhood years or professional career. Then, one day in late 2021, I was involved in a rather heated discussion in Miami with my American-based sister-in-law, Rebecca Francis, on the USA's claim of the "stealing of technology" by China. I told her that I had a different world view from the one she was expounding, since transfer of technology (*via* joint venture arrangements, training of workers, or otherwise) is frequently a part of contractually negotiated performance requirements for entry by foreign firms in the vast and profitable Chinese market and that China could equally accuse US firms (producing in China for exporting back to the USA) of exploiting ('stealing wages') Chinese workers' labour standards by paying them less for a similar task when done in the USA. Rebecca challenged me to write about my experiences that helped to inform my "rather unorthodox" thinking. I later told my wife that perhaps I should indeed take up the challenge, but that I was not sure I had the required stamina to engage in a memoir-type exercise at such a late stage in my life.

But there were three other inhibiting and discouraging factors: *First*, I had not systematically kept reference documents and other material over the years, since I had no plans for doing such a memoir. *Second,* I never kept a diary in which to record significant developments in my life; recollection and recall would therefore be difficult. *Third*, a fire caused by Guyana Power and Light in the year 2000, that began in the master bedroom and adjoining study room of my residence in Georgetown, destroyed some of the research material and documents that I had, by chance, accumulated up to that point in time.

Well, here is the memoir, after a year and-a-half of effort. Writing my life's story involved a constant challenge of deciding what to include and what to exclude; how to be sincere and truthful without being offensive; and how to describe events and persons related thereto, in as objective a manner as possible, while at the same time maintaining thematic relevance.

The story reflects my increasing awareness and social consciousness, and the way in which my academic training and research experience informed my thoughts and the performance of my various obligations and activities as a national, regional and international civil servant.

My writing proved to be a catalyst to an awakening of thoughts and moments from across the years, which also enabled me to express my concern for the injustices and inequalities in the world. The story, then, is about very powerful social, economic and political forces, and how my life interacted with them.

CHAPTER ONE

EARLY AWAKENING (1937-1960)

FAMILY AND SOCIETY

I was born on 7 March 1937 in British Guiana (called Guyana after independence in 1966) one hour before my twin sister, Marva, and therefore, the fifth of eight children (five girls and three boys – Evelyn, Stanley, Jeanne, Norma, Maurice, Marva, Pearl, and Patrick) to James and Isidora Odle. (My father also had a son, Ivan, out of wedlock, but my mother never allowed him to be a close and integral part of the family). The earliest recollection I have of myself is at the age of probably three or four years looking through the window of a small 'bungalow' type house on stilts in Robb Street (near Wellington Street) in the capital Georgetown as the elder siblings trudged to school one early morning. At this tender age, I also remember hiding under a 'Berbice Chair' one night during the Christmas holidays as the apparently bizarrely costumed masquerade band (including acrobatic men on stilts, a 'cow dancer, and a 'mother sally') accompanied by loud and pulsating musical rhythms, pranced down the street, accompanied by hundreds/thousands of joyous followers.

I am told that it is around this time that I miraculously escaped death. One earlier evening, most of the eight children (Patrick, the youngest, was probably not born as yet) were engaged in a pillow fight on top of the bed in the one bedroom they all occupied. During the 'fight', I took a breather by sitting on the sill of the window which suddenly opened-up and I found myself hurtling about fifteen to twenty feet backwards to the ground. Although I must have been very dazed (since I took a rather circuitous route to wend my way up *via* the rear stairway) I was back in the house before any of my shocked siblings could effectively respond. My relieved mother, who had been in the second bedroom of the house, duly gave me a glass of 'sugar water', the traditional treatment for shock. Who knows what may have been the lasting effects of that accident/experience. I am told that I was a very shy person and given to uttering few words and that, after the fall, I became even more introverted.

Life at this time was one of passive social observation. In my household, the fact that my parents occupied one bedroom and all the children the other made for a very tight fit and close physical interaction. The girls slept on the bed in the children's bedroom while the boys slept on the floor. Sleeping on the floor was probably good for one's back, but a problem I encountered was ants crawling into my ear and irritating my eardrums, at which point I would awake screaming until my mother poured cooking oil down my ear. She would then get me to lean my head sideways until the contents came out, ants and all. Adjoining the house to the west was a crowded ghetto-like tenement yard from which emerged loud and colourful language and exuded all the dramas of the daily existence of the 'wretched of the earth'. Two doors away was the Metropole cinema, the crass behaviour of whose cinema goers (led by a character called 'Barney' Johnson) and those loitering outside (without money but hoping to gain entry) were an added dimension to the cellular drama inside. And the notorious "Federation Yard", said to be harbouring young criminals, in Regent Street was only a block away.

My immediate neighbours to the east were the Chapmans of European (Portuguese) ancestry who lived in a three storied building and drove a car, a rarity before the 1950's. One morning, their seven year old son who, in the preceding weeks must have been a close observer of his father's driving skills, sneaked downstairs and managed to move the car along the driveway towards the road with oncoming traffic, before he was spotted by the Chapman's domestic help whose sleeping quarters were on the ground floor. Directly opposite our house

Odle family in the late 1940s. Front row, L-R: Maurice, Marva, James (Father), Pearl, Isidora (Mother) and Patrick. Back row, L-R: Evelyn, Jeanne, Stanley and Norma.

lived another European, a bit of a recluse, whom our family referred to as "Proudy". In the same bloc was a Chinese owned bakery (Tang's) with two sons of my age who lived next door to another Chinese family (in whose yard my elder brother and I regularly practiced cricket with their two sons – Bud and Alan Lee). All four of the Chinese boys became my high school contemporaries at Queen's College and Bud, an excellent ball player, later became a well-known surgeon (one of whose patients was my brother, Stanley). Within the same bloc, but in tenement yards, were some African males (East Indians were mainly in the rural areas and the indigenous Amerindians in the interior of the country); my playmates as youngsters (one of whom was Patsy Peters, later represented Guyana at soccer) whose living conditions were considerably worse than mine, if that was indeed possible. They duly attended primary school, as was mandatory, but never made it to high school, except for Hartley Liverpool, who later distinguished himself as Commander of the troops that expelled the occupying foreign troops in the early 1970s from the New River Triangle region of Guyana, that neighbouring Suriname claimed.

Such was the residential intermingling of the ethnic and class groupings in many parts of Georgetown, although through primary school (and most of my time in secondary school since the history taught was that of Europe) I was too young to understand its origins, dimensions and social significance in the context of the early political stirrings in colonial British Guiana. In any event, communal tolerance prevailed, crime was relatively low, poverty was just bearable and life seemed worth living to the youngster that I was. Only in my teens, did I begin to exercise my independent critical powers.

PRIMARY SCHOOL PRESSURES

I began my primary (elementary) school education when I was five or six years of age (since kindergarten instruction was not available in my era) at Bedford Methodist School, which was opposite Bourda Market (the second largest market in Georgetown). From this early age, my main interest was in playing outdoor games, especially soccer. I was lucky for there was a playing field across the road from the school that was bounded by Robb Street to the south, North Road to the north, Orange Walk to the East, and Bourda Walk to the West. It was after playing there, during one lunch break and arriving in class soaking wet, with perspiration that I could not control for another hour or so, when I first realised that I suffer from what I later learned is called hyperhidrosis. (This Bourda playing field, a few decades later, became an extension to the Bourda market).

My first three to four years at primary school were uneventful, except that I remember achieving first position at the end of year examination in 'First Standard' and a year or two later being the first student in the class who could easily and correctly read out the time of day that was indicated on the clock that was atop the Bourda Market building. It was also at this time that I realised the usefulness of having a twin sister, when we were called upon by the teachers to clean up the avalanche of vomit that our brother, Patrick, four years our junior and a new entrant to the school, had expelled, following his devouring of rotten fruit he had acquired in the Bourda Market during the lunch hour.

By the end of my ninth year, I was catapulted into the class that prepares the so-called brighter pupils (students) for admittance to the elite schools, based on their achievement at a competitive examination (the 'Eleven Plus'). The teacher of this class was the Headmaster himself, one Peter Maurice Augustus Homer, as fearsome and no-nonsense a person (at least to a child's eye) as you can find. He was not averse to meeting out serious corporal punishment to anyone who was committing too many errors in class, which went into late afternoon sessions on weekdays, supplemented by 8.00am to 1.00pm sessions on Saturdays. One Saturday, Homer slammed into the blackboard the head of a student, Eric King, who was in front of the class struggling to solve a mathematical problem. A few days before the dreaded examination, Homer paid my mother a visit to ensure that Marva and I were psychologically ready for the big day and I overheard him casually say that I was "wutless" (creole for worthless) implying that my performance was difficult to predict. (As was then the custom, in his long walk to school, he was usually dressed in a suit, despite the tropical heat, and his military bearing was quite intimidating).

It was also at this stage of my life that I began to realise the very serious personality that was mother. There was never a smile or kind word or any demonstration of affection. She was not averse to telling you (and repeating the same to her friends in graphic detail) how you were. There are three such incidents, in particular, I remember her narrating. One was where I was accused of spoiling a family portrait by hanging my head too low and that, when the family repeated the family portrait a few months later, my head was tilting too much upwards, as a result of over-compensation. A second remembrance related to my having been given the task of 'scrubbing' the back stairway and moving the 'landing' plant pot down each tread, instead of immediately replacing the pot after I had finished scrubbing the landing. A third concerned my supposedly being so timid as to one day, in the scarcities of the latter part of the Second World War, allowing myself to be pushed out of a breadline by desperate adults at Tang's Bakery.

My mother could also dispense rather brutal punishment, on one occasion stripping me naked, for a less than serious misdemeanour. It is not surprising that at this time I began to experience frequent nightmares, whose main theme was that of my enraged mother chasing me in Robb Street and my finding difficulty in eluding or outpacing her. Stress at home and at school was a double whammy.

At the same time, my mother was demonstrating every day how determined she was that her children would have a better chance in life than she had. Adequate food and nutrition was a must. In the absence of refrigeration, her resort was an almost daily trek, before sunrise, to the fish stelling (wharf) and a stop at the fruit market on the way back home. Physical and mental strength/discipline would have been required. Then there was my mother's other daily routine of cooking breakfast before the children departed for school, preparing lunch for when they arrived home for lunch, having a pastry snack for when they arrived home at the end of the school day around 3-4pm, and serving them tea and biscuits around 7pm. She was literally in the kitchen most of the daylight hours, since paid domestic help was unaffordable. Yet the contradiction exists of my mother, from time to time, accusing an offspring, who was lagging with respect to housework, of being fit only for eating food. My contribution to household activities included sometimes accompanying my mother (with hardly a word spoken between us during the journey) to purchase fish and fruit in the morning; cutting up wood for the cooking oven; kneading homemade bread; churning the homemade ice cream can; 'washing' salt out of butter used to make black cake at Christmas; scrubbing the kitchen floor (when a scorpion once bit me); and running various errands, etc.

At the extra-household activity level, my mother was determined that all her eight children would receive at least a basic education. She was therefore particularly pleased when, following the results of the 'Eleven Plus' examination, my twin sister Marva and I were admitted to Bishops High School for girls and Queen's College (founded in 1844) for boys, the two premier secondary schools. There was palpable pride in my mother's face when she and I went to the Portuguese-owned Bettencourt department store to purchase various aspects of the stipulated Queen's College uniform in August 1948, for the commencement of classes the following month.

The underlying tension that existed in my relationship with my mother was mitigated somewhat by a wonderful bond that existed with my godmother, who was sweet beyond words. She was always so glad to see me (along with my twin sister Marva) during the school mid-morning recreation break, since she sold coals and fruit near the western entrance of the Bourda Market that was immediately across the road from the main gate of Bedford Methodist school. She also made sure that she had lots of pastry and other 'goodies' when Marva and I paid our usual afternoon visit, after the prayerful labours of 'Sunday School'. As usual, Marva did most of the talking and I just listened. It was devastating when my godmother later committed suicide (when Marva and I were in our very early teens) as a result, we were told, when her lover jilted her and disappeared with her entire savings. It was devastating to see her in hospital writhing in pain from the poison she had ingested. It was also around this time that the brother of my mother, a kind and generous uncle of her children, died from suffering a snake bite in the interior where he earned a living as a 'porknocker' (small scale gold miner). Soon after, my favourite teacher (a Mr Murray) also committed suicide (most likely because of the torment he suffered, since he was 'gay,' a no-no at the time) and a classmate succumbed from tetanus after being impaled on a zinc sheet. Sadness seemed to be an integral part of life. At a more immediate family level, my elder brother, Stanley, barely survived an asthma attack, after the doctor had said that he may not survive the night. This chronic asthmatic condition badly interfered with his schooling and his physical development.

There are two other things that I particularly remember. One is the induced blackout that occurred whenever German submarines appeared offshore Georgetown, although I was too young and my mother too protective and resourceful for the full force of the World War deprivations to be felt. The second is the "Great Fire" in Georgetown in February 1945 which started about three blocks from where we were living; it was a terrifying sight. My mother had packed all our belongings and was ready to flee and Marva and I found comfort in devouring all the corn pone (a sweet delicacy) that was in the house. The fire in the commercial district downtown raged from mid-afternoon to early next morning (despite the valiant efforts of the local fire fighters and the dropping of sand and river water by members of an American air base stationed twenty-five miles away at Atkinson Field). The next day, the business area of Georgetown looked like a smouldering bombed out city.

At a personal level, I still was not sure who Maurice Odle really was. While I considered myself to be quite shy and timid, I could be given to bouts of youthful exuberance and irrepressible immaturity. For example, one morning, when I was about eight or nine, I woke up early and found myself playing downstairs, in between my house and the tenement yard, when I saw a bird singing sweetly while perched on the electric wire that led to the lamp post on the other side of the street. Some wild instinct caused me to run from the back of the yard, brick in hand, and to hurl same at the bird. Of course, I missed and the brick went hurtling through a glass window of "Proudy's" house that was opposite ours. I immediately dashed up the back stairway, looking very innocent, and soon heard "Proudy" screaming for the police. I told neither my parents nor siblings what really happened, fearing the corporal punishment consequences. Such a bizarre practice was not in vain as, about three years later, I broke the Queen's College 'Under Thirteen' athletics record for throwing the cricket ball. Later on, and without her knowing it, "Proudy" got her revenge when she frequently laughed at my falling down attempts to learn to ride my father's bicycle on the said street.

SECONDARY SCHOOL CHALLENGES

I was eleven and-a-half years old (a few months below the average age) when I was admitted to form 2A at Queen's College, whose hallowed premises were at the eastern extremities of Brickdam Road, next to the premier venue for horse racing. I had not been a student there for more than a couple of months when I had an encounter with the proverbial bully, one Courtney Coltress. Form 2A students had just returned to the class room from mid-morning break and were awaiting the English teacher (Angus Richmond) for the next period (session) when I heard Coltress telling another student (Ian Goring) that he was going to beat-up (or words to that effect) on Odle. I was sitting quietly at the back of the class and in the few seconds it took for Coltress to reach my seat was enough time for me to summon courage and resolve that I would not take any assault from him. I was a bit apprehensive but, nevertheless, ready for him. When Coltress threw the first punch, I grabbed his arm and put him into a wrestler hold which lifted him off his feet. I was obviously getting the better of the exchange. Richmond arrived when the fight was in full flow and, obviously horrified at the spectacle, ordered us to go to the Principal's office. The rest of the story goes like this: Captain Nobbs, an English expatriate, answering the knock on his door asks "Why are you here?" Answer: "Mr Richmond sent us, because we were fighting". Captain Nobbs then invites us into his room, chooses the most sturdy of the canes in his desk drawer, tells us to touch our toes, and then administers six strokes each to our backsides. He thereafter pulls out a "black-book" from another drawer, enters our names, serenely sits back, and then, and only at this late stage, asks us what triggered the fight. That was my first experience of colonial style justice.

However, I became an instant hero to my classmates who had been passively experiencing the torment of the said Coltress. In fact, Coltress thereafter ceased to be such menace as the other classmates stood up to him, in part due to the Odle demonstration effect. I learned a lot about myself from the incident – quiet, but somewhat tough and resolute.

It is not surprising that I did not tell my mother what had transpired in school, since there would have been no sympathy for me, perhaps only more blows from her. Unfortunately, I had a virtually absentee father who, when not at work or imbibing alcohol with his workmates and friends at various rum shops, was secreted in his bedroom sleeping and/or recovering from his exertions. On reflection, it is also not surprising that I did not confide in any of my siblings, given the rather individualistic existences of members of the family. I promised myself that I would in future avoid getting into scrapes or other misdemeanours that might cause me to be expelled from the elite school that Queen's College was and squander a golden opportunity for pursuing a path to personal elevation. Thus, when a senior schoolmate (Horace Von Eden) who was in Form 5, borrowed part of my meagre 'pocket money' one morning while frequenting the school's 'tuck shop' and for weeks repeatedly ignored my requests for repayment, I barely managed to restrain myself from punching him, when he dismissively exclaimed, "little boy, stop molesting me". I resigned myself to the thought of having been conned and began to be aware that not everyone is trustworthy or willing to live up to one's obligations.

Nevertheless, before the end of the first school year, I was caught-up in another school expulsion threatening incident which, again, no member of the family was aware of. It involved some rather immature students of Form1 (entry into which was not based on examination but was reserved for children of expatriates and the privileged). One afternoon, clapping in order to excite certain horses that walked by their Northern playing field on the way to the Durban Park Race Course for a workout, one of the horses, a champion by the name of Ball-o-Fire, panicked, broke loose from his trainer and broke his leg against certain stake barriers at the head of the footpath, resulting in his having to be destroyed. Unfortunately, classmate Geoffrey Sampson and I (students

EARLY AWAKENING (1937-1960)

An enduring symbol of excellence

of the higher Form 2A) were innocent by-standers, who happened to be there in the event that the Form 1 teams were short staffed, such was our fanatical interest in soccer. Both the horse owner/racing authorities and the school Principal were utterly alarmed and word was that the two most senior students on the scene would be expelled. It was the timely pleading with the Principal for mercy by Head Prefect Cunningham, son of an expatriate, that saved our skins.

To this day, there are certain Queen's College alumni who hail out to me *via* the nickname Ball-o-Fire. Another lasting sobriquet I acquired was "Balbus", as a result of being asked while in Form 2A to translate from English into Latin the phrase "Balbus has big hands and big feet". As if those were not enough, some other close friends still call me "Jimmy", owing to certain (mis) perceived similar characteristics to that of my father.

One more incident that occurred during my first year at Queen's College is worth relating. There was a cricket match involving Form 2A members on the Western playing field, after which I was expected by my sister, Jeanne, to purchase, for her benefit, two sweepstake tickets at the nearby Durban Park Race Course, where a horse race meeting (competition) was due to take place that very afternoon. She had given me two shilling coins (the currency was changed to dollars a few years later) for that purpose and, when the cricket match ended at 12.30pm, I went across the street to the race course accompanied by a classmate, Jimmy Ramsahoye, who had recently become my neighbour, my parents having moved house from Robb Street, Lacytown to Light Street, Alberttown. At the entrance to the race course, we observed a 'three card game' in progress and winning seemed so easy to us naïve ones (the three card handler and his accomplice, by sleight of hand, were making it appear so) that Jimmy asked me for one of my two shillings in order to participate in the game. Of course, Jimmy lost and after some expression of remorse and moments of contemplation, asked me for the other shilling so that he could recoup. He duly lost again and, full of anguish, sought out a racing horses' owner (Rahman, I believe, was his name) whom he claimed to know well and from whom he hoped to borrow two shillings.

The rest of the afternoon involved Jimmy trailing (with 'yours truly' in tow) Rahman from the pavilion to paddock, where the latter consulted with his jockey(s) at the beginning of each of the six races scheduled for that afternoon. Jimmy was totally ignored by Rahman and I ended up going home after nightfall without the two shillings and being confronted by angry parents who had earlier gone to the police station to report a 'missing child'. The rather tame but self-protecting explanation I gave my parents was that the money had fallen out of my pocket while playing cricket and that I was searching for it all afternoon. I dared not say that I was a victim of the socially reprehensible three card trick. It is only about sixty years later that I told my sister, Jeanne, the real truth, an account also related in Jimmy's book, *'A Moldy Destiny',* (which is essentially a critique and parody of a book written by a former Guyana Prime Minister/President, Forbes Burnham, entitled 'A Destiny to Mould').

The next few years at Queen's College were not as eventful as the first, although just as enlightening for other reasons. I slowly became more aware of the social and ethnic structure in the school and the extent to which this reflected hierarchical characteristics in the wider society. For example, although Guyana was not a settler colony, the Principal was white (as was the Head Prefect) even though it was said that he was not as qualified as the other senior staff members. A few of the other members of staff were white (British, French and American) although to be fair to them they did not exhibit any sense of superiority or discrimination against non-white (African, East Indian, Chinese and indigenous Amerindian) students, who made up more than ninety percent of the school population.

Also, at least four members of staff were from Barbados: Hilary Beckles, the Deputy Principal (whose nephew some decades later became the Vice Chancellor of the University of the West Indies) Bogus Pilgrim, Victor Rock, and Cameron Tudor who, years later, became the Deputy Prime Minister of Barbados. Our staff and student make-up seemed like a microcosm of the world's population. Such representation (my father was also Barbadian) must have helped to sharpen my sense of regionalism and internationalism. I sensed a mood of harmony in the classroom and in extra-curricular activities (particularly on the playing field). Guyana (and the world) seemed like a happy place.

I was coasting through school without making too much of an academic effort. My main ambition (and enduring satisfaction) was to represent Queen's College at soccer and cricket. I had little interest in academic work and did just enough to be promoted from one class to the next higher class. Not surprisingly, I did not do very well at the General Certificate Examination (GCE) and had to repeat certain subjects in 1953.

It is in that same year that my knowledge and understanding of the nature of the Guyana society and the world at large began to change. In 1953, the British Government, having granted adult suffrage to the people of Guyana, suspended the 'Adult Constitution' within 133 days of the populist and mass based Peoples' Progressive Party (PPP) earning a landslide electoral victory (18 out of 24 seats) on the grounds that the party was exhibiting communist tendencies. British soldiers were dispatched to Guyana and Premier Cheddi Jagan and some of the PPP leaders were imprisoned. We were later to learn that the American Government (led by President Eisenhower) had encouraged the British Government (led by Prime Minister Churchill) to do so in the context of the emerging Cold War. (Interestingly, the previous year I had visited the Jagan-owned dentistry establishment, the cheapest in Guyana at one dollar per tooth extraction, where Cheddi stitched up my bleeding jaw following a bad job of extracting two jaw teeth by his brother, Sirpaul Jagan, the previous day. While waiting in the reception room, I remember perusing a publication placed on the table titled 'Moscow Weekly' and a young receptionist wife, Janet Jagan, keenly observing my intellectual curiosity.

Our history master at the time, Rabindranauth Persaud (who, years later, became an Advisor to the leader of the PPP) took the opportunity to give us a basic understanding of the injustices inherent in a colonial society and cited absurdities such as secondary school viewers of Hollywood cowboy movies loudly cheering the extermination of Red Indians and primary school children being made to sing "God Save the King/Queen" in celebrations on Empire Day. In the same year, I also began to hear on the BBC of "Mau-Mau terrorists" and the "evil" role of Jomo Kenyatta in Kenya, but teacher Persaud's lectures helped to put the struggles for freedom, and against colonialism, in their proper perspective. There was no organised resistance in Guyana to the presence of the British troops but, nevertheless, a loose knit 'gang' (group) of us Queen's College students and neighbourhood friends (the "Goshers") took pride in shouting "Limey Go Home" whenever we spotted them out on patrol. The names of some of the male members of the Goshers group that I remember are Carl Agard, "Squeaky" Agard, Leslie Allen, Havelock Brewster, Courtney Coltress, Vernon Fortune, Leon Fraser, Michael Isaacs, Colin King, Lawrence Mann, Clairmonte Moore, George Munroe, Maurice St Pierre, Junior Surrong, and Clive Thomas. (Of course, some were more core members than others).

By now, I was making a belated entry into Form 6B. But I lasted less than half of the school year before my mother yanked me out of school. It so happened that one day, after formal schooling, I attended a practice music session with the Queen's College-Saint Stanislaus College joint Steel Band, instead of bringing into my mother's yard, in a supposedly timely manner, the lumber that was lying on the parapet (for purpose of repair to the house that she had bought in Middle Street, North Cummingsburg, where we had taken up new residence). In truth, I had intended to deal with the lumber when I returned home from the practice session but, apparently, my mother thought that was not good enough and that I was behaving, as she said, "like a big man" for entertaining such tardiness.

This premature departure from Queen's College was quite a psychological blow for both academic deprivation reasons and the fact that Queen's College students were due to soon travel to Trinidad and Tobago to compete against Queen's Royal College at cricket and soccer. I had been developing a greater interest in cricket (though not rivalling that in soccer) and had interviewed, along with fellow student Geoffrey Chung, the great Clyde Walcott for the student magazine. (Walcott, at the time, was employed by Booker Bros. to develop cricket talent within the sugar estates), I had also been one of the operators of the scoreboard for the Guyana leg of the Australian 1954-55 tour of the West Indies. But all physical and emotional attachment to Queens College, 1948 to 1955, had come to an abrupt end.

Nevertheless, there was a familial and social existence that still had to be navigated. Life in the matrimonial Odle household had continued to be rather strained and the long hours at school and the many extra-curricular activities (mainly sporting) provided a good reason not to be at home. When my mother indicated that I would no longer be attending Queen's College, there were no siblings coming to my rescue. The nature of the household was such that any decision taken by my mother was not to be questioned. In fact, her children were anything but a closely knit bunch and my absences from the household would not have been missed. But I am getting ahead of events.

At week-ends, especially, during the school vacation recesses, I had experienced the comforting companionship of the "Goshers" group

Family home as it appeared in the early 1950s (now the location of law firm Fraser and Housty)

(led by precocious Lawrence "Bonnie" Mann, who lived two doors away from my house in the Alberttown neighbourhood. We tended to engage in mischievously outrageous behaviour and rebellious teenage escapades and took delight in challenging social convention and the established colonial authority. That could have unwanted consequences. For example, one night in 1953, during the emergency period of occupation by British troops, seven of the "Goshers" were arrested by the police, on the road outside Clive Thomas' home, for defying the ruling against public congregation of more than three persons.

Where was my father who, despite being virtually illiterate, rose to become a stevedore foreman (employed by Booker Bros.) when all of the above was going on? As mentioned earlier, he had relinquished the running of the household to my mother. On the limited occasions when he was at home and sober, he said very little although, when he did speak, his booming voice, with an accent that was clearly that out of Barbados (from which he emigrated as a young man) could be a bit intimidating. Deep inside, however, he was rather soft-hearted and my sisters were always able to exploit this to their financial benefit.

Although my father was a rather remote figure, I have rather fond memories of him. For example, I remember his taking me to a boxing match between a Guyana welterweight champion, named 'Tear-Away' Garraway, and a Venezuelan champion, Alfredo Miro, at the then called British Guiana Cricket Club ground. (Boxing was obviously an interest of his, since a very large and proud photograph of the USA heavyweight champion, Joe Louis, known as the "brown bomber", had adorned the walls of our house from the time I was a little boy). He also once took me to an adult party (with full orchestra) when I was only sixteen years old. But what I remember most was his allowing me to accompany him on one of his trips forty miles down the massive Essequibo River to Stampa to collect logs for export to England and giving me the use of the cabin that was assigned to him on the ocean going vessel, Arakaka, while he slept with the general stevedore crew on deck. On that trip, the English 'first mate' (with whom I happened to have a long conversation the day before) drowned one evening when the canoe that was bringing him from shore back to the mother ship capsized. My father had also been invited to the party ashore, but at the last moment declined. Everywhere, danger lurks. I regret not having been able to get closer to my father.

ASPIRING CIVIL SERVANT: GUYANA

With the sudden and premature departure from Queen's College, I soon found refuge in the Guyana Civil Service as from May, 1955. My first position was at the Income Tax Department of the Ministry of Finance. The job was mainly clerical in nature, since I had no accounting qualifications or other financial/economic skills that were required for assessing tax liabilities of companies and individuals. The Commissioner, W.G. Stoll, was a rather stern boss who strode into the office with the air of an emperor, but senior staff, like Jack Ali, Too Chung and Barcellos, and others were quite pleasant. My time in the Income tax department was not very memorable, except for one particular incident, that, though amusing and inconsequential, reflected class divisions in the society. My friend, Claremonte Moore, and I had gone to the Metropole Cinema the evening before and had occupied seats in the cinema's cheapest section ("pit") which was distinctly separate from a more elevated section called "House" and from an even higher and more expensive section called "Balcony". The next morning, when a junior staff member (Patsy Jackson-Rohlehr) who must have been in either "House" or "Balcony", arrived (after me) in the office, she very loudly proclaimed, in an obviously disapproving manner: 'I saw Maurice Odle in pit last night".

There was not much unhappiness on my part when, after a year and-a-half, I was transferred to the Social Welfare Division of the Ministry of Local Government. There I met old classmates Havelock Brewster, who later became a University Professor and United Nations Director, and Wordsworth Mc Andrew, who later became a national poet and folklorist. (A few years later, I was the 'father giver' when Havelock's brother, Erwin, married my younger sister, Pearl). Also among the staff was Frank Pollard (who a decade or so later was a colleague of mine in the Faculty of Social Sciences, University of Guyana) and Cedric Grant (years later, a Guyana Ambassador to the United States). It was Cedric who helped me to draft a reply to an official complaint made to the Commissioner of Local Government, by an obviously frustrated middle-aged female employee, that I tended to expose my underwear when I tidied-up myself in preparation to proceed on my lunch break. (No verbal objection was previously made by her to me). My written and oral defence proved to be adequate but the experience was something of an eye opener. I wondered at the time whether the difference between her Portuguese extraction and my African origin contributed to the complaint being made.

My Social Welfare Division job entailed reviewing prisoners' records and prison warden reports so as to determine whether remission or early release was warranted and the conditions to be attached thereto. If released, the threat of recidivism also had to be taken into account. I found the work quite interesting, as it sharpened my sense of compassion and social consciousness and exposed me to another worldly existence that was seldom ever commented on in the media. In this regard, my colleague, MacAndrew, was of considerable assistance in helping me to formulate, in the required bureaucratic style and fashion, the recommendations I needed to make to my supervisor.

I was therefore very disappointed when I found myself, after only six months, transferred to the Ministry of Works and Hydraulics. My new position involved 'posting' (recording) information, from vouchers onto big clanging machines, relating to daily expenditures on road, sea defence, drainage and irrigation and other capital projects. The work was boring beyond words and I was glad to be re-assigned, within a year, to less boring duties involving calculating the dollar value of travel allowances needed to be paid to the Ministry's engineers, based on the number of miles they recorded in traversing the coastland and the interior. I continued in this assignment until mid-1959, at which point I became eligible for six months' vacation leave (that was required to be spent in England). Such leave, after only four years' service, was originally designed to facilitate expatriates, but union agitation had it extended to Guyanese born. I duly made an application for same, but the Chief Accountant declined to recommend me for receipt of same because he felt that I did not intend to return to Guyana. I resolved to try again, since a number of local civil servants had already made use of the leave facility; moreover, some of my close friends (members of the "Goshers" group) had also emigrated to England.

While work within the Guyana Civil Service lacked stimulation, life in the wider society was becoming more politically volatile and socio-economically competitive in the second half of the 1950s (culminating in a virtual civil war during the early 1960s). I was gaining first-hand knowledge of the concept and practice of racism in Guyana. I was also beginning to learn of the practice of racism on a global scale and related colonial struggles. For example, while I could not quite appreciate the significance of the American involvement in the Korean War or that of the French struggle in Vietnam, I was certainly attuned to the brutality of the 1960 Sharpeville massacre by the white authorities in South Africa.

In addition, I was becoming aware that a sort of "apartheid", however comparatively mild, existed in Guyana. At the time, there were virtually no non-whites in the commercial banks, insurance companies and large department stores. (In fact, my elder sister, Evelyn, was the first non-white person to be employed at that time at the Head office of British-owned Booker Bros. and this was only because her stevedore father was held in such esteem for his services to the company (on the first day in office, her colleagues thought she was the coffee maid). Similarly, the most senior positions in the Civil Service, Public Corporations and the Police were almost invariably occupied by white personnel. In addition, in the bauxite mining town of Mackenzie (later renamed Linden) there was a residential area reserved for employees of the foreign (Canadian) investor, called Watooka, that was out of bounds to non-whites. In effect, there had been more social stratification than my younger self had been able to perceive,

With respect to my household situation, life had become as unstable as that in the workplace. I was evicted from the family home when I failed to give my mother the usual share of my salary after I returned from touring Trinidad and Tobago as a member of the Guyana Volleyball team. (Tension between us had been rising since I no longer gave my mother, as I did in my first year of employment, the entire $68 pay packet, minus five dollars). For a time, I was virtually homeless, sleeping in either the car (PA 675) of a good friend (Lawrence Mann) or under the stilted house of another (Claremonte Moore). In this regard, an interesting and, in retrospect, amusing incident occurred during this period of homelessness. When I was thrown out of the house, I did not take all my clothes with me, since there was nowhere within which to place same. As a result, when the time came to take the person I was dating, Margaret Hutson (who later became my wife) to a friend's party, I did not have appropriate casual wear. I therefore managed to sneak into the family home and wend my way up to the third floor (lower)

Volleyball team on route to Trinidad in 1958. Maurice Odle is pictured far left.

where my party clothes were. But before I could sneak out, my father came home from work (night shift) and I had to wait until he and his wife had finished their gaff session (in which a lot of unflattering things were said about their children). Since they were conversing in the second floor sitting room immediately below where I was hiding, I had to wait until they had vacated that room and repaired to their back bedroom. But before this could occur, a creaking floor board above them made my parents feel that there could be an intruder upstairs. My father came upstairs to look around and found some clothes lying on the floor which they assumed had fallen and caused the sound that they had heard. All the while, I was hiding under the bed. (Eventually, my twin sister, Marva, who earlier had also vacated the family home under unhappy circumstances, I rented an apartment at the corner of Irving and Laluni Streets, Georgetown).

My wife, Margaret, in contemplative mood in London circa 1963

As indicated above, the next year, 1960, I renewed application to my employer for 'long leave'. This time I succeeded. The only problem I had to resolve was whether I should return to Guyana at the end of the vacation period. The Chief Engineer for roads, Philip Allsopp, at my last monthly visit to his office, in order to secure his signature with respect to my calculation of his travel allowance, had strongly suggested that I use the opportunity in England to begin the process of securing a University degree. Moreover, three of my sisters, Evelyn, Jeanne and Norma, had already gone to England to work and/or study, and Marva and Pearl were planning to do so in the near future.

Another factor propelling me to England was in search of medical treatment. A few months after my departure from Queen's College, I severely tore the anterior cruciate ligament in my left knee while playing soccer for YMCA against the Georgetown Football Club. Thereafter, I had been barely able to play even volley-ball and cricket, with my knee heavily strapped-up. At the same time, my siblings had not been doing too badly on the playing field. Stanley had been "called to trials" for possible representation of Guyana at cricket and only the presence of Lance Gibbs (who later became a West Indies and world legend) prevented him from doing so. Norma became a Guyana badminton champion and Marva was once judged as "Basketball Player of the Year". In addition, Patrick represented Queen's College at table tennis.

In retrospect, going to London in May, 1960, proved to be my salvation. I was living an aimless life, with lots of partying and excessive drinking, and being barely able to survive on my meagre Civil Service salary. The only saving grace is that I had developed a steady relationship with a rather attractive young lady, Margaret Hutson, whom I met at a party that I had 'crashed'. She was destined to join me within a year, as a result of my writing her mother and stepfather for her hand. I was slowly developing a sense of identity and purpose. However, there still remained a certain amount of self-doubt.

CHAPTER TWO

INSPIRING LONDON SCHOOL OF ECONOMICS (1961-1966)

FIRST IMPRESSIONS OF EUROPEAN SOCIETY

My trip to England began with a ride on a 'cattle plane' from Guyana to Trinidad and Tobago. From there, I embarked on a thirteen-day boat journey, during which most passengers, including yours truly, were sea-sick during the first few days. The trip was very interesting and educational for a number of reasons. The passengers were almost entirely West Indian, few having been to another Caribbean territory, much less beyond, and an exciting process of bonding and camaraderie took place. The crew of the ocean-going vessel was Spanish and I heard that language for the first time. (Perhaps because France was the main imperialist rival to Britain at the time, French was the only language that was taught in school, besides English).

Before arriving at the port of Southampton in England, the boat made two scheduled stops, the first for a day in Tenerife, one of the Canary Islands off the coast of West Africa, and the second for two days in Vigo, Spain. The boat trip also helped, in a perverse way, to prepare one for the wiles of the metropole. For example, myself and two other passengers, on a stroll downtown in Tenerife, were victims of a swindle in which whisky, sold in the streets in brand-named and perfectly sealed bottles, turned out to be coloured water when we opened same on returning to the boat. And on a 'night clubbing' jaunt in Vigo, it took us some time to realise that we were in a "clip joint" in which the many glasses of vodka the self-invited female Spanish guests at our table were rapidly drinking, and which we were paying for, were really nothing but water.

I was met at Southampton by Michael Isaacs, a "Goshers" member, who had emigrated earlier, and who had arranged rental accommodation for me in West London. My suitcase was nothing but a small grip that was loosening up and I was grateful to be rescued. What I remember clearly is the damp feeling in the apartment and it was already the month of May. I very quickly began to find my way around by way of a map of the street system in Greater London.

Being in the great metropolitan city of London was indeed an eye opener. Everything filled me with awe and wonder – the massively crowded streets downtown; planes constantly flying overhead and leaving a long trail in the sky; the over-head and underground trains forever in motion; the lofty ornate architecture and the famous sites and monuments; the pomp and ceremony outside Buckingham Palace; and last, but not least, given my tropical upbringing, the unpredictable weather (hailstones and all). And on happily exiting my apartment when the sun was shining brightly, I, on more than one occasion, found that my clothing was far too light or that the temperature had suddenly and significantly dropped. It took me some time to learn the art of defensive dressing.

The social dimension was also becoming as interesting as the physical. Soon after my arrival in London, on my way to participate in an anti-apartheid protest outside Grosvenor Hotel, where the South African President (Hendrik Verwoerd) was staying in the summer of 1960, I fell heavily in my hurry to get off the still moving bus, as it approached the bus stop obliquely opposite the hotel. I had obviously arrived in the 'mother country' with an inquiring social consciousness. The truth is that, in Guyana, I had read the book, *'Naught for Your Comfort'*, by Father Trevor Huddleston, on the racial situation in South Africa.

I also began to quickly learn the true nature of British society. While the average citizen was very polite and quick to offer you "Good Morning" or 'Good Evening" greetings, there was a certain class of

Some Odles in London in 1962. Back row, L-R: Maurice, Marva (with baby Marvin) and husband Donald Williams. Front row, L-R: Maud, Norma and Evelyn.

citizens who resented the non-white presence. This class included the landlord owners, some of whom were not averse to posting rental notices that included such alerts as "no Blacks, no Jews, no Dogs". I was also made aware that, in the late 1950s, certain white males, called "Teddy Boys' had been terrorising non-whites in London and it took Jamaican counter vigilantes to restore a certain degree of calm. It also did not escape me at the time that London's underground railway and metro-bus system was quite heavily manned by African, Caribbean and Indian/Pakistani personnel, as was the nursing profession, a sure indication that the wage level was not very high. But I did also notice a few whites doing as menial a job as cleaning the streets, a sight that did not obtain in Guyana.

In the early weeks and months, I considered myself to be on vacation and, therefore, any job in London would do. My first was washing dishes at a large restaurant ('Lions') in the Regent Road downtown area. Not too long after, I secured a somewhat better paying job as a park attendant at Tooting Bec Common. I remember in a letter to my elder brother, Stanley, informing him that one of my tasks involved cleaning the park's public toilets and receiving his reply enquiring "whether the cold has frozen your pride". My boss was a Scotsman, a kind enough person who thought I was hard working. He often engaged me in conversation, but his accent was so deep that I only understood about eighty percent of the words he spoke. In retrospect, the working class experience in Britain, though lasting only a few months, was beneficial in terms of sharpening my social consciousness.

CIVIL SERVANT OF CONVENIENCE: BRITAIN

The time was then approaching for me to return to Guyana as my six months' vacation leave was coming to an end. At first, I had decided that I would return. My eldest sister, Evelyn, who was living in London at the time, agreed with my decision to return to what she described as my "cushy Civil Service job" that awaited me in Guyana. However, after much agonising and, with the active encouragement of two of my secondary school classmates and members of the "Goshers" – Clive Thomas, who was already pursuing a BSc London University degree and Maurice St Pierre, who was sharing an apartment with me in Balham, South London, I reversed my decision and decided to take the plunge and pursue studies in the Economics discipline (putting paid to my mother's wish when I was a youngster that I become an engineer). That was probably the most important decision I have ever made. It was also the most troubling since, for the next couple of months, I would sometimes experience a nightmare involving a scenario of my being back in Guyana, only to realise, after startled awakening, that I was still in London. How stupid of me; the decision to stay should have been a no-brainer.

But first, one had to be successful at the joint Oxford and Cambridge 'General Certificate of Education Advanced Level' (GCE 'A' Level) examination, a more advanced university entry requirement than in the USA, in the relevant subjects, in order to be able to gain admittance to tertiary education in England. I therefore enrolled in night classes for 'mature students' (since I was twenty-three years of age) at the Regent Street Polytechnic and went looking for a job whose remuneration was reasonable, hours of work regular and during daylight hours, and which was not so taxing, either mentally or physically, as to impede my study efforts. That was a tall order. Still lacking in confidence, I also wanted a job that could be the basis for developing a useful working career, in the event I did not gain university entry. Accordingly, I managed to gain employment as a public servant at the Board of Trade in January, 1961, with university entry examinations scheduled a few months later in May.

A herculean effort was required. Maurice St Pierre, also interested in an Economics career, was a good study partner and Clive Thomas an inspiration. I attended classes in the evening, every working day, and did revision or homework most of Saturday and Sunday. The colleagues I interacted with at the Board of Trade were pleasant and the convivial atmosphere was conducive to after-hours study. I studied really hard but I remember Maurice St Pierre telling me that his close friend, Tom Millington, did not think that I would succeed since it was my first attempt at GCE 'A' level, and the preparation time was too short. That made me even more determined. When the examination results were announced, I had done surprisingly well in the Economics, Economic History and British Constitution (Government) subjects, all of which were not offered in the secondary school I attended in Guyana. I was elated and duly resigned from my job at the Board of Trade. During the couple of months before departure, I received a lot of congratulations and good wishes for a successful university career from my Board of Trade colleagues, and, on the day of my departure, I was presented with a parting gift (a book entitled 'Before you Go').

The Board of Trade experience was a happy one, partly because it represented the beginning of a more purposeful life. But I remember one unsettling occurrence while working there. There was a letter from the South African authorities proposing an arrangement whereby goods will be shipped from South Africa to Britain and then re-exported under a British label, so as to evade international sanctions. This knowledge served to increase my understanding of the wiles of the world and the strategies that countries are likely to employ to protect their so-called national interests.

I was called for an interview at the London School of Economics and Political Science (LSE) London University, to which I had months previously applied for admission, pending examination results. I was successful and the school year was scheduled to begin on 6 October, 1961. When I revealed the good news to my friend, Maurice St Pierre, he suggested that I should instead enrol in Regent Street Polytechnic (which offered the London University Degree to external students and to which he was admitted). Why St Pierre made such a ridiculous suggestion I do not know, except that he probably wanted a study partner at Regent Street Polytechnic.

With the school year approaching, my problem was how was I going to be able to pay the LSE annual fees, besides finding money for rent, food, and transportation, *inter alia*. Fortunately, Margaret had by now arrived in London and we had gotten married a month earlier. However, her steno-typist salary was not even sufficient to pay the basic bills. Nevertheless, I started attending classes at LSE without being able to even afford to buy cafeteria meals, instead resorting to taking homemade sandwiches to school where I ashamedly ate same in the toilet. I also could not afford to buy the basic textbooks and so I made full use of the library facilities. If a reference book was not available in the Library, I would go to the Economist Bookshop (which was only about a hundred yards away from the Library) where I would speed-read certain relevant sections of the text and quickly return to my seat in the Library and make notes of as much as I could remember.

All the while, I was hoping that my application to the London County Council, based on my residence in South London, for a university grant, would be successful. When this proved not to be the case, I applied, using my friend Donald Augustin's North London address, for a grant, this time to the Middlesex County Council, giving the latter the hard luck story that my father had suddenly suffered a stroke and would not be able anymore to support me financially. (My father did indeed suffer an incapacitating stroke three years previously, but there was no hope of receiving any assistance from him, even if he were still working). Low and behold, my application was successful and I am eternally grateful for the financial assistance, although I should remind myself that I was a bona fide taxpayer for the one and-a-half years prior to entering LSE.

By now, I was receiving tremendous moral support from my sisters, who all happened to be in Britain, mainly South London, at this time. Marva married Donald Williams and was living in Battersea. Evelyn, who worked in Central London, also lived in Battersea, and would in a couple of years return to Guyana. Pearl had recently gotten married to Erwin Brewster (and I was the 'father giver') with the reception held at Evelyn's apartment (the same place as the wedding reception of Maurice and Margaret, whose residence was also just a couple of miles away in

Among high school mates McKenzie, St Pierre and Thomas, in addition to other buddies at my wedding in London in 1961

Tooting Bec). Jeanne had not yet left London to get married in Nigeria and Norma, who was undergoing medical technology training in Wales, visited her siblings from time to time. This period in alien London seemed to represent the most intense interaction ever among the Odle children.

SOCIO-ECONOMIC AND POLITICAL ENLIGHTENMENT

University life is an exciting journey in anyone's life and being a student in an institution as renowned as LSE made my stay there even more so. Stepping onto the campus for the first time filled me with awe, given its well-founded-reputation as a great place for social science teaching and learning and the many famous people that have graced its halls of learning, particularly in the areas of economics, politics, law and sociology. A number of world leaders, for example John F. Kennedy, had spent part of their university career at LSE and experiencing scholarship there was even more prevalent among Third World statesmen. In the case of the Caribbean, at least five former Prime Ministers – Errol Barrow, Linden Forbes Sampson Burnham, Michael Manley, Percival James Patterson, Eugenia Charles and one current leader, Mia Mottley, spent some time there. It is also interesting to note that Arthur Lewis, a native of the Caribbean island of Saint Lucia, was an LSE lecturer during the 1950s (and later became the third person to earn a Nobel Prize Laureate in Economics).

In the first of my three years as an undergraduate student, I was required to take the three compulsory subjects – Economics, Economic History, and Government and two of the available electives, with my choice being Economic Geography and International Relations. The content of each of the subjects was to serve me in good stead. Economics greatly enhanced my rudimentary understanding of basic economic theory and market principles. The principal professor for this course was R.G. Lipsey, who later expanded his lecture notes and produced a first year best seller, comparable to that of the American, Paul Samuelson. In fact, the 1961-62 student body, of which I was a member, was the guinea-pig class to whom the lectures inspired the conversion into a book. Economic History included developments on the American continent and was not traditionally restricted to the European experience. Similarly, the lectures and tutorials relating to the subject, Government, were an eye opener in that the course covered not only governmental principles (supplemented the next year by a course on History of Political Thought) but, also, institutional, social and cultural issues. What struck me at the time was the reverence with which the lecturer spoke of the royal family, their embodiment of "purity" and their national unifying role, despite the hereditary and essentially undemocratic nature of that institution. A non-native could not understand how important tradition was to the English. Given my radical thinking at the time, I made sure that I did not, in the end of my first year examination, answer any question dealing with the role of the monarchy; perhaps, that was also the reason why, years later, I failed to attend the MSc. graduation ceremony at which the 'Queen Mother' was slated to present certificates. All in all, I felt that I was being grounded in the essence of political economy.

With respect to the required two optional subjects, the choice significantly broadened my education and general knowledge of the world. 'Economic Geography' dealt with issues related to the environment and sustainable development at a time when such issues were not very fashionable and, in discussing exploration and frontier activity, pointedly posed the pertinent question as to "whether man is a product of his environment or master of his environment". At that time, it also occurred to me that the weather might have been a contributory factor to the level of material development of societies, in that most countries in the Northern Hemisphere (including Japan) had attained a high level of development whereas most of those in the tropical Southern Hemisphere, that did not require the acquiring of engineering and similar scientific skills to erect sturdy buildings (that led to other types of sophisticated construction projects) and thick protective clothing that stimulated manufacturing activity, did not. (In later years, my intellectual curiosity was not followed up with research on the history of development, but with research on factors that would promote future development in the Third World). The other optional subject that I chose, International Relations, was just as interesting, since it dealt with concepts and practices such as "balance of power" and great power rivalry, in addition to the makings of international law and rules/rights relating to traversing the seas, *inter alia*. But perhaps not every student found the first year as interesting as I did, since Mick Jagger did not proceed any further and launched into a famously successful pop singing career.

The next two years of the first degree course of study were one of consolidation and specialisation in the economic discipline, proper. The area of specialisation I chose was Monetary Economics. The two main lecturers were Professors Reginald Sayers and Alan Day, both of whom had written books on the subject area and had also participated in providing evidence and expertise towards the findings of the Radcliffe Report, that the British Government had commissioned a couple of years earlier on the workings of the money, banking and financial system. The essence of the findings was that "near money" assets were becoming increasingly important in the modern economy. While my path through these matters of high finance was fairly smooth and rather uneventful, there was one interesting observation that was made by a classmate from Ghana who had been a member of the country's central bank since its formation on attaining independence from Britain in 1957 and had arrived at LSE in order to sharpen his skills. All of the six students who had been asked by Professor Sayers to make presentations to the plenary class during 1962-64 were white and probably just out of high school, but he was not chosen, even though he had central banking experience.

Very soon after graduating in 1964, I had a meeting with Professor Sayers, my 'personal tutor/advisor' and, when I told him that I was still in the process of deciding what I wanted to do next, he exclaimed that I was behaving in a "feckless manner" (first time I heard the term) and that I should apply for a job in the banking system. However, I felt that I needed to attain a higher degree (MSc.) to further enhance my economics and econometric skills. I therefore submitted an application to the LSE/London University authorities. But how was I going to pay the school fees. I accordingly applied, in hope rather than successful expectation, to the Middlesex County Council and was pleasantly surprised when they agreed to extend my grant. I originally chose International Economics to be my speciality but, within a couple of weeks of the term, I realised that it was not to my liking and switched to Development Economics, since I thought that the latter was more relevant to the situation existing in Guyana and the Caribbean, to which I eventually intended to return. The didactic content of the course of study was a disappointment, in that there was not enough normative emphasis on "big push" and other dynamic requirements of economic transformation. It was as if all that was required was for Third World countries to do what activities they were currently engaged in more efficiently. On reflection, this conservative approach is not surprising since the "economic miracles" of Singapore and certain other South-East Asian countries had not yet occurred to provide the required demonstration effect.

While throughout the 1961-1966 years, my focus was on what was going on in the classroom, LSE spawned a number of extra-curricular activities on campus and reactions to events off campus, both nationally and internationally. Lively discussions on local, national and international issues were the norm at campus coffee tables, lunch rooms and Friday night student parties. The social debates were particularly furious among the West Indian student contingent that included a number of "island scholars" (i.e. the particular persons who achieved the best 'A level' performance in a particular year). For example, from Guyana, alone, there were "Guyana scholars" Herman Mackenzie, Haslyn Parris and Patricia Robinson. In addition, from Guyana, there were Lawrence Mann (who later became Ambassador to the United States) and Chandra Singh (who became a World Bank official). At this same time, other LSE students from the Islands who later distinguished themselves included Jamaicans P.J. Patterson (multiple term Prime Minister of Jamaica), Norman Girvan (Professor and Secretary-General of the

Association of Caribbean States) and Orlando Patterson (Harvard Professor); Barbadian David Simmons (Minister and Chief Justice). In addition, there was Bert Commissiong from St Vincent and the Grenadines and, also from Jamaica, Adolf Edwards and John Maxwell.

The vibrant West Indian Society (of which I was Secretary for a period of a year) organised the occasional guest speaker forum (at which the entire LSE student body was invited). Guest speakers included Forbes Burnham and Cheddi Jagan who were in London in October 1963 for discussion with UK Minister Duncan Sandys for the latter to determine whether the election (in 1964) to precede independence should be on a 'first past the post' or 'proportional representation' system. The Burnham arguments for proportional representation (by showing the wide discrepancy between votes cast and seats earned at the previous election in 1961) was particularly convincing but, even so, it was obvious that the eventual Sandys preference (actively supported by the USA Government and the CIA) was really designed to oust the radical incumbent Premier, Cheddi Jagan.

Another invitee of the West Indian Society at the time was Malcolm X, who was on his way back to the United States from participating in the Mecca experience in Jeddah, Saudi Arabia. At the Friday evening session, held at LSE's packed Large Lecture Theatre, Malcolm X was his usual brilliant and captivating self. After the speech, the West Indian Society had a cocktail party in his honour and the close interaction with the great man was a memorable one. It was therefore something of a shock to turn on the TV two evenings later to learn that he had been assassinated. The feeling was one of extreme sadness, especially since I considered him to be addressing the racial situation in the USA more vigorously and directly than Martin Luther King Jr.

On a lighter note, the BBC (its building, Bush House, was obliquely across the Strand road from LSE) once asked the West Indian Society to organise a party, so that they can record the sound (and dance movements) reflecting the musical transition from blue beat – rock steady – ska – and, finally, reggae. At the party, I drank a little too much and had to be carried home, much to the annoyance and displeasure of the awakened landlady (Hiller) and my wife, Margaret.

It would also be remiss of me if I did not mention cricket, an activity for which the West Indies was probably even more well-known and admired than reggae music. The second Test Match of the West Indies tour of England was to be held at Lord's Cricket Ground in a couple of days and the visiting team was staying at the Savoy Hotel in Strand road, a few hundred yards from LSE. Myself and David Simmons, paid them a visit, courtesy of Lance Gibbs, and my sister Jeanne and I were at the test match a few days later to witness the century of our countryman Basil Butcher. I was also at the last Test Match of the 1966 tour (at the Oval Cricket Ground) when Garfield Sobers was adjudged the best player of the cricket series. What was particularly memorable during the 1963 and 1966 tours was the ecstatic and nationalistically proud behaviour of the West Indians in the crowd at the successful batting and bowling performances of the visiting team. (A decade later, in 1975, the West Indies won the first 50-over final at Lord's cricket ground, on the back of a century by Clive Lloyd, who along with Vivian Richards, led a winning series streak from 1980 to 1994).

Beyond the boundary, cricket had become an integral and foremost part of West Indian nationalism. Nationalism was being fostered by the writings of socialist commentators living in London like C.L.R. James, who was also the leader of a Friday night West Indian discussion group that was held at his home and which included a number of LSE and other London University students, such as Cherita Bent, Margaret Carter, Adolf Edwards, Stanley French, Norman Girvan, Walton Look-Lai, John Maxwell, Maurice Odle, Orlando Patterson, Joan Rainford, Walter Rodney and Richard Small. At this time, the West Indian Student Centre, situated at Earl's Court in west London, had also become a lively meeting place, especially at weekends, for discussions on the socio-economic path that should be taken by the emerging independent nations in the 1960s.

West Indians at LSE and their friends and associates were not the only ones with a socio-economic consciousness. The other students of various nationalities had their own Societies/Clubs and contributed to the political ferment that existed outside of the classroom in the 1960s. Many luminaries of a mostly leftist persuasion were invited to speak to the student body on various issues of the day. For example, when President Kennedy was assassinated, the American author of 'Rush to Judgment' was invited to expound on his views that the official verdict relating to the manner of his shooting, and those responsible, contained elements of a conspiracy. Such was the benefit of the campus being situated in Central London. Another notable speaker was the philosopher Bertrand Russell who was engaging in ardent opposition to the American involvement in the Vietnam Civil War, and the brutal bombardment (including use of chemical weapons) of the North Vietnamese. (Over three million Vietnamese and fifty-three thousand Americans eventually died). A group of LSE students, *inter alia*, volunteered to go to Vietnam to participate in the resistance, but we were told by the North Vietnamese that they would prefer to receive material and vocal support, rather than physical bodies. My horizon was broadening and the exposure was making me a citizen of the world.

OFF-CAMPUS SOCIAL SPILL-OVERS

Whenever I was physically on campus, I felt like being part of one big family of students from every part of the globe. Interacting with them was an education in itself and gave me a good appreciation of our human commonality and the possibility of attaining liberty and fraternity on a universal scale. However, whenever I stepped outside of the campus, I immediately became aware of the cold reality and the need to be on guard. Some encounters are worth relating.

Because I could not afford to buy text books, I tended to make use of LSE's library facilities until the 10.00pm closing time. One late evening, a few months after I became an LSE student, I was wearily walking to the nearby Aldwych underground station to catch the train(s) on the way home, when a police patrol car slowly drove by and stopped about forty yards further on. Out jumped one of the two officers, who began to walk on the pavement purposefully towards me. His first words in my recollection went like this: "pardon, but could you tell me what is in your bag". I immediately began to open my dark brown briefcase but he stopped me in mid-motion, saying "first tell me what is inside". I told him that school books were in the briefcase to which he then said "okay, open and let me see". After he verified what I was telling him, he calmly said "I am so sorry to disturb you sir, have a good evening", and cheerily walked back to his car; a clear case of profiling.

A more interesting, and probably more socially significant, encounter occurred when Ian Smith, the Premier of Southern Rhodesia, a colony of Britain, made a 'Unilateral Declaration of Independence' (UDI) in 1965. The morning that the LSE students heard of the declaration, about three thousands of them poured out of the campus and marched down the Strand road to Rhodesia House, which was situated a few hundred yards away. The crowd's opposition to the declaration and anger at the reluctance of the British Prime Minister, Harold Wilson, to forestall same by his "kith and kin", was reflected in loud sloganeering at the scene. The police soon arrived and, probably intimidated by the size and vigour of the crowd, decided to arrest exactly ten persons whom they considered to be either the leaders or most vocal, in what was up to then a very peaceful demonstration. I was one of those arrested and taken to Bow Street police station a mile away. I am not claustrophobic but, when the four-inch thick door of my jail cell was slammed shut, I feared for my safety, in the event of a fire. Early the next morning, I was placed on an arcane charge of "wilful obstruction" and released under my own recognisance. I was due to appear in court in a month's time and, in the intervening period, I was coached by certain Professors at LSE on the basic aspects of the law relating to such a charge, as I intended to represent myself, being somewhat of a pauper. Perhaps I should have studied Law, instead of Economics.

When the day came for me to appear in court, I put the police officer, who had arrested me, on the witness stand and confused him totally. I was granted a "conditional discharge", with the requirement that I am not arrested on a similar charge within the next six months. (It would take another fifteen years of struggle, and hundreds of thousands of lives lost, before Southern Rhodesia became independent Zimbabwe; and I was destined to be involved in two other encounters concerning that country, in the 1980s, when I was a United Nations official).

Involvement in one other protest is worth relating. There was a club (called Whisky a Go-Go) in the Soho area in West London, frequented by some white LSE students, who found out that it was practicing racial discrimination. They therefore asked me (now known in LSE for my UDI protest action) if I was willing to be involved in a sting operation designed to expose the company. I agreed, and also contacted my friend Maurice St Pierre. When we arrived at the club one evening, we were denied entry as expected. But, immediately after, some white LSE students were admitted. Nightly anti-discrimination picketing, reported in *The Guardian* newspaper, resulted in the club eventually relenting and abandoning its practice of racial discrimination. During this period of protest action, the LSE Principal, Sydney Caine, did request an audience with me, but his only advice was to "be careful".

These LSE related experiences were informing and reinforcing my political beliefs and political loyalties. I had become a supporter of the Labour Party and had voted for it in the victorious 1962 elections. But later commentary in *The Guardian* and *Daily Worker* newspapers and the speakers at Hyde Park Corner in Central London, *inter alia*, convinced me that the Government was not doing enough for the less well-off sections of society. Their performance was rather disappointing, with significant deviation from certain progressive stances, both at home and abroad. At the next election, I therefore voted for the Workers' Party.

I was living a very hectic student and social life and I was grateful to my wife, Margaret, for permitting me the required space for participating in the various activities. My first son, Ronnie, was born in 1963 and, even though this engendered a lot of happiness, it was an added financial burden to my meagre student existence. It was therefore necessary for me to work during the vacation periods. Summer jobs included working, at various times, in a furniture store; a cocktail bar; an office doing data entry; preparing meals at Lord's Cricket Ground; and at LSE tabulating vehicular transport statistics for a Lecturer that was doing research. In the winter, sorting or delivering mail for the postal services provided a few weeks of pay. But the money earned was not enough in the circumstances and so, during the later MSc. course of studies, I resorted to doing 'supply teaching' at secondary schools where teachers were temporarily absent. One day, a persistently unruly female student (a Jamaican craving for attention and identity) threw a biology lab chair at me and nearly broke my arm – a case of 'To Sir, **Without** Love'. I also taught part-time, at Ealing Technical College, those students who were studying for the BSc (Econ,) examination. Doing so required my dashing out of LSE during the day (in between lectures and tutorial classes) and travelling by subway to the very Western end of London. But it was worth the strenuous effort, since a couple of my students did so well at their undergraduate studies as to be later admitted into the MSc course of studies at LSE. I, myself, was to later secure a PhD from London University, but the travails of academic and political activism conspired to delay the securing of same before 1973, as shall be described in the next chapter.

CHAPTER THREE

ACADEMIA AND ACTIVISM (1966-1980)

UNEVENTFUL LECTURESHIP AT MIDDLESEX UNIVERSITY

After passing the MSc Examination at LSE, I was able to secure a lectureship at Enfield College of Technology, later named Middlesex University. As a result, my financial situation was significantly improved. I was able to move residence from Muswell Hill to an apartment a few miles away in Finsbury Park. I was even able to buy a second hand Ford car from my former "Goshers" and LSE colleague for the princely sum of twenty-five pounds sterling. What, at the time, I thought was a good deal turned out to be a disaster since the car was in terrible operational condition (and I was not aware that it used to be disparagingly referred to as the "goady"). Even in the summer, there was sometimes need to tinker under the bonnet in order to get the car to start in the morning and, in the winter, I used to have to park the car at the top of the hill on which my apartment building was located, release the hand brake and put the car in downhill motion before the engine would turn over. Moreover, the car was only fit to be driven relatively short distances.

One morning, I was late in catching the bus that was hired to transport certain students and myself, and another of the lecturers, to the headquarters of the South East England gas and electricity company on an educational field visit. My colleague proceeded to depart without me in the hope that I would follow by car. It was a harrowing trip for three reasons. First, on the A1, en route to the M1, in my desperate hurry I tried to overtake at a bend and nearly collided with an oncoming truck. Second, on the M1, the conditions were far from ideal and the gusting winds swayed the rather light Ford car dangerously from side to side, the faster I drove. Third, the piston rings of the engine were in such bad condition that blue-grey smoke billowed from the exhaust and I was concerned that I would have to stop in order to replace the lubricating oil that I was losing fast. When I arrived at the electricity company, the host official was not too pleased at my arriving late. It was not my first experience of how a stickler the English are for adhering to time and timeliness of behaviour.

Overall, my year as a Lecturer at Middlesex University was a very pleasant one. The Principal, George Brosan, was very energetic in his desire for the college to earn a good reputation. My colleagues were just as keen and included two who had just graduated with an MSc (Econ) from LSE in the same year (1966) as I did. My very first lecture was on the economic theorising of Marx, partly because the staff wanted to excite the imagination of the students beyond the classical learnings in high school, and partly because I had been infected with the LSE brand of radicalism, to the extent of my having paid a visit a couple of years earlier to the Karl Marx tomb in Highgate Cemetery, North London.

Nevertheless, after a 1966-67 year of comforting full-time work, the call of home became irresistible. Guyana had become politically independent a year earlier and exciting prospects of participating in nation building beckoned. It was always my intention, even after graduation, to return to Guyana (or another part of the Caribbean) rather than attempt to build a meaningful career in England, such that I did not even seek to acquire UK citizenship, as my twin sister, Marva, had successfully done, before the descent of the Union Jack flag and the ascent of the Golden Arrowhead flag of Guyana on 26 May, 1966.

But I had to make a choice as to what work establishments in Guyana I should target. In September, 1966, Prime Minister Forbes Burnham had attended his first Commonwealth Heads of Government Conference, which was held in Marlborough House and, during his stay in London, had actively encouraged graduates to return home and make their contribution to the economic and social development of Guyana. I was one of those who had met Burnham and the exchange between us was such a rather disturbing one, that it is worth relating.

A few days before my encounter with Burnham, I had been to a West Indian Student Society forum (at which Walter Rodney spoke) where a London PPP overseas supporter had gratuitously thrust an interim membership card of the PPP into my hand. On my way in a taxi to the Meeting with Burnham, with my friend Maurice St Pierre and the Chairman of the London PNC overseas support group, Bertram Abrams, I related the card incident as an example of a crude marketing practice by a supposedly serious political party. When we got to the hotel at which Burnham was staying, he had not yet returned from a BBC television interview involving certain other Commonwealth Heads of Government.

On his return to the hotel an hour or so later, Burnham walked straight to his room, curiously closely followed by Abrams. When he emerged a few minutes later, his first words were: "Odle, when are you going to leave the PPP"? Very surprised, my emphatic response was: "I am not a member of the PPP. Burnham's retort was: "Then you are a member of the PNC". Further, nonplussed at the 'grand charge', my response was: "I am neither a member of the PNC". For the next forty minutes or so, Burnham wanted to know why I was not a member of the PNC and what would I recommend other than what the PNC was currently doing in order to better serve Guyana as a whole. In response, I took the opportunity to propose the "power sharing" strategy that the New World Group publication had recommended a few months earlier as being appropriate in a very politically partisan, socio-economically divided and dangerously unstable Guyana society. (In 1962-64, there had been a mini ethnic civil war in Guyana between African supporters of the PNC and East Indian supporters of the ruling PPP). Burnham responded that he was not prepared to go that route so early in his term of office (which began in 1964) and that what his African supporters expect was a period of consolidation and furtherance of their interests, which had been neglected by the development strategies of both Premier Jagan and the previous colonial system. He added, very pointedly that, if the PPP were ever to regain office, its pro Indian economic policies would surely return. What Burnham was saying was surely not only for my benefit. In the hotel room were about a dozen of his supporters who acted as an 'amen chorus (including Sydney King who, by then, may or may not have changed his name to Eusi Kwayana).

I was so shaken up by Burnham's views, that when I returned home that evening I found great difficulty in falling asleep. I did not realise that race relations in the plural Guyana society had deteriorated to such an extent during my six years of absence from its shores. Little did I know at the time that the encounter with Burnham in the London hotel was to be a rather mild forerunner of what was to befall me when I returned to Guyana.

I applied to both the University of Guyana and the Central Bank of Guyana. I was interviewed by Professor Lytleton Ramsahoye, the fourth ranked academic at the University and Hans Brockleman, the German born Governor at the Central Bank. I decided to accept the university position, rather than the banking job, partly because I had already acquired a bit of lecturing experience and partly because I thought it would allow me a little more freedom for engaging in extra-curricular social activity. The salary offered was much lower than what I had been receiving at Middlesex University, but it did not matter; the non-monetary benefits were expected to be significant.

The journey to Guyana was a non-stop nine-day trip by boat, compared with the thirteen-day voyage to England seven years earlier. The journey was a pleasant one and, also, one full of proud expectations, as I was returning home as a fairly well-qualified professional (at a time when a relatively small number of such persons existed in the country}. But there was one occurrence on board that signalled a permanent health condition that I was not aware of. One evening, there was a party on deck that included lots of shell fish, among other foodstuff. During the evening, I felt uncomfortable and returned to my cabin for a change of clothing because I thought that my suit was too tight. I did not realise that I was severely allergic to shell fish and that during the party revelry I was 'swelling-up'. It was months later that the allergy condition was confirmed.

GUYANA UNIVERSITY – A CAULDRON OF ACTIVITY

The yearning was over. It was a good feeling to be back home, although there might have been lurking fears as to how easily and quickly I would be able to insert myself back into the Guyana society, after a seven-year absence. What helped to ease the transition was that my two brothers, Stanley and Patrick, were still in Guyana and that two of my sisters, Evelyn and Norma, had returned home from England. They assisted me in finding accommodation, firstly in Prashad Nagar, a lower middle income suburb, a couple of miles from downtown Georgetown, the capital. I soon learned that I had indeed lost touch with the Guyana society, its ambience and its rustic quaintness. I would be awakened in the morning with the sound of cocks crowing and, throughout the day, one would be subjected to the frequent barking of dogs and strong odour of Guyanese dishes being cooked by neighbours, in addition to loud animated conversation emanating from nearby houses or passing pedestrians.

But what stood out the most was the heat. While the coastland's all year temperature, cooled by North-East trade winds, was a relatively mild average of 86 degrees, the climate in England had caused me to grow unaccustomed to the tropics. I therefore needed to quickly get rid of the long sleeved shirts that I had worn in England for something shorter and of less thick fabric. The purchase of a car became high on my 'to do' list and a Portuguese company salesman facilitated the purchase.

My wife, Margaret, was also glad to be in Guyana, as she had not seen or spoken to her parents and siblings since 1961, given that the only affordable form of communication was writing letters. My son

Ronnie, four years old in 1967, was a source of attraction, since he had a very distinct cockney accent and everyone he met encouraged him to speak, so as to hear the quaint English sounds coming from his African lips. An immediate need was to get Ronnie settled into a kindergarten school. This turned out to be an interesting exercise. Every day I took Ronnie to school, I would have to remain in the class with him for a while until he became distracted and I would then slip out. A more normal exit tended to produce hysterical crying. I always wondered whether this crying was because, in England, he was put in the daytime care of a white nanny (who had particularly curious neighbours) when he was only six weeks old, while his mother went to work and his father attended college.

When I arrived in Guyana in 1967, the University of Guyana (UG) had already been in existence since 1963 and teaching took place at night on the campus of the premier high school, Queen's College. The University had been mockingly described by Forbes Burnham, when he was Parliamentary Opposition Leader, as "Jagan's Night School", partly because he felt that the latter should have made the University of Guyana an integral part of the regional University of the West Indies system, rather than an independent institution. Burnham's view was that racial separation was the motivation of Jagan, since the Caribbean region was predominantly African, and that similar partisanship had led Jagan to decide to remain outside of the newly formed West Indies Federation in 1958 and which contributed to its collapse in 1962. The night school stigma persisted for a while, even with the physical movement in 1970 to a pristine day and night campus (whose hours of teaching were designed to suit public and private sector employees). Political and racial division, even in educational matters, has continued to haunt Guyana.

In my early years as a staff member, it was clear to me that, even on campus, there were clear divisions, along both racial and ideological lines, among academic staff members. Hierarchy wise, the Vice Chancellor and most of the Deans were white (partly because of the low stock of available renowned Caribbean and Third World scholars at the time) and the bulk of the staff were mainly of Guyanese African or East Indian origin (The Chancellor, Justice Kenneth Stoby, was also Guyanese, but his was a merely ceremonial, rather than executive position). Also, the very senior academic staff seemed to have two distinct socio-political positions, not surprisingly, given the very partisan nature of Guyana society. Among the very senior staff in the late 1960s, the views of Professors Harry Drayton and Lytleton Ramsahoye seemed to be more radical than those of the expatriates and such locals as Bertrand Collins and Kenneth Stoby.

With respect to the general academic community, there were also divisions within and between Faculties. Most Social Science faculty members tended to be very liberal and they included economists Clive Thomas, Compton Bourne, Aubrey Armstrong, Wilfred David and Maurice Odle; political scientists such as Harold Lutchman, Paul Singh and Perry Mars; and lawyers Arthur Alexander and Rudy James. But some radical elements were also in the other Faculties and these included historian Trembley, Arts lecturers Bill Carr and Derek Bickerton and natural scientists Malcolm Rodrigues and Zinul Bacchus, who were among those struggling for socio-economic change in a newly independent Guyana.

It is this vibrant academic community in which I happened to find myself immersed. I was assigned to teach two subjects – Intermediate Economics and Monetary Economics and, later on, Development Economics. Many of the incoming students were particularly bright (even though the entry requirements were relatively low) partly because Guyana's secondary school system was arguably the best in the Caribbean, and partly because there was a stock of well qualified persons who, prior to 1963, did not have the opportunity to go to a local university and, invariably, did not have the wherewithal to go abroad and attend classes in a foreign institution.

Within two years, I was asked to take on the responsibility of being Head of the Department of Economics. The following year, I was persuaded by the members of the Social Sciences Faculty to assume the duties of Dean of the Faculty. This arose as a result of the members deciding, at a specially convened meeting, to not endorse a new term of office for the incumbent expatriate Dean. A strong feeling of nationalism was pervading the campus, following Guyana's attainment of independence from the British in 1966.

Despite my heavy teaching and administrative responsibilities, I soon found myself engrossed in various extracurricular activities. These included pro-bono and, to a lesser extent, paid consultancies, in addition to a certain amount of political activism. That activism was to have certain unintended consequences.

For example, I happened to write a series of articles (one of which had the title *'Guyana Caught in an IMF Trap'*) in the country's daily newspaper, critically analysing the Government's 1968 budget, and this brought me a lot of attention. *First*, my reference to the rather low benefits accruing to the local economy from foreign investment in the sugar industry (which produced as much as 345,000 tons the previous year) prompted the virtually monopolistic Booker Sugar Company to invite me to spend a day interacting with their administrative and operational staff, with the obvious intension of getting me to modify my views. On the appointed day, I was picked up at my residence early in the morning by the Public Relations Officer, Ms Dianne McTurk, who later became well known for her caring love of otters and other animals at her ranch in the Rupununi region, adjoining Brazil. First stop was the bulk loading operations at the company's wharf and related facilities. Then, I was chauffeured to the Enmore Estate to have lunch with the Chairman and Chief Executive Officer (CEO), Mr Jock Campbell. (There I learned the art of eating a five course meal with the finest dinner ware one can imagine). I was later taken to the Head Office in Georgetown to interact with the accountancy staff, with the aim of convincing me that the company was neither very profitable and exploitative of its sugar employees nor engaged in depriving the nation's Treasury of its deserving tax take. This concern for the plight of the ordinary worker endeared me to the labour movement and, Joseph Pollydore, the then president of the Trades Union Congress (TUC) asked me to provide pro-bono advisory services to the organisation, as Chairman of the Fiscal Advisory Committee of the TUC, 1968-69.

Second, the budget articles also captured the attention of Prime Minister Burnham who, at a public reception came up to me and said that, if I had views on government economic policies, it would be nice and well appreciated if I would seek him out and express same, rather than air my views in public. Obviously, he felt that the Parliamentary Opposition would be able to use any criticism of mine against his Government. I also suspect that he had not forgotten that rather tense exchange of views in the hotel in London in 1966 when he was there for a Commonwealth Heads of Government Conference.

Third, the Permanent Secretary to the Ministry of Works and Hydraulics, George Williams, invited me to be a consultant to that organisation. I ended up doing two major reports – 'Sea Defence: Cost-Benefit Analysis' (jointly with Prem Arjune) and 'The Economic Justification for a Toll Road in Guyana' relating to the Soesdyke-Mackenzie/Linden highway that was under construction. Having completed those studies, I felt I needed to part company with the Ministry because I was finding it difficult to devote enough time to both my core university teaching and research activities and an increasing amount of political activism. But I decided to retain, in a private arrangement, the services of Ms Joan Arthur, for the typing of university related research that I was involved in. By now I had probably been deemed by the Government to be a politically dangerous person and so, when the Minister with the Works and Hydraulics portfolio, Hamilton Green, in enquiring why Maurice Odle was in the Ministry's compound, found out about the typing arrangement, he immediately fired Ms Arthur. (This development arose when, in taking some of my research work to the Ministry for Joan Arthur to type, I had hurriedly parked my car in the bay reserved for the Minister, who turned up very soon after, took umbrage to the intrusion and threatened to shoot people like me). However, with a bit of effort, I was subsequently able to secure employment for Ms Arthur as a Secretary in the University of Guyana's Faculty of Social Sciences.

Fourth, I was a Member of the Burnham Government Committee that, in 1968, recommended the 'Phasing Out of the Railways'. For years, the railways had been incurring huge losses because they were no longer used to transport bulk sugar (that was their original purpose) to the docks for export, preferring to use coastal shipping (and, to a lesser extent, the improving, but fragile, road transportation system) and therefore relying on meagre revenue from passenger (mainly school children) traffic. The Committee recommended that the Government authorities decree that transportation of sugar should be solely *via* the railway network but the Government did not find favour with that alternative. The international oil price hike a few years later increased the price of road transportation and the railway phasing out became rather unpopular, partly because the decision to phase out was not properly explained to the public. To this day, one can hear adverse comments about the recommendations of the 'wise' Committee Members that were made in the 'Report of the Committee which investigated the Phasing out of the Railways'.

At the same time, political activism was increasing among UG academics. I was persuaded to become President of the UG Staff Association (UGSA). Walter Green became Secretary to the UGSA and, fairly soon after, he changed his name to Omawale, in keeping with the budding Africa origin consciousness trend of post-independence Guyana, to be rid of slave owner names. A decision was soon taken to convert the UGSA into a union, but the formal registration only succeeded with the assistance of influential George De Peana (who at that time was President of the Clerical and Commercial Workers Union – CCWU) since Prime Minister Burnham, ominously, was not happy with this supposedly radical initiative.

Another development of more far reaching consequences was also occurring at the national level. Because the coalition between Burnham's African based People's National Congress (PNC) and Portuguese Peter

D'Aguiar's United Force (UF) party had collapsed on the eve of a national election in 1968, and lacking significant Indian ethnic support, Burnham, in order to stand a chance of winning the 1968 election, decided to introduce an overseas voting element in the electoral system, but one which would attempt to exclude diaspora Indians and those Africans that were suspected of not being PNC supporters. When I reported to a local newspaper columnist (Rickey Singh) the difficulty that Clive Thomas, a Guyanese lecturer at the University of the West Indies (UWI) Mona Campus in Jamaica was experiencing, Burnham was obviously unhappy with this revelation. One day, when I visited Parliament to listen to the debate concerning the Bill that was being debated on the abovementioned toll road, Burnham introduced me in the corridors to his Minister of Foreign Affairs (Shridath Ramphal) thus: "Meet Maurice Odle; Black people are the fair fair-minded people in the world" – a subtle appeal to kith and kin, in the presence of an unlikely bystander. (Burnham had been told by my friend Lawrence Mann, then Permanent Secretary in the Ministry of Trade, and political confidant of Burnham, that I was the person who informed Rickey Singh that only PNC supporters were being registered overseas). Other more blatant acts of electoral rigging enabled Burnham to retain the Presidency in 1968 and, realising that he did not really have majority support, he was forced to take increasingly oppressive measures against organisations and persons who were perceived to be opposed to his regime, sometimes in the guise of supposedly creating a benign socialist State.

 The UG academic resistance to what was considered an emerging authoritarian Government soon began to receive governmental pushback. A public meeting arranged by the UG Union and held on Parade Ground playing field, a well-known site for political campaigns, came to an abrupt end when the speech of invitee Parliamentary Opposition Leader, Cheddi Jagan, was interrupted by thugs attacking him and his bodyguards. The main daily newspaper reported the next day that Burnham was critical of the UG Union for providing Jagan with a political platform and receptive crowd.

A hard hitting pamphlet was created around this time by certain radical academics and called 'Ratoon', in keeping with the historical dominance of the sugar industry in the lives of the Guyanese people. The industry's historically oppressive and exploitative aspects were reflected in the publication's masthead, which was designed by my brother, Stanley. In the first year of its weekly publication, I was the principal editor, but by 1970/71, Josh Ramsammy took over the country-wide distribution duties. This prominence of the Ramsammy role would have infuriated the Government and may have contributed to the regime's attempt to put an end to his life in October, 1971. One mid-morning, in downtown Georgetown, men in a vehicle that was said to include the third highest ranking of the PNC leaders, opened fire on Ramsammy, who barely survived with significant lung damage, after being in a coma for several days.

But, though rattled, this did not deter the radical academics from continuing with their various politicking activities. In order to further extend their influence beyond the campus and strengthen their support base, they formed an organisation called Movement Against Oppression (MAO) whose headquarters was sited in Tiger Bay, one of the depressed, but centrally and strategically located areas in the capital, Georgetown. There were also moves to link up with other radical international and regional movements. For example, one of the USA student leaders, Stokely Carmichael, who I had met in London, was invited by the Ratoon group of academics to pay Guyana a visit. I was responsible for receiving him on his arrival at the airport and I found him quite engaging. Unfortunately, the central theme of his Black Power message, which posited that Blacks should politically organise separately and only when they reach a critical level of sufficient strength should they collaborate with other ethnic groups, did not resonate too well in the country's ethnically plural society. But the singing of his wife, the celebrated South African Miriam Makeba, at a public concert organised by the Ratoon group and MAO, was very well received.

The academics went on to challenge the Government's position on a number of socio-economic issues and their stance began to attract a number of supporters and sympathisers in the wider community. In this regard, the academics also began to agitate on behalf of the poor and disadvantaged, the inhabitants of whose neighbourhoods were frequently harassed by the police.

NEXUS WITH CARIBBEAN POLITICAL ECONOMY

Radicalism in the Caribbean and at its regional university (UWI) was also an important influence on developments that were taking place in Guyana's university. The major English speaking Caribbean countries had newly become independent and were attracted to the socialist ideological construct or some form of egalitarian political economy, given the exploitative form of foreign dominated capitalism that had been their experience. Genuine socio-economic transformation was on the agenda. National political leaders: Forbes Burnham of Guyana, Eric Williams of Trinidad and Tobago, Errol Barrow of Barbados and Vere Bird of Antigua and Barbuda formed in 1968 the Caribbean Free Trade Area, which was followed in 1973 by the Caribbean Common Market. Another leader, Jamaican, Michael Manley (son of previous Premier Norman Manley) was one of the signatories in 1973 of this radical group, but he was to later receive fierce opposition from conservatives in the Opposition Party, such as Alexander Bustamante, Hugh Shearer and Edward Seaga.

The national and regional struggle at the political level was equally intense at the university level (similar to what was obtaining academically in Guyana) particularly on the campuses of Mona in Jamaica and Saint Augustine in Trinidad and Tobago. The Faculty of Economics at Mona and Saint Augustine campuses was becoming a School of Dependency Economics. The pre-independence society in the Caribbean was likened to one vast Plantation (the periphery) in which foreign capital historically extracted maximum profits for holders of capital in the metropolitan centres abroad, with minimum or subsistence level benefits remaining for host country workers and the local treasury. This, according to Professor George Beckford, led to a situation of "persistent poverty" in the Caribbean. Thus arose academic writings on structural transformation (including economic integration) and regular discussions (which I participated in when I was in Jamaica on research fellowships in 1970 and 1973-1974 and, later on, in connection with joint UG-UWI research projects). Some of the Mona campus economists spearheading the new paradigm included George Beckford, Norman Girvan, Alister McIntyre, Owen Jefferson, Clive Thomas, Havelock Brewster, Alfred Francis and Steve de Castro, and socio-political scientists included Vaughan Lewis, Eddie Greene, Carl Stone, Edwin Jones, Louis Lindsay and Trevor Munroe. On the Saint Augustine campus, the analytical crusade was being conducted by scholars like Lloyd Best and James Millette. The scholars were known as the New World Group which had a liked named publication on socio-economic and political issues. There was also a related 'Abeng' Group, named after the bugle like instrument that the slaves had used to communicate over long distances, including sounding the call for rebellious action.

The Jamaican Government was prepared to fight back against the radical current. In early 1968, the passport of UWI lecturer, George Beckford, was seized, when he returned from a trip to Cuba. It was therefore not entirely surprising when history lecturer, Walter Rodney (a non-Jamaican) was banned from re-entering Jamaica after returning from a history conference in Montreal, Canada. In the previous year, Walter had engaged in intensive discussions with Rastafarian inhabitants of disadvantaged areas in Kingston, Jamaica about their wretched living conditions and related social inequalities (as he later described in the publication, *'Groundings with My Brothers'*). It seemed as though the Jamaican Government feared that Rodney was inciting an insurrection. As the news of the banning spread, rioting broke out and lasted for a number of days in Kingston, Jamaica. The Mona campus staff also staged a number of protest meetings, to which the Government of Jamaica reacted by instituting a state of emergency and banning from Jamaica a fellow Mona campus lecturer, Guyanese Clive Thomas. Academic freedom was under siege. These two bannings would later have a significant impact on political events in Guyana in the second half of the 1970s.

Clive Thomas returned to Guyana and took up an appointment at UG but Walter Rodney did not seriously consider the urgings of myself and certain other UG staff members for him to seek employment in his native Guyana, because he felt the racially divided situation was not conducive to the expression of liberal thought. He therefore returned to Tanzania, where he had spent two years teaching at the national university, after graduating with a PhD in 1964 from the School of Oriental and African Studies, London University.

In Guyana, with the rigging of the 1968 election out of the way, the political situation had settled down somewhat and the Burnham Government felt it could further undermine the PPP opposition by showing that his Party, the PNC, was even more radical and socialist inclined. In the early 1970s, he therefore embarked on a programme of nationalisation of the "commanding heights of the economy" (sugar, bauxite/alumina, etc.) and an economic policy of "feed, clothe and house" the nation. This seemingly progressive strategy also seemed to partly quell the level of agitation emanating from the UG academics. I took advantage of this lull in political activism to concentrate more on my teaching and research activities. But this relative respite was to be the calm before the storm.

UNIVERSITY/GUYANA GOVERNMENT DENIES WALTER RODNEY PROFESSORSHIP AND CONSEQUENCES

After a long absence, Walter Rodney returned to Guyana in mid-1974 from his near six-year sojourn at the University of Dar es Salaam, Tanzania. Clive Thomas had spent a sabbatical year at Dar in 1973 and is said to have partly influenced Rodney into returning to Guyana. The Head of UG's history department (Bobby Moore) had recently emigrated to Canada (as Ambassador) and it was felt that Rodney stood a very good chance of being appointed Professor, given his outstanding biography. The History Department (and Faculty of Arts) duly recommended his appointment to the approving Academic Board, but, when it went before the University's Board of Governors (later called Council) for the usual mere pro forma approval, the appointment was denied.

At the time, I was Dean of the Faculty of Social Sciences and, therefore, a Member of the University's Board of Governors. The reason for the denial was of course political and was facilitated by the significant presence of political appointees in the membership of the Board. At the meeting, the argument for denial was led by Minister Hamilton Green; the reasons proffered by him were anything but convincing. Immediately after, Haslyn Parris, the Chief Executive Officer (CEO) of the then nationalised bauxite industry (and the Government's ideological guru) took the floor and gave a very long and meandering speech in support of the Minister's position. I found this very surprising, since Parris was a contemporary of Rodney during their high school and university (UWI) undergraduate years. (The truth is that the PNC saw the charismatic Rodney as a potential political threat). As is usual in cases when an organisation is failing to reach consensus, the Chairman recommended the formation of a Committee comprising Government and academic representatives, to review and help resolve the matter.

The Government representatives were Viola Burnham, the wife of the Prime Minister, Desiree Bernard, High Court Judge and later Chancellor of the Judiciary, and Oscar Johnson, Principal of the Critchlow Labour College. Representing the academics were Maurice Odle, Dean of the Faculty of Social Sciences, Perry Mars, Political Scientist, and Arthur Alexander, Lawyer. The discussions, though very cordial, amounted to nothing; it was an exercise in futility. The UG Board did not formally appoint Rodney as Professor.

Rodney thus found himself in somewhat of a dilemma; he was without prospects of a job in an area in which he was trained and eminently qualified. At the same time, he was not willing to seek employment abroad since, as he puts it, he was not prepared to be a refugee from his own country. What is to be done? Although Rodney was subsequently able to secure stipends for occasional lectures abroad and one or two small grants from overseas-based institutions for research purposes, his financial situation was rather precarious and non-sustainable.

Accordingly, I was able to help the situation by securing funds from UWI's Institute of Social and Economic Research for Rodney to be able to do research of interest to the Caribbean, while based in Guyana. I was also able to use my good offices, as newly appointed Director of UG's Institute of Development Studies (IDS), to employ his wife, Patricia, as my Research Assistant. It was fortunate that, at this time, UG had as liberal minded a Vice Chancellor as Dennis Irvine, who was prepared to defend the academic freedom of his staff.

Because Rodney only needed to work on his personal research and did not have burdensome teaching assignments, he was able to devote a considerable amount of time to political activism against a creeping dictatorship. As he once described the situation he found himself in, Burnham had made him into a near full time politician. At the beginning, Rodney was not well known in Guyana, and his street corner and town hall meetings were not very well attended, even with the subsequent return to Guyana of school colleague, Rupert Roopnarine, who had graduated from Cambridge University in the UK and Cornel University in the USA. However, this situation changed dramatically, when the Government building housing the "Ministry of National Mobilisation and General-Secretary of the PNC" was destroyed by a fire that started around midnight. This development was to have very serious consequences.

Even before daybreak, the Government of Guyana had begun a round-up of the leaders of the Working People's Alliance (WPA). Omawale phoned me around 5.00am to say that police were at the door of his house and asked for my advice as to how to respond to their wish for him to accompany them to police headquarters. I hurriedly got dressed and drove to police headquarters, only to be surprised by the sight, in a holding room, of five executive members of the WPA – Rupert Roopnarine, Bonita Bone, Karen De Souza, Kwame Apatha and Omawale. I soon left the building and quickly drove down to Rodney's residence to alert him, only to find that the police were already there conducting a search of his house. I managed to have a very quiet, but brief, discussion with Rodney about security matters before the police requested him to accompany them to the La Penitence Police Station. In my discussion with Rodney, he had also asked me to take two of his children to school, as they were already dressed and ready to depart. I readily agreed and as I was driving past the La Penitence Police Station, the logical route, an unidentified car with three men inside, blocked my path. (They were obviously plain clothes intelligence officers who were keeping an eye on my movements after my visit to Rodney's house). They said that I was under arrest and should go into the police station with one of the officers, and the other two officers would safely take the children to school. I had no alternative, given the absence of cell phones in that era. When I entered the police station, there I found seated in one of the security rooms no other than a pensive looking Walter Rodney. I had been caught up in the dragnet, either accidentally or because I was a known executive member of the WPA.

In the detention room, I tried to communicate with Rodney who was about ten feet away from me, by hand signals and improvised code language, mindful that the room may have contained hidden cameras and secreted listening devices. I also disposed of a sensitive slip of paper, piece by piece, that I had in my pocket, by surreptitiously swallowing same. I was suddenly released around midnight (but Rodney, Roopnarine and Omawale) remained in the lockups (De Souza, Bone and Apatha having been earlier released) for another few days until appearance in court to answer the State's charge of larceny and destruction. During the court hearing, there was commotion among the large crowd that was outside the building and Father Darke was stabbed to death by a group of thugs, led by one Rabbi Washington, that had been recruited

Dr Walter Rodney: The people's hero

by the Burnham Government. Father Darke, who was white, was seemingly mistaken for the real target, his white colleague, Father Morrison, who was the Editor of a weekly newspaper, *Catholic Standard*, that was a thorn in the flesh of the PNC Government, at a time when the Government had deliberately made it difficult for daily newspapers and other outlets to import adequate supplies of newsprint.

When the defendants were released, they immediately proceeded to the home, randomly chosen, of my brother (Stanley) in Bel Air housing scheme, in a suburb of Georgetown, where they had a drink and discussions among themselves. I was there. A few days later, the police raided my brother's home in the dead of night looking, in vain, for arms. The political situation was getting more tense and some of its ramifications were getting closer to home.

That a group of political activists might have been involved (never proven) in an act that amounted to challenging the authority of the

Burnham Government, which by that time was exhibiting increasing dictatorial tendencies and claiming PNC paramountcy, excited a majority of the population and anti-Burnham sentiment and support for the WPA grew by leaps and bounds. Encouraged by such support, a decision was taken to merge the Ratoon/MAO group with three other groups – Association of Cultural Relations with Independent Africa (ASCRIA) led by Kwayana, Indian Revolutionary People's Association (IRPA) led by Moses Bhagwan and Socialist Vanguard Party (SVP) led by Brindley Benn, to form an organisation called Working People's Alliance (WPA). The WPA's message at street corner meetings, conveyed mainly by Rodney and Roopnarine (but supported by Moses Bhagwan, Eusi Kwayana, Clive Thomas, and Josh Ramsammy, *inter alia*) became hugely popular, as judged by the enormous crowd turnouts. Rodney's favourite slogan was "People's Power, No Dictator" and, in one memorable speech, likened Burnham to "King Kong".

A few months later, further encouraged by the huge public following, a decision was taken by the WPA to change their status from being a mere movement to that of a full-fledged political party, and to so declare at the next public meeting. Rodney and myself, drafted the proposed public announcement on the afternoon of the night-time meeting. But I suspected that Burnham would employ a dirty trick of triggering a blackout during the course of the public meeting and so I prepared for such an eventuality/contingency. When the blackout came, I quickly went to the trunk of my nearby parked car and took out a very large battery operated French camping light (that I had recently bought on a trip abroad) which brightly illuminated a large part of the crowd and the meeting proceeded without any further interruption.

At this stage, Burnham felt really threatened, partly because a failing socialist experiment and shortages associated with scarce foreign exchange, were making him loose the support of even his African base. Burnham, therefore, went on the offensive. He ordered his intelligence agencies to produce a "Recognition Booklet" containing the photograph and physical characteristics of WPA Executive Members and declared that each should "make his will" since "our steel is sharper now." He also declared that the letters of the acronym WPA really stood politically for the words "worst possible alternative". The 'death squad' arm of the police force was let loose. They would try to seize WPA's public speaking equipment when street corner meetings were held and I was once involved in a tug-of-war with one of the saboteurs.

There were also countless rumours of imminent danger. Rodney recruited a bodyguard by the name of Edward Dublin. Twice they tried to kidnap Clive Thomas, who resorted to sleeping at the closely guarded Roman Catholic Vestry, opposite the Brickdam Cathedral, rather than his usual residence. I identified a number of sympathisers who were willing to have me spend the night and I therefore tended to have a number of different door keys in my pocket, not sure which I would utilise in an emergency. I once went into hiding in a senior CARICOM official's (Byron Blake) residence, in a middle class neighbourhood, for a whole week-end. Four WPA Executive members engaged in protest action found themselves in prison. Casual supporters of the WPA were also targeted, and some lost their jobs in the public sector for such supposed infractions as being identified among the crowd at a WPA public meeting, making a casual criticism of the Government in the presence of a PNC diehard, not following irrational orders to hire a PNC comrade, or failing to fire a civil servant who is out of PNC Party favour.

The security situation inevitably got worse for the WPA. A key member, Ohene Koama, who managed the WPA office, was gunned down by the police. Some months later, Rodney's bodyguard, Edward Dublin, was murdered in Linden, a mining town sixty-five miles south of Georgetown. Rodney is not allowed by the authorities to travel out of Guyana and so, I am asked to travel to Port-of-Spain, Trinidad to discuss with George Weekes, Head of the Oil Field Workers Union, *inter alia*, the dire security situation facing the WPA. That meeting took place in the dead of night. Rodney eventually manages to leave Guyana, through backdoor channels, in order to attend a non-aligned conference in Lusaka, Zambia. Burnham had also been invited to the conference. When

Burnham saw the irrepressible Rodney at the conference, his mind was probably made up. Rodney had to be eliminated. There was need for further implementation of the threats he had been making. The die was cast.

Rodney's assassination on Friday, 13 June, 1980 left the WPA, Guyana and the progressive world in a state of total shock. The WPA had been infiltrated by an army intelligence agent, Gregory Smith, who had led Rodney to believe that he could use his electronic skills to construct a makeshift walkie-talkie system for use by executive members of the Party. When the time came for testing same, unknown to Rodney it was filled with explosives which nearly decapitated him and badly injured his brother who was the driver of the car that Rodney was in when the explosion occurred. It had been widely thought that the Burnham regime would not dare to kill Rodney because of the latter's huge popularity, at home and abroad, and the expected backlash. But Rodney (not to mention the rest of the WPA leaders) was riding a tiger, and in this slow moving tragedy there was something almost inevitable about the outcome. Mass appeal is not enough to oust an unpopular regime.

Two hours or so before his death, Rodney had been attending a WPA executive meeting and, during same, had asked to be excused in order to tend to an unspecified matter. With the meeting finally over, I went home and was having dinner when two executive members (Kwayana and Bhagwan) came and informed me that "something terrible" had happened to Walter and that there was need for executive members to engage in an emergency meeting. A number of other members and certain key supporters were rounded up and a "safe house" found in the Prashad Nagar suburb. At the end of an emotionally painful meeting, a decision was taken not to violently retaliate to what everyone assumed to be a Government orchestrated killing. The inability or unwillingness of the WPA to defend itself against the crossing of a 'red line' was a surprise to the general public. On the other hand, the greatest surprise of all was the reaction of Parliamentary Opposition leader.

Cheddi Jagan, whose PPP the WPA had thought of as an ally, but who proudly proclaimed on radio the next morning, in an indirect rebuke of the WPA, that his Party was wise enough not to choose the path of "insurrection", in opposing Burnham. That was a time for mourning, not strategic vindication.

At the open air public funeral ceremony in the Merriman Mall (later called Rodney Mall), the skies opened as though the Gods were weeping over this tragedy. It was an exceedingly painful period for me and I remember silently resolving that I will finance the construction of a Walter Rodney Memorial (which I later did with the pro-bono assistance of engineer Bert Carter around a plinth provided by the organisation 'Red Thread' at a site on Hadfield Street, near where he was killed). There, I also remember handing over the keys to my house to my sister Norma, who was standing next to me, since a strong rumour was circulating that the WPA executive members were to be rounded up and placed in the lock-up immediately after the funeral. My wife, Margaret, had surprisingly died (9 June) of hepatitis in the public hospital (whose treatment there was suspiciously non-aggressive), just four days before Rodney's assassination (13 June) and my two sons had to be taken care of in the event of my absence from home. The round up did not take place but, a few decades later, the long awaited Commission of Inquiry found the Burnham regime culpable, as reflected in the following Findings:

SIGNIFICANT FINDINGS

7.35 In the end it is clear to us that the Police were unprofessional, extremely inefficient in turning a blind eye to the obvious, or deliberately botched the investigation in Dr Rodney's killing or were complicit with others, including the GDF in hiding or shielding Gregory Smith from facing the brunt of the law for having murdered Dr Walter Rodney

7.36 Given all the relevant facts, events and circumstances set out in the Report, we unhesitatingly conclude that Gregory Smith was not acting <u>alone</u> but had the active and full support, participation and encouragement of, and/or was aided and abetted by the GPF, the GDF, agencies of the State, and the political directorate in the killing of Dr Walter Rodney.

7.37 Dr Walter Rodney was a man of large and significant stature both in Guyana and beyond at the time of his death. He could only have been killed in what we find to be a State organised assassination with the knowledge of Prime Minister Burnham in Guyana of that period. It was a controlled society and Burnham had a large and detailed knowledge of whatever was being done by the State and its agencies.

7.38 Mr Laurie Lewis, then Head of Special Branch and later Commissioner of Police is dead. We find, however, that there is prima facie evidence that he, along with Major General, Norman McClean (Ret'd), then Chief of Staff of the GDF and Mr Cecil 'Skip' Roberts, the Deputy Commissioner of Police and Crime Chief, had significant roles to play in the conspiracy to kill Dr Walter Rodney and the subsequent attempt to conceal the circumstances surrounding his death.

7.39 Further, given the manner in which the country was run, coupled with the threats issued by Prime Minister Burnham to the members of the WPA and the evidence of Mr Robert Allan Gates, we conclude that Prime Minister Burnham knew of the plan and was part of the conspiracy to assassinate Dr Walter Rodney".

In at least one other part of the Caribbean, Jamaica, the radical social democratic thrust was also experiencing setbacks and the economy was floundering, partly owing to low bauxite/alumina export prices and CIA inspired disturbances. The progressive Michael Manley Government of the second half of the 1970s had, by 1980, found itself vigorously trying to devise an alternative economic recovery and development plan that would studiously avoid entanglement with the International Monetary Fund (IMF) and the latter's well known structural adjustment (recessionary) policies. Manley was to lose office later that year to the incoming Seaga Government, which was critical of Manley's reluctance to have dealings with the IMF and, in campaigning, effectively interpreted the letters of that international financial institution to mean: "Is Manley Fault". The fortunes of the Left in the Caribbean were receiving a serious setback.

RESEARCH AS REFUGE

Despite the intense level of political and social agitation during the 1960s (late 1960s as far as my involvement was concerned) and throughout the 1970s, I still managed to devote sufficient time and effort to my academic duties. I remember comrade Andaiye once asking me how it is that I am able to academically focus despite all the turmoil. I even once forgot to pick-up my son from school, until hours later, such was my immersion in research. But I had been made aware of the adage "publish or perish". Research probably also served as an emotional anchor and a form of therapeutic retreat to tranquillity, at a time of extreme political stress.

There were five main areas of research in which I was involved. *First*, since Monetary Economics was the area that I specialised in for my first degree at LSE, it seemed natural for me to want to continue to have an interest in the subject. It therefore seemed fortunate for Wilfred David and Maurice Odle of UG to be co-founders, jointly along with Alistair McIntyre and others of UWI of a Regional Monetary Studies Programme in January 1968, on the occasion of a 'Regional Conference on Devaluation' that was held on the UWI Mona campus in Jamaica. The leading article of the Fifteen Conference Papers on the experiences of the Caribbean territories published by UWI's Institute of Social and Economic Research was the one by W.L. David and M.A. Odle, entitled *'Devaluation: The Case of the Guyanese Economy'*.

This Regional Monetary Studies Programme has remained very active over the next fifty years. At the outset, the programme, financed by the Central Banks in the Caribbean, provided me with a Research

Assistant, Asgar Ali (who in the early 1990s became the Minister of Finance in Guyana) and I had generous access to regional data and logistical and other support. Emanating from this particular project was a book I wrote titled *'Significance of Non-Bank Financial Intermediaries'* that was published by the UWI Press in 1970. A term spent as Visiting Fellow on UWI's Mona campus facilitated completion of same. I was also the Coordinator of the research programme for a couple of years and, in the mid-1970s, produced a UWI published book on *'Pension Funds in a Labour Surplus Economy'*, and a monograph in the UWI Working Paper Series (No. 24) on *'Multinational Insurance Companies Dependency Operations: The Trinidad Experience'*.. I also wrote a book on *'Transnational Banks and Underdevelopment'* that was published by the New York based Pergamon Press in 1981. The staff at the Central Bank of Trinidad and Tobago, particularly Gerry Hospidales and Patricia Robinson, were a very willing and useful source of data and information.

Second, I was working towards submission of a PhD thesis to London University. I was registered as an external PhD student, having returned to Guyana in 1967, and was determined not to be too distracted from the task at hand. I submitted the thesis on *'Public Expenditure in Small, Open, Dependent Economies'* in 1972, but was asked to revise same along certain specified lines. I was paying the price of not ever having a single session with a supervisor. However, in 1973, I re-submitted and, at a 'viva' at LSE, involving Professor Maurice Peston (one of the Lecturers in my MSc. course during 1965-66) and Professor A.R. Prest, the latter a world authority on Public Finance. I made a successful defence of the thesis. The thesis was later published by UWI's Press. The significant number of publications contributed to my becoming a Senior Lecturer in 1971 and a full Professor and Director of UG's Institute of Development Studies (IDS), following a one year Professorial Fellowship at UWI in 1974. As Director of IDS, I was relieved of major teaching responsibility.

Third, as Director of IDS, I also needed to pay less attention to my own research and to devote most of my energy into giving strategic direction to socio-economic research being conducted by other IDS members of staff, which included Henry Jeffrey, Prem Misir and Ms Nan Bardouille. Academics are individualistic characters, imbued with little team spirit, and managing them can be a bit contentious. Bardouille's output suffered as a result of the untimely death of her husband, who was also a lecturer in UG's History Department. Henry Jeffrey, who was doing research on the developmental role of Cooperatives, resigned (with little prior notice) to head the Government-owned Kuru Kuru Cooperative College, at a time when Cooperative Socialism was the country's official ideology. (Henry Jeffrey later became a Minister for about twenty years in the post 1992 PPP Government). Prem Misir was dogged in his research and, a couple of decades later, became the Pro Chancellor of the University of Guyana, and Director of Public Information in the PPP's Government, among other official positions held.

Fourth, research in the area of Technology Transfer and Technology Development became an important activity and was funded by Canada's International Development and Research Centre (IDRC). As Director of IDS, I initiated that particular research programme and sought the collaboration of UWI. About a dozen monographs relating to various sectors and themes came out of the programme. For example, I co-authored a UWI publication with Owen Arthur (who later became a three term Prime Minister of Barbados) entitled '*Commercialisation of Technology and Underdevelopment*'. Following the success of this technology research programme, the IDRC was approached by me in the late 1970s for funding in another subject area, this time dealing with the Developmental Role of State Enterprises, in keeping with the ideological tendencies in certain Caribbean countries at that time. (Another reason is that I had acquired an interest in the subject area having had an article of mine entitled *'Conflicting Attitudes Towards Public Enterprises: The Commonwealth Caribbean'* published in Lok Udyog, Monthly Journal of the Bureau of Public Enterprises and the Public Sector, India, Vol.1X, No. 6, Sept., 1975). The research output from this Caribbean public enterprises project was again considerable. For example, I produced a monograph entitled *'State-Owned Enterprises and the Development of a Technological Capability'*.

Fifth, research on Transnational Corporations (TNCs) was a popular subject area, partly because foreign multinational companies accounted for a significant proportion of national activity in both the real and financial sectors in Guyana, as in the rest of the Caribbean and many other developing countries. In this regard, I produced two monographs, one entitled *'MNCs in the Caribbean'* and another, entitled *'Expropriations on a World Scale'*. For the latter Study, I decided to pay a data collection trip to Africa and, on the way there, I made a stopover in New York to see what data existed in the archives of the United Nations Centre on Transnational Corporations (UNCTC). In doing so, I made known to one Sylvanus Tiewul the work that I had done on TNCs.in the Caribbean and he asked me to do a Study for the UNCTC elaborating on certain peculiar characteristics of the operations of TNCs. I accordingly produced a Report in March 1980, entitled *'Structural Practices of Transnational Corporations in Selected Economies'*. The beginning of the Preface could very well have been written today, as some of the problems remain endemic, and read as follows:

> *Although there has been in recent years a great deal of discussion about the need for a New International Economic Order, concrete information on the actual operations of the transnational (a key institution in any new restructuring) is not readily available. The transnationals, themselves tend to publish only global figures for obvious reasons, and the host governments, saddled with archaic disclosure laws and excessive fears of transnational reprisal and/ or non-cooperation do not publish disaggregated data on the activities of individual corporations; the most that the researcher can hope for is aggregated sectoral information under some such broad heading as "foreign companies" and only when the individual firms cannot be easily identified. This not only makes*

the ferreting out task of the investigator particularly difficult but, also, causes there to be wide variations between countries in the quality of data coverage in any comparative research exercise.

Ideally, governments (who frequently pay lip service to the need for foreign companies to be 'better corporate citizens') should not only make as much information as possible on the transnationals available to researchers but should also exchange as much of this information among themselves so as to acquire a clearer understanding of the workings of the transnationals, perceive where the national operation fits into the latter's global strategy, and learn from the policy experiences of others in trying to cope with, and partially counteract, the socially adverse practices of the various corporations. As it is, the ignorance is so great that very few host countries can even claim "most favoured nation" treatment in their bargaining with the transnationals. However, the transnationals are frequently in a position to demand "most favoured company" status. The underdeveloped countries are their own worst enemies.

Lo and behold, a couple of months later, I received a long telex from UNCTC offering me a job at the Professional P5 level (Principal Officer). This offer, made late June 1980, came as a real surprise, since I had not for a moment thought of seeking employment at the United Nations. Tiewul had obviously recommended me to his supervising Director (a Peruvian) and the Assistant Secretary-General (a Finn) without even finding out whether I was available. Coincidentally, I was planning to go on sabbatical leave later in the year and so I decided, without too much hesitation, that UNCTC should be the location.

There is an interesting foot note to the abovementioned trip to Africa. In Zambia, the Guyanese Ambassador, Cedric Joseph, had asked his chauffeur to take me to the airport at the end of my research visit. On the way, I asked the chauffeur to drive by a certain building, a discovered hideout of Mugabe/Nkomo guerrillas across the border from Southern

Rhodesia that Ian Smith's army had bombed. When we arrived at the building, I took out my camera and, as I was about to take a photograph, I noticed through the viewer an AK 47 pointing straight at me. I froze. Fortunately, the chauffeur was able to explain the situation and dispel any fears of my being a spy of Ian Smith. (Little did I know that, about a dozen years later, I would be involved in another frightening incident, this time on a UN technical assistance mission in Tashkent, Uzbekistan where, out sightseeing, I was accosted by soldiers for attempting to take a picture of a military parade).

On the plane to London, en route to Guyana, things became equally interesting, but for more pleasant reasons. At about 2.00am on the overnight flight to London, I found myself still awake, perhaps because the AK 47 near miss was still on my mind, and requested the air hostess to tell the Captain that I would like to spend a little time in the cockpit (The Captain had hours earlier made such an offer to anyone finding difficulty in sleeping but there had been no takers). The Captain agreed and I found myself strapped into the "jump seat" of the jumbo jet for the next couple of hours until the plane made an unscheduled stop in Rome to refuel, because it had been battling serious head winds and using up more fuel than expected. During the entire period, the Captain took the trouble to explain to me what actions and related manoeuvres were being conducted in the cockpit. What an experience, which would not be possible in today's terrorism fearful world.

CHAPTER FOUR

ENLIGHTENING UNITED NATIONS (1980-1997)

PHYSICAL AND EMOTIONAL DISLOCATION

I planned to leave Guyana on 23 October, 1980 to take up the job at the United Nations Centre on Transnational Corporations (UNCTC) in New York. Since my wife, Margaret, had died four months earlier, I made arrangements for my two children, Ronnie and Akanni (seventeen and ten years old, respectively) to stay at the residence of my sister, Norma, during my expected one year absence in New York. Both Ronnie and Akanni were attending the premier boy's school, Queen's College, and I did not want to interrupt their education, unnecessarily. Moreover, Ronnie was a champion high school athlete. However, Norma found relating to Ronnie increasingly difficult, and so my elder brother, Stanley, later took on the responsibility of accommodating the children.

Meanwhile, I was also finding settling-in not very easy. After a brief stay in a rather expensive hotel, a Guyanese, Ms Hazel Scott, who was working at the UNDP headquarters in New York, kindly offered me a room in her Manhattan apartment. I was keen to find my own apartment, but rent in New York City was rather prohibitive. Fortunately, job facilitator, Sylvanus Tiewul, had moved to the suburbs, but had retained the lease on his strategically located Manhattan apartment (Waterside Plaza) and I duly persuaded him to let me sub-let (without building management's knowledge) his apartment.

With Christmas approaching, I arranged for my two sons to spend their school vacation with me in New York. We were invited to Christmas day lunch in Brooklyn at my deceased wife's sister, who had also invited her visiting parents from Guyana; it was a severe winter's day. As we exited my apartment, Akanni visibly and audibly shivered when he experienced a cold blast of wind, even though I thought I had provided him with sufficiently warm clothing; I felt for him. The day was quite relaxing, and everyone was glad to see the children, but I detected a certain lack of real warmth towards me. I was to find out later that they thought I had not paid enough attention to my wife, both before and during her month long hospitalisation. I found such erroneous beliefs rather upsetting.

Early the next year, I struck up an amorous relationship with one Brenda Do Harris, who was a teacher at the premier girl's high school in Guyana and, having been fired by the Burnham Government for political activism, had migrated a few months before to join her mother in Brooklyn, New York. The relationship was not a smooth one, partly because there was frequently a clash of two strong personalities. Moreover, I had left behind in Guyana a young lady, Valerie Alleyne, with whom I had developed a loving relationship before my departure from Guyana. The situation became more complicated because, before departing, I had promised to invite Valerie to spend time with me in the summer of 1981. I found myself in the ridiculous situation of arranging for her to stay in a UNCTC colleague's nearby vacant apartment, on the pretext that my two sons were in the rather small apartment spending the summer with me. (A couple of months before, I had spent a few days with Valerie in Trinidad and Tobago but did not reveal to her that I was also having a relationship with Brenda, even though she suspected that something was amiss). I eventually confided to Valerie while transporting her to the airport that our relationship was over and she was utterly devastated. It was also heart breaking on my part to see her so unhappy. In hindsight, it was a bad decision.

My children, Akanni in particular, were not happy with the thought of returning to Guyana. Therefore, I had to find a university for Ronnie and a high school for Akanni. Ronnie wanted to go to any college that was well known for its athletic programme but, after consultation with my friends as to the value of such an education, I persuaded him, with some difficulty, that he should pursue entry to a more academically acclaimed college and that I could afford same, with the help of the traditional UN education grant. Ronnie failed to gain entry into Columbia University and somehow found himself in Adelphi University. But when I realised how lowly rated academically Adelphi was, I pulled Ronnie out after a couple of weeks and gained entry for him in New York University. For his part, Akanni gained entry into the UN School in New York City.

Soon after, Brenda took up residence in the apartment with me, but things slowly began to dis-integrate. Quarrels between myself and Brenda occurred more frequently. In addition, Ronnie, who had been quite attached to his mother, Margaret, began to show his displeasure at Brenda's presence. The small size of the apartment did not help the situation.

In 1982, the sub-letting was exposed and I reluctantly moved from Waterside Plaza to a bigger apartment in what was called Gateway Plaza, a newly constructed residential tower opposite the World Trade Center (WTC) that was a few miles further away from the UN headquarters. But greater living space did not make any difference to the tension at home. I was due to participate (in my private, rather than UN, capacity) as a lecturer in an International Development Research Centre (IDRC) financed Technology Transfer Training Workshop in West Africa and, before departing, begged Brenda to stay out of Ronnie's way. On return, I was told of serious conflict between Ronnie and Brenda that obtained while I was away. I immediately decided that the two had to be physically separated. Ronnie was persuaded to take up residence with his aunt in Brooklyn and I proceeded to continue financing his education, in addition to giving him a monthly stipend for his general upkeep and miscellaneous expenses. But my relationship with Brenda did not significantly improve. Nevertheless, we were married a few months later.

In 1984, Brenda and I bought a house in Elmont, Long Island, New York. This meant that Akanni had to travel a considerable distance to get to the UN School, but we thought it made financial sense to be a home owner, rather than renting an apartment. This was my introduction to the racial intricacies of housing separation in the USA. Ronnie helped with the physical moving-in but, thereafter, I would only see him when he met me at Citibank in Manhattan to collect his monthly stipend. On graduating in 1985, he proceeded to inform me that he was emigrating to England (where he was born). When I enquired "why", he stated that he was still interested in athletics and, being a middle distance runner, he wanted to go to a country that had (at the time) the best middle distance runners. I responded that the quality of the coaching system was more important. I failed to dissuade him from going to London, where he was to be accommodated by my twin sister, Marva.

In 1987, Brenda and I moved from the modest 'starter home' in Long Island to a larger house in White Plains, Westchester, New York State. None of the neighbours (all white) ever spoke to me. When one of the next door neighbours hurriedly moved out, they were replaced by a young Korean family, who were very sociable and proved the exception. One bit of racism (or simple fear) stands out in my memory. A hurricane had struck the Eastern Seashore and had knocked down trees and electric lamp poles. One night, alone in the darkness, Brenda, was endeavouring to walk from the bus stop to her house, but tripped over one of the fallen trees and badly busted up her mouth. She knocked on the nearest door and the white man who peered through an opening in the window curtains merely shrugged his shoulders and walked away.

By now, it was time for Akanni to go to university and I asked him what was his choice of career. He seemed not to have given the matter much thought and so I suggested medicine. He emphatically said no, because, according to him, he felt uneasy handling blood. Wherein, I suggested (as in the case of his brother) economics and business as a fairly useful course of studies when one is not sure of a choice of career. (I regret not having pressed him a bit harder on the subject of a medical career). Akanni proceeded to apply to a number of universities. One of them was Harvard for which he had an interview at an alumni that was living in the far eastern reaches of Long Island. He was unsuccessful and finally settled on the University of Pennsylvania.

Brenda subsequently moved to Maryland, so as to pursue post-graduate studies in Washington, DC at Howard University, whose staff she later joined. To see each other, there was need to engage in a strenuous commute of 220 odd miles each way by either car or train. The marriage was just about holding up. So much so, that, with the death of the fearful autocrat Forbes Burnham in 1985, we could safely contemplate making a trip to Guyana when next I was eligible for 'home leave' entitlement. (Since 1980, I was reluctant to pay a visit to Guyana because, right after Rodney's assassination, I had received an anonymous letter through the post, with a picture of me in the company of someone, who was an obvious intelligence plant, stating that my "balls" will be cut off, etc.). I made the first return trip in 1988 and I was astounded at the decrepit and unpainted nature of the capital city, Georgetown, a product of the decade-long economic depression. We were part of an Odle family reunion.

Soon after the return to the USA, relations with Brenda made a turn for the worse. A few months later, after a quarrel, I walked out of Brenda's Maryland apartment, never to return. She filed for divorce late 1989 and the settlement was eventually completed in 1993; it was not a pleasant experience. During this period, Valerie and I had renewed acquaintances and this helped me to maintain my sanity.

Such was the familial context and stressful situation within which I was operating while employed at the UNCTC in New York for the period 1980 to 1993, after which I was stationed at the United Nations Conference on Trade and Development (UNCTAD) in Geneva, Switzerland. It must have had an adverse effect on my professional performance (not to mention the impact on my two children) even though I was promoted to one of the Director positions.

POLICY RESEARCH ON THE OPERATIONS OF TRANSNATIONAL CORPORATIONS

The UNCTC was established in 1977 at a time when developing countries (particularly the newly independent) were engaged in a struggle to derive greater benefits from foreign investment activities in their host countries. Failure on the part of the Transnational Corporations (TNCs) to adequately respond to these wishes for a more equitable relationship was invariably forcing the developing countries to take more drastic action. This was the case in Chile, where The Salvador Allende Government threatened to nationalise the branch operations of the International Telephone and Telegraph (ITT) Company and, to counter, there was a CIA inspired coup that resulted in the death of the President. In the words of the USA Secretary of State, Henry Kissinger, the USA was "saving Chile from itself". A military dictatorship was established. Most countries (particularly the developing ones) were livid and, as a result, the United Nations decided to set up a New York based agency to deal with the workings and impact of transnational corporations.

I was recruited in 1980 to be a member of UNCTC's Research Division. Professionals in this Division were about 20 strong (with the Technical Assistance Division having a similar number of staff). About half of the staff were from the developing countries, but the Assistant Secretary-Generals, from the inception to the time of the agency's incorporation into UNCTAD, was from the developed (Western) world – Klaus Saghren – from Finland, Sidney Dell from Britain and Peter Hansen from Denmark. This may have given the agency a conservative bent.

I soon came to this realisation. Within a few months in the job, in reviewing a draft monograph on Transnational Banks (TNBs) for which I was the responsible officer, ASG Saghren found problems with the analytical nature of the document, destined for publication, and, for example, accused me of using, in his own words, a "militaristic term such as strategy" in describing the TNB's approach to profit maximisation. On another occasion, in introducing the newly-appointed

UN Secretary-General, Javier Perez de Cuellar, to individual members of UNCTC staff, Saghren, rather disparagingly, referred to me as an "egg-head". In the early years, I continued to be frustrated with the extent to which UNCTC analyses strove, in the crafting of conclusions and policy recommendations in their monographs and working papers, to be supposedly 'even handed', in pursuit of the declared mission of making foreign investment more development-oriented and less non-equitable in the distribution of benefits. I was experiencing an ideological clash between the emerging radical Third World economic tradition and the more conservative UN approach that was pursued, also, by Directors Kawamura of Japan and, to a lesser extent, Diogo de Gaspar of Brazil. Some balance was restored when Pedro Malan (who, years later, became Brazil's Minister of Finance under the Fernando Cardoso Government) became the Director responsible for policy analysis and research.

Some of the policy analysis and research projects in which I was directly involved included studies on 'Regulation and Control of Transnational Banks'; 'External Lending of Transnational Banks to Developing Countries'; 'Transnational Corporations and Technology Transfer'; and 'Technology Relations between State-owned Enterprises'.

As a result of its policy and research activities, the UNCTC made an enormous contribution towards the understanding of the phenomenon of Transnational Corporations. Besides amassing and assembling a tremendous amount of data and information on TNCs, the UNCTC's conceptual innovations are reflected in the use, and popularisation in the literature, of such analytical terms as: home and host countries; inward and outward investment; South-South investment; intra-firm and arms-length investment; and new forms (non-equity) of investment. But, conceptually, the most far reaching was the 'eclectic theory of production' espoused by the UNCTC consultant, John Dunning, who showed that, for the role of TNCs in the world economy to be understood, dimensions such as ownership, location and internalisation advantages need to be taken into account, in addition to technological innovation and related business strategies. This theorising concerning the complex interaction among TNCs and their affiliates and between TNCs and local suppliers ("spaghetti bowl effect") was an important forerunner to the understanding of today's 'global supply chain' phenomenon.

UNCTC's flagship publication in the early years was a periodical study of *'Transnational Corporations in World Development: Trends and Issues'*. This document, rich in data and analysis, benefitted from the inputs of both staff members and outside consultants. (One of the consultants who I recommended, my old university colleague, Norman Girvan, spent a year as an in-house advisor for the Third Survey in 1983). I was responsible, along with the Assistant Secretary-General, for reviewing drafts of Chapters for the publication. It was a very stimulating and satisfying experience and the document made a genuine contribution to knowledge. Mainly, as a result of the drive and initiative of my colleague, Karl Sauvant, the publication (later called 'World Investment Report') was annualised in 1991, partly because the rapid pace of internationalisation of economies (later termed globalisation by UNCTC and others) required more regular and intensive treatment. The focal themes for each of the years 1991 to my retirement in 1997 were 'The Triad in Foreign Direct Investment'; Transnational Corporations as Engines of Growth'; 'Transnational Corporations and Integrated International Production; 'Transnational Corporations, Employment and the Workplace; 'Transnational Corporations and Competitiveness'; 'Investment, Trade and International Policy Arrangements; and 'Transnational Corporations, Market Structure and Competition Policy'.

A publication, called 'CTC Reporter', was also morphed into a Journal called 'Transnational Corporations'. In Volume 2, Number 2, August 1993, is an Article by Maurice Odle entitled, *'Foreign Investment as Part of the Privatisation Process'*. Partly fuelling the globalisation process was the Washington Consensus inspired privatisation in developing countries (and in post-Soviet emerging economies) of state-owned enterprises, in which TNCs found useful opportunities for investment and re-investment.

However, when the still rather conservative UNCTC was absorbed into UNCTAD in 1993, there arose something of an ideological clash. Most of my colleagues felt that the real intention of the absorption, that was enthusiastically promoted by the West, was to get rid of UNCTC altogether, since the institution was damaging the interests of the TNCs. The official rationale for the insertion into UNCTAD was, firstly, an economising one and, secondly, that there was a nexus between investment (which subject area was dealt with by UNCTC) and trade (which was handled by UNCTAD). But, ever since the 1960s impact of Argentinian Raoul Prebish, UNCTAD's Secretary-General at the time, and his import substituting strategy for economic development, that institution had developed a radical position on transformation issues, as reflected in their annual flagship 'Trade and Development' publication. UNCTAD had also adopted a critical approach to the developmental and stabilising role of the International Financial Institutions and, also, the international private capital market system. Tension among staff members, therefore, arose between the two conflicting approaches to policy research in the one institution and strenuous efforts were made to satisfactorily resolve the matter.

In this regard, I also saw it fit to maintain contact with other economic and social agencies of the UN, so as to enhance my understanding of the roles of that unique organisation and broaden my world view. Accordingly, at various times, I was a Member of UNESCO Expert Group on Higher Education (1984); Member of UNDP (TCDC) Expert Group on South-South Cooperation on Trade, Investment and Finance (1996); and Member of UNIDO Expert Group on Alliance for Africa's Industrialisation (1997).

During my period as a UN official, I also tried to maintain contact with academia and related activities. For example, I participated in a 'Third World Economists Conference' that was held in Havana, Cuba, in 1981 and which was hosted by Fidel Castro, who delivered a rousing opening address and hosted the participants at an evening reception. A couple of days later, I was one of Castro's guests on the reviewing stand at the very impressive May Day military parade. I also accepted speaking engagements on the role and impact of TNCs at tertiary institutions in the New York area, including New York University and Columbia University and, also, City University where a joint presentation was made of a paper by Norman Girvan and myself, entitled *'The Role of Transnational Corporations in the Economies of Caribbean Countries'*.

But the greatest involvement, while at the UN, was with the Caribbean universities. Before arriving at the UN, I had provided External Examiner services to UWI in the subject areas of Public Policy – MSc (1977-80); Caribbean Economic Problems (1971-1980); and Public Finance – BSc and MSc (1971-1980). I therefore continued to do so while at the UN, as follows: Development Economics – MSc (1980-1985); Economic Theory (1985-1986); Economics of Technology Policy (1985-1991); Caribbean Economic Problems (1986-1991); Industrial Planning (1988-1991); Social Security Economics – MSc (1992-1994); and Economic Development – MSc (1994-1996). I was also sought an opinion with respect to PhD theses in the areas of Monetary Economics and Public Finance. In keeping with my abovementioned keen interest in technology transfer and development, I also presented a Paper on *'The Caribbean Experience re Technology Contracting'* at a Workshop on Strategies for Technology Transfer and Development in the Caribbean that was held in Kingston, Jamaica in 1986. In the case of UG, I was the External Examiner for the course on Public Enterprises. In addition, I maintained an interest in the Caribbean Regional Monetary Studies Programme and, besides making the Adlith Brown Memorial Address in Saint Kitts and Nevis in 1986, presented a paper at the Annual Monetary Studies Conference (that has existed since 1968) that was held in Belize, entitled *'Privatisation and the International Experience: The Foreign Investment Dimension'* and another at the 1998 Annual Conference in The Bahamas, entitled *'Banking, Finance and Caribbean Development'*.

ENLIGHTENING UNITED NATIONS (1980-1997)

Maurice Odle (back row, ninth from right), Compton Bourne, Gobin Ganga and other stalwarts at a typical annual Monetary Studies Conference

TECHNICAL ASSISTANCE TO HOST COUNTRIES

My shift in 1986 from an emphasis on research to a focus on technical assistance was as a result of a promotion. Sam Asante, a Lawyer and Senior UNCTC Director from Ghana, became my new immediate boss. A major area of technical assistance related to assisting host countries in formulating appropriate policies, legislation and regulations; negotiating mutually beneficial contracts and agreements; and training government and other local officials in know-how related to the abovementioned issues. In this regard, since joint venture arrangements are important, there was, also, a spin-off entrepreneurship training programme called EMPRETEC. A second technical assistance area related to the formulation of a framework and draft text for United Nations Member States' negotiation of an International Code of Conduct on Transnational Corporations.

With respect to traditional technical assistance on TNCs, the legislation programme of activities included drafting and/or giving advice on basic legislative structure and critical safeguard clauses in contracts, as well as an appropriate risk/reward strategy relating to incentives. The natural resource sector was the most frequent recipient of such assistance.

For contracts and agreements, the focus of advice was on avoiding the adverse tax revenue effects of transfer pricing, relating to both wholly-owned and joint venture activities involving the State. Concerning natural resource projects, another concern was the tendency of the foreign investor to employ a high rate of capitalisation and debt to equity gearing ratio, where there was tax minimisation opportunity, and to cite high interest rates on borrowing from affiliate companies. Services contracts, such as hotel agreements, also required scrutiny, since TNCs avoided the costly and risky area of construction and ownership. Instead, they concentrated on the non-equity aspect of fees for use of their brand name and provision of management, purchasing and marketing services related to running a hotel.

During my seventeen years in the UN System, many dozens of advisory projects were executed, some of which involved my direct participation. For example, in 1992 the UNCTC and the Association of Southeast Asian Nations (ASEAN) Committee on Finance and Banking jointly published a 336-page monograph on *'Modern Management and Supervision of Financial Institutions'* in which there was an overview by editors Maurice Odle, Jacinto de Vera and Kovit Poshyananda, entitled *'Overview and Update on Recent Developments: Modern Management and Supervision of Financial Institutions'*. The concluding paragraph of that Overview contains words that are prescient to the financial crisis that was to occur a decade-and-a-half later:

> *For financial institutions, self-regulation is necessary but not sufficient. Managers do not always maintain the fine balance between prudence and profits. While managers are interested in safe and sound practices that safeguard the funds deposited with them, the profit maximisation objective, along with changing economic circumstances, are continuously propelling them, especially in the new climate of financial liberalisation, in pursuit of innovative ways for satisfying the needs of their clients. But new instruments and practices bring new opportunities for finding loopholes in what remains in the regulatory system and new temptations for indulging in speculation and excessive risk taking. The supervisory authorities are continuously playing "catch-up" for want of an adequate monitoring system.*

In 1993, one of the many UNCTC advisory projects in progress related to a request from the newly elected President of Guyana, Cheddi Jagan, for me to conduct a UNCTC review of certain important natural resource projects that the previous Government had initiated, one of which was a majority-owned Canadian gold mining venture involving Cambior Inc (60%); Golden Star Resources (35%); and the Government (5%). The UNCTC review members were staff members Maurice Odle (Team

Leader) Rory Alan, and John Gara, along with Carney Johnson of Horizon Group Inc. The Team found that the Mining Agreement was tilted in favour of the foreign investors, partly because the depressing state of the economy at the time had reduced the Government bargaining powers, and included a high gearing ratio clause that allowed the foreign partner to contract very high interest loans, (most likely from an affiliate) thus minimising government tax revenue. Lessons are not easily learnt, since such a clause is repeated in the current petroleum contract with Exxon partners.

In this regard, UNCTC had published in 1987 an advisory study on 'Natural Gas Clauses in Petroleum Arrangements' and UNCTAD, in May 1995, had published a monograph, "under the direction of Mr Maurice Odle", entitled *'Comparative Analysis of Petroleum Exploration Contracts'*, at a time when advisory work in this important subject area was not very fashionable. (By 1993, I was working at UNCTAD in Geneva, because UNCTC's mandate and related operations had been incorporated in 1993 into the former institution).

Besides advisory projects, national and regional training workshops were a very important feature of the technical assistance programme in the 1980s. One that is worth mentioning, because of the nostalgia associated with it, occurred as far back as June,1988. I had been arrested in London for protesting the November 1965 Unilateral Declaration of Independence (UDI) of Ian Smith and, since then, was keen to see what the country Zimbabwe (formerly South Rhodesia) looked like. The opportunity came when I led a mission there as a UN official in June, 1988. As I was about to present my written "Opening Remarks" at a UNCTC organised African Regional Technology Workshop in Harare, I made an unscripted comment about the November 1965 arrest and, according to my then wife, Brenda, who had accompanied me, the stir and whispering among the whites in the audience suggested that I was not very welcomed and that they were still unhappy about regime change. What I did later observe, on a guided tour around the capital, was the vast developmental difference between the neighbourhoods of the whites (who were 5% of the population but owned 70 percent of the country's arable land) and those of the black community. (Every white home seemed to have a swimming pool). On recent re-reading of my speech, I am surprised how devoid it is of polemics, in the circumstances:

> *On behalf of the United Nations Centre on Transnational Corporations, let me straightaway thank the Government of Zimbabwe for so graciously agreeing to host this regional workshop and for providing such excellent conference facilities.*
>
> *The decision to make new technologies the focus of this workshop on technology transfer could hardly have been more appropriate. According to many analysts the series of recent changes in production and organisation, based on new technological advances in microelectronics, genetic-engineering, materials science and factory management amount to a veritable Third Industrial Revolution. The purpose of this workshop, then, is not only to sensitise the countries of Africa to the importance of these technological changes but also, to examine what policy changes are necessary in order to more rapidly and effectively absorb these new frontline technologies into the production process in those industries which are vital for the transformation of Africa. However, the task will not be an easy one. A couple of weeks ago, May 22 to be exact, there was an article in the Sunday New York Times by the President of the Overseas Development Council, which stated that most developing countries (except those in East Asia, India and parts of Latin America) will gain little from the new technologies because of (1) a lack of highly trained scientists and engineers, (2) a lack of access to financial capital markets that could provide investible funds for these new technologies, (3) a lack of foreign exchange due to declining revenue from exports of raw materials, and (4) the new technologies are labour displacing and would aggravate an already acute unemployment problem. Our challenge, Mr*

Chairman, is to prove the President of the Overseas Development Council and other doubting Thomases wrong.

Nevertheless, there is no denying that the technological and industrial gaps are increasing both between African and the developed countries and between Africa and other developing countries. This crisis in development is the basic reason for the launching of the United Nations Programme of Action for African Economic Recovery and Development. This Programme of Action involves all the key United Nations agencies and encompasses a broad range of activities.

Mr Chairman,
This workshop in Harare can be seen as just another contribution to the Programme of Action in the area of technology policy, but with specific references to transnational corporations. It is a follow-up to other assistance that our Centre has recently rendered to African countries in the area of technology policy, including advisory projects in Kenya and Ivory Coast, national workshops in Nigeria and regional workshops in Sierra Leone and Senegal. But technology is only one, albeit important, area in which the Centre provides technical assistance to developing countries in Africa and other continents. For example, during 1987 the Centre provided technical assistance in 40 advisory, information and training projects in 21 African countries covering such subject areas as revision of policies, laws and regulations towards foreign investment, streamlining the investment approval machinery and assisting governments in negotiating deals in specific sectors and industries. These activities will be intensified during 1988 and subsequent years as part of the Centre's contribution to the African Recovery Programme. Enough about the Centre for the moment, but an opportunity will be taken during this workshop to give a more comprehensive briefing on the nature of the Centre's activities so that more effective use can be made of same.

Mr Chairman,

The new technologies are not widely available and so far only readily accessed by the process of investment by transnational corporations. However, Africa faces a dilemma in that the level of foreign direct investment in the last decade has been low not only in traditional sectors but, also, in those industries in which the rate of technological progress has been fastest. As part of the African Recovery Programme, our Centre was asked by the Intergovernmental Commission on Transnational Corporations to prepare a report by the end of July this year on ways and means of increasing foreign direct investment in Africa. Last week I was also in Addis attending a meeting of a United Nations task force which discussed this capital resources crisis and other matters related to the African Recovery Programme. But despite all the domestic and international efforts, the prognosis is not very good and so it is incumbent on a workshop like this to devise policies for not only making the transfer of new technologies more effective when transnational corporations are involved but also to map out a non-equity related strategy for acquiring and absorbing such technologies even when foreign direct investment is not involved.

In seeking solutions to this problem, we fortunately have a faculty of workshop lecturers that is up to the task. During the course of the next two weeks we are going to be exposed to international and regional experts who have vast knowledge of these new technological developments and who will engage us in a no doubt stimulating discussion of ways in which these technologies can be applied to the particular circumstances of the African economies and to those critical sectors that are the key to any meaningful recovery effort. We are thankful that they took time off from their very busy schedules to make the long trek to Zimbabwe for this workshop.

We are also grateful to have as participants at this workshop not only important host country technicians and officials from some sister UN agencies but, also, high level representatives from at least 14 other African countries who can bring their own peculiar country experiences to bear on the deliberations. We hope that this interchange and interaction will enrich the workshop experience and will give rise to firm recommendations for an effective acquisition strategy and regional co-operation with respect to the new technologies and the key production sector.

Finally, I once again wish to thank the Government of Zimbabwe for hosting this workshop and for the hard work put in by the Ministry of Industry and Technology officials in making various logistical arrangements, including those relating to certain field trips.

In the 1990s, there was a continuation of the workshop programme, with the organisers operating from the new Geneva location. For example, on 24-27 June 1996, there was an 'International Conference on Reviving Private Investment in Africa: Partnerships for Growth and Development' at which I presented a Paper on *'Foreign Investment Opportunities in Africa'*. The Workshop was memorable for more reasons than one. I took the opportunity (accompanied by my newly-wed, Valerie) to pay a visit to the Dutch-built 'Elmina Castle', a major holding station for captured would-be slaves embarking on the horrendous cross Atlantic journey. It was a very sad and sobering visit and a reminder of the pertinence and incisiveness of Eric Williams' book, *'Capitalism and Slavery'* and how unjust the system continues to be. Three months later, on 23-25 September, I organised a 'Training Workshop for ASEAN Investment Policy Making Officials on International Investment Scenario and International Business Practices' (sponsored by the ASEAN Secretariat, in cooperation with UNCTAD and supported by the Philippine Board of Investment). I presented a Paper on *'ASEAN's Place in Global Foreign Investment Trends'*. During this training workshop, I was presented with an Award by the Philippine Government.

Maurice Odle, lecturers and participants at a memorable ASEAN Investment Policy Workshop, Manila, Philippines, 1996

This ASEAN Workshop (and the abovementioned Ghana workshop) signalled a significant change in sentiment against emphasis on careful scrutiny of the operations of TNCs and, instead, a greater focus on attracting increased flows of foreign investment, in order to enhance economic growth prospects, in keeping with neo-liberal economic thought and the "Washington Consensus". Accordingly, a decision was made to pivot more towards investment promotion activities. The Division on Investment, Technology and Enterprise Development in UNCTAD (now made up of transferred UNCTC colleagues) initiated the creation of Regional Investment Promotion Associations as part of my founding of the World Association of Investment Promotion Agencies (WAIPA) relating to which John Gara and Paul Wessendorp also played an important role) and conferences were held annually to exchange information and best practice ideas about effective investment promotion.

With assistance from the South African branch of the International Chamber of Commerce, I subsequently led the UNCTC organisation to an international and continent-wide conference, of over 500 participants,

At a moving ASEAN Award Ceremony, Manila, Philippines, 1996

called 'Africa Connect", in Johannesburg, South Africa (co-hosted by the South African Chamber of Commerce) during 2-4 May 1996, in which there was a very significant TNC presence on every sectoral panel, and a great deal of networking and project initiating also took place. Other participants included national investment promotion agencies. My optimistic opening remarks, as Conference Director, were justified by the obviously successful nature of the Conference. On the last day of the Conference, there was a "Johannesburg Declaration" and Communiqué, which suggested that the experience was a defining moment in the investment climate in Africa and investment flows began to gradually rise so that, in association with other determining factors, average growth rates began to approach the 5% rate it is today. The Conference was destined to be my last major activity at UNCTAD, as retirement beckoned.

But not before the UNCTAD Secretary-General had one last request to make of me. "Africa Connect" had been such an exciting event, that he wanted to know what follow-up developments were likely to follow. A few months later, I was invited by UNCTAD to make a presentation at one of their annual Meetings, and when I arrived in Geneva on 25 September, I promptly sent him the following missive:

Dear Mr Ricupero,
On the eve of my departure from Geneva on retirement, you had asked me to send you a note, after I had settled into my new job in Guyana, on ways and means in which WAIPA could make a contribution to realisation of the Midrand concept of a "Partnership for Growth and Development". Having come to Geneva to participate in the Expert Meeting on 'Investment Promotion and Development Objectives', I thought that I should not leave without letting you have such a note, as attached.

"The Midrand Declaration indicates that partnership involves more than cooperation between countries and their IPAs. It also involves a "dialogue and common action between Governments

and civil society (and) partnerships between the public and private sector..." (Midrand Declaration. P.4). Civil society can probably include representatives of labour, consumer organisations and other NGOs. Such a tripartite partnership (involving government, business and the civil society) recognises that development needs to involve all these stakeholders in order for economic growth not only to be effectively pursued but, also, for bringing about a more equitable and sustainable existence.

The purpose of the dialogue would be to enhance the greater good of all by maximising the benefits in areas of common interest and minimising any negative effects in areas of potential conflict. The composition of the dialogue partners suggests that the objective will be maximisation of the public welfare, via benefits from foreign capital, rather than the maximisation of foreign investment inflows, per se.

Certain issues may be of particular concern to each tripartite constituency. For example, governments may be keen to include in the agenda for dialogue the issue of the harmonisation of fiscal and financial incentives to reduce the tendency towards bidding wars, which have adverse consequences for budgetary revenue. Two other issues that might be of considerable interest to governments include the transfer of technology and development. On the one hand, the foreign business community may have a special interest in the issue of the right of establishment and the length and complexity of the investment approval process, while local firms and their representative business associations may be especially interested in the issue of the development of meaningful joint venture arrangements with foreign capital. Civil society would also have an agenda. For example, labour may want to initiate a dialogue on training and skill development and, also, employment maximisation, whereas general welfare and poverty issues, particularly in this era of competitiveness, might be of concern to consumer associations and other NGOs.

The fora for the dialogue can take certain forms. First, UNCTAD's annual <u>international</u> Expert Group Meeting, timed to deliberately coincide with Annual Conference of WAIPA, can be one occasion at which formal dialogue can take place. Second, the meetings of the <u>Regional</u> Chapters of WAIPA in their particular regional locations can be another occasion for dialogue if there can be inclusion of such an item in their agenda proceedings. Third, an attempt should be made to encourage existing <u>sub-regional</u> economic integration groupings (e.g. Asean, Mercosur, SADCC) to include a business forum (in collaboration with UNCTAD, WAIPA and possibly others) in their annual summit activities. This would be appropriate given the nexus between trade and investment.

Since UNIDO and MIGA (World Bank) have been strengthening their involvement as support agencies of WAIPA, it would be appropriate if those agencies could also have as a standing agenda item or parallel event, (in the form of either a business forum or round table) the convening of an annual Pro-Invest Dialogue.

The above-mentioned fora are neither mutually exclusive nor exhaustive and can be effectively used to synergistically complement one other as instruments of investment partnership and business development.

The technical assistance experience at the United Nations was a very exciting one. Besides the satisfaction of rendering directly tangible assistance in a subject area of vital importance for development purposes, it gave me the opportunity of meeting many leaders and high level government officials and employees in a variety of locations and cultural settings. (This complemented the experience of working in New York and Geneva with colleagues from almost every conceivable part of the world). The technical assistance programme involved very many dozens of missions (some extra-budgetary financed). The countries to which I personally led an advisory mission, in some cases more than one such

At a Transfer of Technology Workshop in Kenya, Africa, with expert Constantine Vaitsos (second from right) and others, 1990

mission, included Antigua and Barbuda, China, Colombia, Egypt, Ethiopia, Ghana, Guyana, Indonesia, Ivory Coast, Jamaica, Kenya, Malaysia, Namibia, Philippines, Saint Kitts and Nevis, South Africa, Thailand, Uzbekistan and Zimbabwe.

Perhaps the most memorable technical assistance project was that concerning South Africa. Since the decision was made that sanctions, including divestment and disinvestment, had to be imposed on the South Africa apartheid regime, UNCTC had been engaged in writing an annual report on the effectiveness of such sanctions. One year after Nelson Mandela was released from political prison in 1990, the African National Congress (ANC) sent a communication to the UN Secretary-General requesting that a mission be sent to South Africa for discussion of a plan of action with respect to how TNCs operating in South Africa could be made to better serve the interests of the masses, including the formation of joint ventures with local partners, particularly black entrepreneurs. The Secretary-General duly consulted with the Assistant Secretary-General heading UNCTC and I was selected to lead such a mission. Intensive preparations immediately began to take place. When the white authorities in the capital, Pretoria, heard of the plans for such

Interacting with Chinese hosts at a massive telecommunications complex under construction in Shanghai, 1990

a mission, they immediately telephoned me in New York seeking details and requested that I find time during the course of the ANC-focused mission, to have audience with them. Two experts accompanied me on the mission in 1992, one of whom was an in-house UNCTC consultant named Roland Brown, a British lawyer with wide developing country policy experience. The day after arrival in Johannesburg, we met in Mandela's office and discussed the purpose and objectives in general terms, including certain political logistics. What struck me most is how charming a person Mandela was and how relaxed he seemed for someone who had spent twenty-seven and-a-half years in prison.

The next day, the Pretoria Government duly sent a driver to pick up Roland Brown and myself at our Johannesburg hotel. When we arrived at Government headquarters in Pretoria, we were ushered into a small conference room where a number of high level officials were seated awaiting the arrival of their Minister. When he did arrive, he walked by me and greeted Roland Brown, more than six feet further away with the words: *"Good Day, Mr Odle, I am very pleased to see you"*. Roland Brown calmly pointed in my direction and said *"this is Mr Odle, Head*

Economic Policy Strategy Session with Nelson Mandela in 1991

of Mission". The embarrassed white South African could not have imagined that the New York based senior official he had spoken to, a few days earlier, was black. It reminded me of a sight I witnessed a year previously at the Johannesburg airport where a German shepherd dog, in the company of a policeman patrolling a corridor, ignored all passers-by until it came upon a black person attempting to go by; the dog responded with a leap and a growl, testing the strength of the restraining policeman. The dog had apparently been trained to recognise blacks as the enemy, as was the South African Minister.

Technical Assistance and the Role of WAIPA

Early Developments

By the beginning of the 1990s, the technical assistance programme of the UNCTC had developed to the stage where over one hundred advisory projects and about 20 training workshops were being conducted annually in developing countries and the transitional economies of Eastern Europe (the Soviet Union having collapsed) and China (post Mao), inter alia. The main type of advisory and training activities tended to relate to the formulation of foreign investment legislation; structuring and negotiation of petroleum and mining contracts; the crafting of appropriate joint venture arrangements; encouraging transfer of technology (both equity and non-equity related) by TNCs; and safeguards against transfer pricing for tax avoidance purposes. Much later in the period, technical assistance related to privatisation also assumed some importance.

The effectiveness of the technical assistance programme was enhanced by existence of a productive parallel UNCTC programme of research. Synergy lay in the fact that the research programme sought to focus on developmental and other spin-off benefits that could be associated with, and coaxed out from, the operations of TNCs, such as inter-sectoral linkages, employment creation, the dissemination of management and marketing skills, and tax revenue generation. Capital was not the only attribute associated with foreign investment flows.

The very large number of countries that sought the technical assistance services is perhaps a testament to the effectiveness of the advice and training rendered by UNCTC. Many technical assistance recipients made repeated requests over the years. Moreover, the host countries most likely took comfort from the existence of the technical assistance programme and became more inclined to opening up their economies to foreign investment. The more beneficial the results from one encounter the greater the disposition to enter into another. A major highlight of the programme was the assistance rendered to China which sought out the UNCTC when it made the decision in the second half of the 1980s to open up its economy to foreign investment inflows. A few dozens of advisory projects and training workshops followed, and today China is the largest recipient of foreign investment and a major supplier of foreign investment, itself. Another highlight worth mentioning is the technical assistance rendered to South Africa when Mandela was released, sanctions against investment in South Africa were relaxed, and the ANC requested UNCTC advice on policies towards TNCs in the new social dispensation.

Evolution to a WAIPA Oriented TA Programme

By the second half of 1993, the traditional programme of technical assistance (TA) was in serious decline, as a result of a constellation of factors. First, a liberal economic paradigm was in the ascendancy and countries were beginning to subject TNC entry to less scrutiny. Second, the 1980s were something of a loss decade, from a GDP growth point of view, for a number of developing countries who had vainly substituted foreign public debt for private equity in their economic transformation efforts. Third, host countries had over the years become more knowledgeable about the workings of TNCs. Fourth, there had been speculation for over a year that UNCTC might be disbanded and this eventually led to a drying-up of the technical assistance funds, which had been donated mainly by the Scandinavian countries. It is at this time that the technical assistance programme, along with the other areas, of the UNCTC organisation (except the suspended Code of Conduct operations) were incorporated under the UNCTAD umbrella.

Lack of funds required a more focused technical assistance programme. And the prevailing international ideological and socio-economic environment dictated that there should be a greater emphasis on the promotion, rather than strict scrutiny, of foreign investment. It is in this context, and as a result of the initiative of the TA Director, Maurice Odle, in cooperation with a Steering Committee of six IPAs from Canada, Ireland, Peru, The Philippines, Poland and Uganda, that there was born a World Association of Investment Promotion Agencies (WAIPA). Over the years, UNCTC had been receiving requests for TA from investment promotion agencies, inter alia, and had been engaging them with respect to both advisory and training projects. The training workshops, in turn, while focusing on issues related as to how to minimise costs and maximise benefits, was also indirectly involved in helping these organisations to improve both their analytical and intelligence capacities. This was reinforced in regional workshops (SADCC; ASEAN; CARICOM, etc.) where information and experiences were exchanged and networking achieved. The process was contributing to a levelling of the playing field vis-à-vis TNCs.

WAIPA was established at an UNCTAD organised Meeting in Geneva attended by the representatives of 59 IPAs in April, 1995. The Meeting agreed that its main objectives should be to share experiences in attracting foreign investment, strengthen mechanisms for the exchange of information, and to network with the international business community. The Meeting also established a Working Group of IPA representatives, under the Chairmanship of Paid Mc Menamin, Managing Director of International Development Ireland Ltd, to develop the Statute and Work Programme of WAIPA. This Working Group, along with co-support agencies UNCTAD and UNIDO agreed on the structures and provisions of the WAIPA statute at its Meeting in the Philippines in October, 1995.

There followed a spate of activity over the next ten years. In 1996, a WAIPA Newsletter called Pro-Invest and an IPA World Directory appeared in print. Other institution building activities included the establishment of a Regional Chapter in Africa and a Regional Chapter in Asia. Later on, Regional Chapters were established in Latin America and the Caribbean and in Eastern and Central Europe. The World Bank's Multilateral Investment Guarantee Agency also became a support agency of WAIPA. Numerous conferences and other activities took place over the years involving the exchange of IPA experiences.

One particular highlight in this early period was the regional conference, held in Johannesburg on 2-4 May 1996, that was called 'Africa Connect: Doing Business in Africa' and which gave birth to the formation of the first Regional Chapter of WAIPA. "Over the course of the three days, approximately 500 African and international participants from firms and business organisations, including national investment promotion agencies, chambers of commerce, manufacturers associations and international economic agencies, supported by ministerial officials and other key Government representatives, exchanged experiences on doing business in Africa in various sectors and industries in the context of improving investment and trade environment, initiated very numerous deals among themselves, and committed themselves to various other proactive measures in order to make Africa 'the dragon of the 21st century'". Johannesburg Declaration: Africa is Ready for Business, United Nations, New York and Geneva, 1996, p.1). This conference is said to have resulted in a spurt of foreign investment in the relatively low income economies of Africa and this momentum has tended to be maintained.

Excerpt from article **"Technical Assistance and the Role of WAIPA"** by Maurice Odle, appearing in 'United Nations Centre on Transnational Corporations: Corporate Conduct and the Public Interest', Edited by Khalil Hamdani and Lorraine Ruffing, Routledge Publishers (Global Institutions Series) 2015

CONTENTIOUS CODE OF CONDUCT

The third area of technical assistance was that relating to a Code of Conduct with respect to TNCs. Efforts at negotiating such a Code began ever since the establishment of UNCTC in the late1970s, but the process was suspended in 1990 and effectively abandoned in 1992. UNCTC was primarily involved in assisting the preparation of a Draft Text for negotiation at international forum meetings between home and host countries. The Text amounted to a set of global rules that were considerably stronger than mere measures relating to corporate social responsibility, and the UNCTC stood ready to assist the developing countries in the negotiation process, where necessary.

From the outset, the intent of representatives of the main home countries appeared to be to water-down the rules. My observation of Meetings of diplomatic and other representatives of the various countries was that the air bristled with Cold War ideological tension and it was interesting to witness the diametrically opposed positions adopted early on by, for example, Western and Eastern Germany. With the collapse of the Soviet Union, the developed Western countries sought the opportunity to not only remove prescriptions encouraging TNC technology transfer but, also, to introduce rules restricting developing countries ability to adopt import substituting measures. Thus arose rules relating to Trade Related Intellectual Property Rights (TRIPS) and Trade Related Investment Measures (TRIMS). There was a permanent stalemate. Globalisation could proceed on the TNC's own terms.

During the lengthy negotiation period, a Code that was supposed to be a constraint on the behaviour of the transnationals was transformed into a Code that contained rights and obligations with respect to both transnationals and host governments, as a result of the hard bargaining of the developed countries. Later on, the balance shifted even more in favour of the transnationals. Eventually, the negotiations process failed, partly because of the increasingly liberalising nature of the global economic environment. The developed countries recognised that they did not need a Code to protect their cross-border investments and exercise global corporate reach, and could do so *via* an even more favourable Bilateral Investment Treaty (BIT) type of instrument. The developing countries did not protest the abandonment of the negotiations too vigorously, partly because of fatigue, and partly because economic exigencies had made them increasingly vulnerable to entrapment to the economic doctrines of the Washington Consensus. (Somewhat more successful, and complementary to the Code's requirements on the disclosure of information, was the effort to formulate International Standards on Accounting and Reporting (ISAR) through an intergovernmental expert group of Government Finance Authorities, Lawyers, Chief Executive Officers (CEOs) and Professional Accountants and Auditors).

The developed country members of the Organisation for Economic Cooperation and Development (OECD) had posited an alternative to the United Nations Code of Conduct, in the form of a 'Multilateral Agreement on Investment' (MAI), but this also eventually foundered. But the Code did have a catalytic effect on similar regulatory/ guideline efforts elsewhere, such as by the International Labour Organisation (ILO).

Nevertheless, UNCTC, and later UNCTAD, continued to provide policy advice and organise training activities, geared towards capacity building in developing countries, so that the latter could effectively participate in international investment rule-making at the bilateral, regional, plurilateral and multilateral levels. Such activities covered the following topics, *inter alia*: admission and establishment; competition; dispute settlement (investor-State); dispute settlement (State-State); employment; environment; fair and equitable treatment; foreign direct investment and development; funds transfer; home country measures; host country operational measures; illicit payments; incentives; investment-related trade measures; modalities and implementation issues; most- favoured-nation-treatment; national treatment; social responsibility; State contracts; taking of property; taxation; transfer of technology; transfer pricing; and transparency.

ASSESSING THE EXPERIENCE

My seventeen years in the service of the United Nations, thirteen in New York and four in Geneva, were both interesting and enlightening. Working with colleagues from so many different countries shattered a lot of the stereotypes that might have been acquired in one's younger days. Since my previous professional experience was essentially that of an academic, as an official at the United Nations I gained significantly better understanding of the real world, greater appreciation of business economics and finance, and enhanced depth of knowledge with respect to global trade and investment relations. As an economist, I learned a lot from colleague lawyers and financial analysts.

The dynamic and ever evolving nature of inter-state activity in which, for example, in one generation, foreign investment-led development could give way to nationalisation and then quickly revert full circle to liberalisation and privatisation (with TNCs playing a prominent role) was indeed a paradigmal eye opener. Above all, I experienced a great amount of satisfaction helping developing and emerging economies acquire an increased capacity for promulgating policy, cum regulatory measures and utilising effective negotiating strategies for dealing with TNCs, towards levelling the playing field.

The UNCTC was the genuine pioneer in the provision of technical assistance on foreign direct investment to developing countries as the World Bank and other agencies were latecomers. In fact, the World Bank only began technical assistance in this area after two ex-UNCTC staff members joined their staff and transferred the technical assistance model. UNCTC was also a front runner to providing advisory and training assistance to China in its opening-up and early dealings with TNCs and I was a lecturer at Shanghai University in July 1992 on TNC issues.

However, despite the increasing capacity for dealing with TNCs to the benefit of the developing countries, at the broader level, the UN economic system, as a whole, has not generated sufficient synergy to effect significant change in global power relations. The world has not

My wife and I with UNCTAD Deputy Secretary General Carlos Fortin and colleagues celebrating successful UNCTAD IX/Africa Connect Conferences, Midrand, South Africa, 1996

become a much better place, but organisations like UNCTC and UNCTAD have continued to carry out their mandate. Since its incorporation into UNCTAD, the UNCTC-type operations partly shifted focus from a concentration on the actors (i.e. TNCs) to activities (investment, technology and skills transfer).

From a personal point of view, the level of social activity in Geneva, Switzerland, also brings back very pleasant memories. Whereas, in New York, at the end of the working day you almost invariably never saw any of your colleagues until the next morning, partly because of the anonymous nature of a large metropolis, the considerable distance between staff residences, and the bustling workaholic culture. In slower moving Geneva, however, there was much more 'after work' and weekend social interaction among staff at their various homes. Valerie, for her part, had to be restrained by me for wanting to entertain guests virtually every quarter. There were also group trips to surrounding cities/towns and countries.

But there is not always a happy ending to revelry, as I was to find out. A German colleague, Joerg Simon, was eager to pay a visit to Mont

Blanc, the highest mountain peak in Europe, and persuaded me to accompany him. On the Saturday before the designated Sunday for making the trip, while in the office working, I began to feel that a bout of flu (accompanied by a sore-throat) was on its way and was tempted to ring Joerg and suggest a postponement, but decided I would spare him the disappointment. I was also hoping that he would have forgotten about the arrangement. However, the next morning, Joerg, with true German precision, arrived at my apartment at the agreed 10.00am time.

It was a very cold winter's day, and we arrived at the top of Mont Blanc, *via* a ski lift. Unfortunately, I did not have enough protective covering around my neck and head. (I should have been wearing the thick woollen winter hat that my Russian colleague, Nikolai Zaitzev, had gifted me after return from one of his trips back home). I spent the next day in bed. My right ear had become swollen and turned black and I was in excruciating pain, that was so constant, I could hardly sleep. The right side of my face became paralysed and the doctors later told me that I was suffering from Bell's palsy. The virus that was in my throat had gravitated to my cold and vulnerable ear *via* the Eustachian canal. I was away from work for about a month, during which time I had comforting visits from my 'wife-to-be'/ 'fiancée, Valerie, and my twin sister, Marva. A few months later, after a rather painful divorce from Brenda, Valerie and I became married at a wedding that was held in Georgetown, Guyana, and she soon after joined me in Geneva. I was very happy to have her with me, since she is a consummate 'social animal' and made my stay in Geneva a very enjoyable one, when I originally had a lot of misgivings about the transference there, from New York.

Since age sixty was, in my opinion, too early to go into full retirement, I had to determine what to do in the remaining years of my life. Re-joining academia seemed like the most obvious occupational/vocational choice, especially since I had been encouraged by the economists at the University of the West Indies (UWI), Mona campus in Jamaica, to contemplate taking up a Professorship there. This seemed like a tempting offer. (As I indicated earlier, I had not lost track of academia and contemporary issues, while at the UN).

An alternative source of employment was probably with the PPP Government in some advisory capacity, but I had burnt my bridges when, about four years earlier, I had declined their offer, conveyed to me one Saturday morning, in 1993, by Roger Luncheon (Chef de Cabinet/Head of the Presidential Secretariat with Ministerial rank) for me to succeed Clarence Ellis, a good friend of mine, as Caribbean Regional Director at the Inter-American Development Bank – IDB (a rotating position among officials of CARICOM Member States). Clarence had been keeping me informed of the difficulties he had been experiencing in trying to convince President Jagan that the lease of a large portion of land, that the previous PNC Government had made to Kayman Sankar, a rice producer, should not be revoked. The reason for the PPP's intent to fire Clarence was ostensibly ideological, smaller plots to many farmers being preferred, but Clarence was of the view that the PPP felt that any Indian that had relations with the PNC was a 'traitor'. In the circumstances, I could not accept the offer and that did not seem to endear me to the PPP. Cheddi Jagan said to me: "You academics are oh so objective and principled". However, Havelock Brewster, a Director at UNCTAD at the time, accepted the offer of the position at IDB. I remained at UNCTC and, later that year, the latter institution was merged into UNCTAD. I was learning more about the Guyana society and polity. Life has lots of twists and turns. (It is ironic that Jagan might have thought that I was being too conservative and favouring wealthy Guyanese land owners, whereas at UNCTC I was considered too radical).

There was a third option. It involved working as an Economic Adviser at the Caribbean Community (CARICOM) Secretariat, which was located in my home country, Guyana. Moreover, my wife, Valerie, was working at the same institution and the situation there was comparable to what I had enjoyed at the United Nations, in terms of emoluments, with tax free and duty free benefits, and generous vacation leave. The best of all worlds.

CHAPTER FIVE

CARICOM EXTERNAL NEGOTIATIONS (1997-2008)

RETURNING HOME (ONCE AGAIN)

As expected, reaching the United Nations retirement age of sixty made for a rather mixed set of feelings. At one level, there is gratitude at being relieved of the daily grind and eagerly looking forward to having much more time for relaxation and enjoying the little pleasures of life. On the other hand, besides fear of boredom, there is a natural uneasiness as to whether one has accumulated enough savings for one's old age. In addition, my pension would be based on a relatively short period of service – seventeen years. Any post-retirement activity, therefore, would preferably not be pro bono.

In fact, during the weeks leading up to retirement, a friend of mine, Claremonte Kirton, who was a Senior Lecturer at the UWI Mona campus in Jamaica, had contacted me to enquire whether I was interested in a professorial position there. I had not pursued the matter, owing to a nostalgic preference for wanting to spend as many of the remaining years of my life in my home country, Guyana. Moreover, my wife, Valerie, was expecting to resume working at the Caribbean Community (CARICOM) Secretariat, which is situated in Guyana.

Employment at the UG campus was a possibility, but the prospect did not fill me with excitement, partly because I had heard that the academic standards had fallen well below the halcyon days of the 1960s and 1970s. In addition, the economic depression in Guyana,

The CARICOM Secretariat proudly houses staff from fifteen Member States

during the 1980s, had caused serious deterioration in the campus infrastructure and other physical facilities. Fortunately, just before leaving Geneva, I received a call from the CARICOM Secretariat, offering me a position of Technical Advisor to the Regional Negotiating Machinery (RNM).

FREE TRADE AREA OF THE AMERICAS

The Free Trade Area of the Americas (FTAA) negotiating process reflected a grand experiment in hemispheric liberalisation. Its origins lay in the Enterprise for the Americas Initiative of 1990 and the example of a successfully concluded North American Free Trade Agreement in 1992. I returned to Guyana once again, in 1997, to find preparations in full flow for the beginning of plurilateral and WTO plus negotiations, with all hemispheric countries participating, except US embargoed Cuba. The major substantive areas included market access, investment, anti-dumping measures, agricultural subsidies, competition policy, intellectual property, government procurement, dispute settlement, and services. I was primarily responsible for negotiating investment and financial services on behalf of the Caribbean, and the other subject areas had been assigned to other professionals in the Region, under the aegis of a Regional Negotiating Machinery (RNM). Hemispheric negotiations began in earnest in 1998.

The pace of negotiations was very hectic, as the process was scheduled to conclude in 2005. It also involved my making a number of trips to Panama City, Panama and Mexico during the first two years. One experience is memorable, not for the intellectual challenge, but for its association with a calamitous personal event in 2003. I had left Guyana early one morning for Panama and, when I arrived at the hotel, I was told at the reception desk that my wife had left a message indicating that a rather serious fire had taken place at my residence in Guyana. I immediately turned around and headed back home. A fire of high voltage electric origin had started in my master bedroom, and had spread to the adjoining study, resulting in my losing, through both fire and water damage, a very significant proportion of my published and unpublished monographs, articles, photographs and other memorabilia, *inter alia*. This was a rather sad and depressing experience and I found myself spending the next few weeks (including Christmas) at the home of a CARICOM colleague, Marilyn Trotz, who was on vacation at the time and had kindly given my wife Valerie and I permission to occupy her house, while she was away. Surprisingly, this was my second fire encounter. Almost exactly thirty years earlier, I returned home one evening to find a fire of electric origin in progress around the light in the ceiling of my bathroom and I was fortunate, with the assistance of my then wife, Margaret, and son Ronnie, to extinguish same before the arrival of the fire brigade. (Perhaps my schoolboy false name, "Ball-o-Fire", was something of a bad omen. But I am getting ahead of the core narrative).

When I joined the CARICOM staff in May 1997, I immediately began to do background research of relevance to the Proposed FTAA. Examples of papers that I produced were the following:

(i) Comments on the ECLAC Paper, Regional Integration Fund of the Free Trade Area of the Americas, 15 August, 1997;

(ii) Commentary on the European Union Green Paper, with particular Reference to Promoting Investment and Supply Capacities (1997);

(iii) Notes on TRIMS, Investment Policy and Competition Policy in the Caribbean (presented at the Commonwealth Caribbean Workshop on Legal Issues Arising from the Uruguay Agreements, Port-of-Spain, Trinidad and Tobago, 18-22 August, 1997);

(iv) Guyana's Foreign Policy: Perspectives for the 21st Century, prepared for Discussion Panel of the Guyana Institute of International Affairs, 9 July 1998; and;

(v) The Free Trade Area of the Americas (FTAA) Process, Regional Rules on Investment and the CARICOM Experience (presented at Regional Workshop on 'Investment Agreements and the Caribbean', sponsored by the Caribbean Regional Negotiating Machinery and the Organisation of American States, 25-26 October 1999, Barbados).

The FTAA process began with a spurt, with a number of preliminary and full-fledged negotiating sessions in the first couple of years, but then things began to slow down, as the major negotiating partners got around to tackling the more difficult issues. CARICOM also had its own particular concerns.

Selected Aspects of Concern to CARICOM of the FTAA Investment Agreement in Process of Negotiations

Core Negotiating	Selected Major Areas of Contention
1. Basic Definitions	Should portfolio investment be included? Should real estate assets, which are not part of a productive process, be included?
2. Scope of Application	Should investments "controlled" by third parties be included? Should investments in force prior to the Agreement be recognised? Should all central and provincial levels of a Federal State (for example in Brazil, Canada and the USA) be subject to the Agreement?
3. National Treatment	Should the national treatment concept be qualified by the term "in like circumstances?" (If accepted, this would allow discrimination on the basis of size, location and other objective considerations).
4. Most-Favoured Nation Treatment	Most of the countries in the Hemisphere are members of a regional integration movement and therefore are desirous for an exception to be made on this basis. However, Panama, which is not a member of a sub-regional free trade arrangement, objects.
5. Fair and Equitable Treatment	There is debate as to whether a foreigner would be able to demand conditions better than national treatment.
6. Expropriation and Compensation	Should the concept of "creeping" (virtual) expropriation be entertained. (Creeping expropriation refers to the impact of an increase in taxation or other adverse regulatory change).
7. Compensation for Losses	In emergency situations of flood, hurricane, earthquake, etc., should a host government be permitted to compensate its nationals to a greater degree than foreigners, thus providing an exception to national treatment and fair and equitable treatment?

8. Key Personnel	How elastic should be the terms "key personnel", in keeping with the need for efficiency of operations and maintenance of control?
9. Transfers	In addition to such cases as criminal violations, bankruptcies and other such financial circumstances, should transfers be subject to balance of payments exigencies? (Fixed Exchange Rate Regimes).
10. Performance Requirements	In addition to the performance requirements that are prohibited under the WTO rules of the game, should there be NAFTA type prescriptions, such as in relation to technology transfers?
11. General Exceptions and Reservations	Should exceptions related to double taxation treaty status, membership of a free trade movement, and security concerns, *inter alia*, be part of the NGIN Chapter, or should these be part of a general (horizontal) Chapter in the FTAA Agreement? To what extent should exceptions be accorded to smaller economies? What should be the maximum level of sectoral and other reservations? What should be the duration/time limitation of transition periods? Is it possible to reconcile a "negative list" approach in the investment negotiations with a "positive list" approach in the Services negotiations?
12. Dispute Settlements	In order to give comfort to prospective investors, is there need to go beyond what is contained in traditional bilateral investment treaties? Should both State-State and Investor-State disputes be settled in accordance with horizontal procedures determined by the Negotiating Group on Dispute Settlements and applicable throughout the FTAA Agreement or should there be separate procedures for the Investment Chapter?

Source: Paper presented by Maurice Odle to CARICOM Council on Finance and Planning, Sept. 2001

CARICOM Submission on Special and Differential Treatment on FTAA Investment Issues

Article 1: Scope

Whatever the scope of the Agreement reached with respect to pre-FTAA investments, smaller economies will have the right to negotiate coverage of such investments on a case-by-case basis.

Article 2: National Treatment

While admitting the general applicability of the concept of national treatment with respect to the establishment, acquisition, expansion, management, conduct, operation, or sale of an investment, in certain special circumstances, e.g. the threat of economic instability stemming from vulnerability, prudential measures employed by a smaller economy may be allowed to fall less heavily on domestic companies than on foreign companies.

Article 3: Most-Favoured-Nation Treatment

While recognising the generality of the MFN principle, a smaller economy may be exempted from same in those circumstances where it extends more favourable treatment to investors/investments from other smaller economies in the hemisphere

Article 4: Exceptions to National Treatment and Most-Favoured-Nation Treatment

Special arrangements between smaller economies, who constitute a common market, shall not be obligated to be extended to Third Parties.

Article 5: Standard of Treatment

While each Party shall be expected to accord to investors/investments of another Party the better of national treatment or most-favoured-nation treatment, exceptions can be made with respect to treatment favouring small and medium-size domestic enterprises.

Article 6: Fair and Equitable Treatment

While a smaller economy shall extend fair and equitable treatment to foreign investors at all times, any treatment less favourable than that extended to investors of other smaller economies shall not constitute an abrogation of this principle.

Article 7: Performance Requirements

Smaller economies may exercise the right to impose certain development-related performance requirements, provided these are WTO compatible.

Article 8: Key Personnel

Smaller economies should be able to require in appropriate circumstances, that a certain percentage of key personnel at the executive and managerial levels be hired locally, since this could act as a form of technical training and transfer of know-how and organisational technology.

Article 9: Transfers

In addition to the usual restrictions on free transfers of capital to take account of non-payment of taxation, findings of adjudicatory proceedings, and protection of the rights of creditors, smaller economies, which are susceptible to export income volatility, would be allowed to exercise flexibility with respect to the provision that such transfers be made without delay. This would be effected on a case-by-case negotiations basis with the investor, and be influenced by any existing foreign exchange control laws and the potential for exchange rate movement when the reserves situation is significantly impacted.

Article 10: Expropriation and Compensation

In the event of an expropriation occurring at a time of impending foreign exchange crisis, smaller economies may be granted flexibility with respect to "prompt, adequate and effective" compensation and therefore a longer time period for payment, with a waiver from payment of interest rates during the extension.

Article 11: Compensation for Losses

In the event of catastrophic loss, natural or man-made, smaller economies may not be obliged to compensate foreign investors to the same extent that they do domestic enterprises.

Article 12: General Exceptions and Reservations

Smaller economies shall be entitled to maintain reservations as are necessary to achieve their national development objectives, including those designed to protect small enterprises and sensitive industries, and will be allowed to remove such reservations at a slower pace than other parties.

Article 13: Dispute Settlement

Smaller economies shall be allowed access to technical assistance and an extended time period, where necessary, for dealing with state-to-state and investor-state disputes.

Article 14: State-to-State Disputes

Where a large or developed State submits a dispute to the general settlement mechanism, at least half of the legal costs incurred by the smaller economy State should be borne by a Regional Integration Fund or some other hemispheric technical assistance/cooperation scheme.

Article 15: Investor-State Disputes

Where an investor of a large or developed economy is involved in a dispute with a smaller economy State and the matter is submitted to arbitration, at least half of the legal costs incurred by the State should be borne out of a Regional Integration Fund.

Article 16: Commitment Not to Relax Domestic Labour Laws to Attract Investment

For smaller economies, a commitment not to relax domestic labour laws should be allied with compensating access to the Regional Integration Fund for the training of workers to make them more productive and the associated enterprises more competitive.

Article 17: Commitment Not to Relax Domestic Environmental Laws to Attract Investment

For smaller economies, a commitment not to relax domestic environmental laws should be allied with compensating access to the Regional Integration Fund for the purpose of introducing more modern machinery and industrial practices that would better protect the environment.

Source: Maurice Odle, FTAA Negotiations, 2002

The FTAA negotiation process finally collapsed in 2005, partly because Latin America and the Caribbean, led by Brazil, were unhappy with respect to USA's insistence on maintaining that country's regime of significant agricultural subsidies. There was also displeasure with the USA's negotiation position, and related provisions, concerning services and intellectual property rights. Argentina, Bolivia and Venezuela, *inter alia*, were in support of Brazil.

The FTAA process, involving 35 countries in North, Central and South America had lessons for the small Caribbean countries. *First*, there needed to be a lot of learning and catching-up since, as a Grouping, the Caribbean's only previous experiences were bilaterally with Colombia, Dominican Republic, Mexico and Venezuela and, plurilaterally, as part of the African, Caribbean and Pacific (ACP) countries, with the UK and the European Union (EU), and those arrangements were essentially non-reciprocal and non-competitive in nature.

Second, associating with a considerable number of partners, almost all of whom were larger and economically stronger, meant that the scope and tempo of the negotiations were dictated by those countries, as well as the outcome. Although ground-breaking Drafts of an agreement were produced in July 2001 and November 2002, the dynamics of the negotiation process was such that the USA and twelve (12) other States wanted an "ambitious" agreement, like the North American Free Trade Agreement (NAFTA), but Mercosur was only interested in a "possible" and more modest FTAA. The Caribbean countries were effectively onlookers and observers.

Third, there was need to become acquainted with certain new negotiating concepts that were underpinning many of the main areas of negotiation: market access; investment services; government procurement; dispute settlement; agriculture; intellectual property rights; subsidies; anti-dumping; and countervailing duties, which were lifted almost verbatim from the completed 1993 NAFTA negotiations. Particularly problematic was dispute settlement, since an attempt was being made by the USA to introduce "Investor-State" relations (in addition to "State-State" relations) so as to allow transnational corporations to be treated as legal entities, like people, with the power to sue Governments for profits lost (due to sovereign laws enacted post the Agreement to protect consumers, workers and the environment) and which development is claimed to be "creeping expropriation", as the USA had done in its Bilateral Investment Treaties and NAFTA. Brazil and Argentina wanted this Investor-State matter taken up in the WTO, instead. Another new concept that the Caribbean had to grapple with was intellectual property rights, that was introduced by the USA for maintaining its technological superiority and competitive advantage and delaying technology acquisition and transfer. Since the WTO was not reaching agreement very easily with respect to these concepts, the strategy of the USA was to promote its interests through other avenues.

Fourth, like at the WTO, there was a struggle by the small economies against the 'one size fits all' approach. The FTAA dealt with the issue of Treatment of the Differences in the Levels of Development and Size of Economies *via* a specially formed Consultative Group on Smaller Economies. However, despite many guidelines issued by the Group, in keeping with the mandates of the Ministers, there was very little translation of those guidelines into concrete reservations, exceptions and transitional periods in the draft negotiated texts of the nine negotiated areas. There was also no fleshing out of the subscription to the proposed idea of a Hemispheric Cooperation Program of technical assistance. In this regard, I did produce a Paper, dated 15 August 1997, commenting critically on the ECLAC proposed Regional Integration Fund of the Free Trade Area of the Americas.

ECONOMIC PARTNERSHIP AGREEMENT (WITH THE EU)

Another negotiation was beginning to engage the attention of the RNM at the time. It was an Economic Partnership Agreement with the European Union (EU) for which purpose I produced a Background Paper on *'International Openness in the Area of Financial Services Trade Agreements*: *The CARICOM Experience'* (presented at the Third High-

Level Meeting on the Reforms of the Financial Systems in Latin America and the Caribbean, Madrid, Spain, 27-29 May 1998); a Paper entitled *'Information Technology and Freedom of Trade in Financial Services'* (that was presented at AIIC's Second Annual Caribbean Insurance Conference, Saint Lucia, 8-10 November, 1998).; and a May 1999 Paper for CARIBINVEST publication issue of Euromoney Institutional Investor, entitled: *'Inward Investment Opportunities in the Caribbean for European Union Investors'*. The RNM had decided in August 1997 that nine (9) sectoral studies should be undertaken for buttressing the negotiation process, one of which was designated as 'Services Sector Policy with Particular Reference to Financial Services and Accounting Services', with Maurice Odle as Lead Author and other members of the sectoral group being Laurence Clarke (Coordinator of the Regional Monetary Studies Programme); Trevor Carmichael (UWI Professor of Law) and Compton Bourne (Professor of Economics and Principal of the UWI Saint Augustine campus in Trinidad). It was a formidable team of intellectuals.

That Study began in October 1997 and a Draft was presented to the RNM Working Group on Global Trade and Economic Issues in March 1998. It was around this time that I came into administrative conflict/difficulties with the RNM system. Shridath Ramphal had been approached by the CARICOM Secretary-General with the offer of a position of Chief RNM Negotiator, who felt, however, that the Secretariat was not the most appropriate mechanism through which to supervise and report on the EPA negotiations. He therefore persuaded a Heads of Government Conference that he should report to a Prime Ministerial Sub-Committee (with P.J. Patterson of Jamaica as Chairman) and that Alister McIntyre would be his Chief Technical Advisor.

The result was that Shridath Ramphal would set up his own autonomous unit and hire consultants to do eight of the required nine background Studies, The ninth Study, on Financial Services, would be done by Maurice Odle, operating out of the Secretariat, and all would be servicing the RNM. There was therefore room for administrative

Secretary-General (SG) Carrington, ASG Greene, DSG Applewhaite, ASG (and future SG) La Rocque and Special Economic Adviser Odle, on the occasion of SG's retirement farewell function, 13 December 2010

and supervisory misunderstanding. The problem began with an inquiry of mine on 16 April 1998, to the CARICOM Assistant Secretary-General (ASG) responsible for Regional Trade and Economic Integration, Byron Blake, for "Clarification on the Status of the RNM Studies" and the unclear nature of the transition to the new supervisory system, as follows:

> *During the last few weeks, I was hoping to have a word with you to seek clarification on the abovementioned matter, but you seemed to have been on mission most of the time. I am therefore resorting to writing because I am increasingly not sure of the extent of my responsibilities with respect to the RNM programme of Studies.*
>
> *2. In July 1997, after review and revision by the RNM of seven project proposals and the subsequent addition of two others, a programme of nine (9) General Studies was agreed on. However, the Commonwealth Secretariat indicated that it was prepared to provide funding for only three of the Studies.*

3. Recently, it was brought to my attention that CRISP funding may be available to initiate work on one or two of the other Studies. It was in this context that I encouraged you to have a meeting with Duke Pollard and myself to discuss Competition Policy. That discussion proved to be quite useful. The subsequent Trinidad Meeting of the Working Group on Global Trade and Economic Issues, including WTO issues, confirmed that a Region-oriented economic analysis should complement (and underpin) the legal work that had already been initiated by Ms Geraldine Foster. Immediately after the Trinidad Meeting, we discussed the matter in your hotel room and we agreed on general terms of reference for myself and two consultants (both of whom had been identified and written to since mid-1997). It was therefore with utter consternation and dismay that I learnt, on return to Guyana from Trinidad, that, since 8 December 1997, a fax had been sent from Arnold McIntyre (on UWI letterhead) to Glenda Itiaba indicating significant revision in the composition of the teams for the nine Studies. More significantly, my name had been removed from the Competition Policy Study. Also, I had been removed as Team Leader of Study 6 on the WTO (and was not even named as a member of the Team). On enquiry, I was informed by Ms Itiaba that the new list was official and that the changes had been made at a Policy Advisory Group Meeting, chaired by Alister McIntyre, earlier that month in Jamaica.

4. From the above, it would appear that there has been a fundamental breakdown in communication. Also, some prospective consultants, to whom letters were written in August/September enquiring as to their availability, have not been informed that their services are no longer required. In fact, I actually had discussions with two of them in Trinidad on the erroneous assumption that they were still expected to be team members when their Studies eventually get off the ground.

> *However, one prospective consultant, whose name has remained on the list for the Competition Policy Study, is Ms Taimoon Stewart. You may wish to respond to her attached letter in your capacity as "Technical Coordinator for the RNM", since I am no longer expected to be involved in that subject area.*
>
> *5. Finally, in SG Carrington's letter of 12 March 1998 to P.M. Owen Arthur, it is stated that "Sir Alister McIntyre, on demitting office (as Vice Chancellor of UWI) would take over responsibility for the organisation and general management of the Studies". Perhaps I can be informed whether you, as Technical Coordinator for the RNM are responsible until Sir Alister retires from UWI (in September 1998, I am told) and contractually assumes his new office. That way, I will know to whom to address the final version of the Study on 'Competitiveness of Caribbean Financial Services and WTO Negotiating Strategies'. Please let me know, also, whether I should begin work on any of the Special (not General) Policy Studies (e.g. on Investment) or whether I need to wait until September.*

The ASG, in turn, wrote the Secretary-General on 8 May on the subject of "Dr Odle's Memorandum on Status of RNM Studies".

> *Kindly see attached copy of a memorandum from Dr Odle, RNM Technical Adviser, to me.*
>
> *2. I understand and share Dr Odle's concerns and consternation. I have pondered over his memorandum but, unfortunately, I am unable to respond to him for two reasons.*
>
> *3. First, I have noted that in the organogram and the description of RNM arrangements submitted by this Secretariat to Barbados and transmitted to the IDB, the position of CARICOM*

Secretariat's Technical Coordinator was omitted. This was a lynchpin position in the original RNM structure approved by the Prime Ministerial Sub-Committee and the Conference in Antigua and Barbuda. The omission, at this critical juncture, by the Secretariat could mean that I have no locus standi to respond to Dr Odle or, indeed, to coordinate the Secretariat's Technical Secretaries.

4. Second, I did not understand the communication from Dr Arnold McIntyre of what emerged from an "informal" meeting in Jamaica on 8 or 8-9 December 1997 as constituting agreed changes, either to the terms of reference or to the proposed study teams. (To the best of my knowledge, and I readily admit this to be very imperfect knowledge, the meeting in Jamaica was not even a meeting of the Chief Negotiator's Advisory Group.) My understanding of the information therefore was that it constituted recommendations which would be taken into account when teams for the individual studies were being constituted by the Secretariat.

5. Indeed, this information could enjoy no higher status, since those who were making the recommendations would have been unaware of:

(a) any commitments which might already have been made by the Secretariat; and
(b) the rationale for the selection or non-selection of persons for these teams.

For example, in composing the teams, the Secretariat had expressly applied the principle that <u>high-level</u>, <u>high-profile</u>, <u>full-time</u> government employees would not be <u>employed</u> to undertake the studies but could be members of review teams for the studies so that the process benefitted from their expertise. The rationale *for this principle was that a Member State could object to its "employee" being so diverted without its consent or other Member States might request explanation as to why their "employees", similarly placed, were not used and, most importantly, donors could query such persons being paid from their resources. Additionally, there was the real issue as to whether such officials could be held to deliver within fixed timeframes, given their commitments. The principle might have been wrong and could have been discussed and we might have even been convinced. In the event we agonised over it and decided not to include any of the many full-time Ambassadors/High Commissioners who were originally suggested. Many of these names re-emerged among the recommendations.*

6. I am not sure whether you are in any better position to relieve Dr Odle's anxieties.

A couple of months later, at a Meeting held at the Secretariat (chaired by Shridath Ramphal) to review the status of the RNM Studies, the Chief Technical Adviser (Alister McIntyre) accused Maurice Odle of failing to live up to his obligations. In reply, Maurice Odle began by invoking the biblical adage, "seek and you shall find" and went on to say that the Study for which he was the designated Lead Author was completed months ago.

The tension was not to abate. On 13 November 1998, Byron Blake wrote Alister McIntyre concerning the comments he (McIntyre) made to a Meeting of the Council on Trade and Economic Development (COTED) on the Studies commissioned by the Secretariat. Apparently, McIntyre was very unhappy with Byron Blake's communication and found that its "tone and language are completely unacceptable and without precedent in my communications with the Secretariat" and, in complaining bitterly to his boss, Shridath Ramphal, he also referred to "the rather rude response of Dr Odle to a request from the Chairman of

COTED to clarify the status of his Paper on Financial Services". The full text of McIntyre's letter reads as follows -

> *"You would have seen a copy of the letter from Assistant Secretary General Byron Blake to me of November 13, 1998, concerning the comments made about the studies commissioned by the Secretariat in the note which I presented to the Second Special meeting of COTED.*
>
> *Setting aside the fact that the material contained in his letter and appendices confirm rather than rebut the content of my statement, I have to say that the tone and language of his letter are completely unacceptable and without precedent in my communications with the Secretariat.*
>
> *This comes after the rather rude response of Dr Odle to a request from the Chairman of COTED to clarify the status of his paper on financial services. I did not reply to Dr Odle, neither shall I reply to Mr Blake. But I must protest through you to the Secretary General about the evident discourtesy if not insolence of these two officials. If you think it appropriate I shall raise the matter at the next meeting of the Prime Ministerial Sub-committee, reluctant as I am to take up the time of busy Prime Ministers with lapses in the conduct of Secretariat officials.*
>
> *At the very least, I must insist that any further communication to me from the Secretariat on RNM matters be routed through the Secretary General. I am sure you would agree that this is the least that can be done in the circumstances".*

On the same 19 November, the CARICOM Secretary-General (SG) wrote Sir Alister McIntyre informing him that a Draft entitled *'Competitiveness of Caribbean Financial Services'* had been presented to an RNM Working Group as early as March 1998, and, had been subsequently reviewed by Senior Finance Officials and other Technical Experts in April 1998 and, by Finance Officials and Ministers of the Council for

Finance and Planning (COFAP) in June 1998. The SG ended his letter by stating that "in submitting this final report, the CARICOM Secretariat feels that it has now discharged its responsibilities". The full text of the SG's letter is as follows:

As you are aware, one of the three (of the original nine) studies that the Commonwealth Secretariat agreed to finance was that on "Services Sector Policy with Particular Reference to Financial Services and Accounting Services". On immediate review of the matter, it was decided to separate Financial Services from Accounting Services and to make the research two distinct studies. The Commonwealth Secretariat duly issued contracts to Drs Compton Bourne, Trevor Carmichael and Laurence Clarke, in connection with the Financial Services Study, and to Dr Bhoendradatt Tewarie, in relation to the Accounting Services Study.

The Study, 'Competitiveness of Caribbean Financial Services and WTO Related Strategies' began in October 1997, with the team led by Dr Maurice Odle, RNM Technical Adviser. A draft of the Study was presented to the RNM Working Group on Global Trade and Economic Issues in Port-of-Spain in March 1998. The Group recommended that a Special Meeting of Senior Finance Officials and Other Technical Experts be convened to further evaluate same and this took place in Bridgetown in April 1998. The main findings and recommendations of the Study were then presented to a Meeting of Finance Officials Preparatory to the First Meeting of the Council on Finance and Planning (COFAP). The deliberations were reported to the COFAP Meeting that took place in Castries on 29 June 1998. Comments that were later received from certain CARICOM Member Countries and the Commonwealth Secretariat have been taken into account in the attached revised version.

The Study of Accounting Services began in March 1998. Completion of the Study was delayed by, inter alia, the rather poor response to the questionnaire that was sent to the Institutes of Chartered Accountants in the various CARICOM Member Countries. Nevertheless, for the purpose of handing over duties to you, we requested the Consultant, Dr Bhoendradatt Tewarie, of UWI's Institute of Business (St Augustine), to submit work completed to date. The major shortcoming of his attached draft is the failure to analyse and indicate "the extent to which the operating rules and regulations are consistent with a WTO-inspired liberal global regime of trade in such services" (as per the terms of reference). You may want to ask the consultant to address this matter, particularly from the point of view of GATS Article VI.4 (Domestic Regulation – Necessary Disciplines) and the overlapping Articles XVI (Market Access), XVII (National Treatment) and II (Most Favoured Nation Treatment). Also, more use could probably have been made of both WTO 'offers' data and the information contained in the questionnaire; to assist this process, and based on the available data and information, Maurice Odle has constructed 21 Annex Tables, attached hereto.

In submitting this final report, the CARICOM Secretariat feels that it has now discharged its responsibilities with respect to the abovementioned studies.

But the matter was probably not yet at rest. Sir Shridath Ramphal sent the following communication to the Secretary-General (copied to Sir Alister McIntyre; All COTED Ministers; Ms C. Constantine, PS, OPM Jamaica; Director-General, OECS; Dr Maurice Odle and Dr Arnold McIntyre) referring to Byron Blake's letter of 13 November 1998 to Sir Alister McIntyre and stating that he had cause to "share Sir Alister's astonishment and indignation" and called for "greater civility and an absence of temper and petulance". Interestingly, Shridath Ramphal's letter ends by stating that "I must affirm Sir Alister's request that communications to him, and I must add to me, from the Secretariat on

RNM matters be routed through you". Status counts. The full text of Shridath Ramphal's letter is as follows:

> *I write to you with some distress in the context of Mr Byron Blake's letter of 13 November 1998 to Sir Alister McIntyre. I send to you a copy of the letter which Sir Alister has written to me on this matter and I hope you will agree that it is only right that I should copy this communication and Sir Alister's reply to all those to whom Mr Blake sent his original letter. I share Sir Alister's astonishment and indignation. If we cannot conduct our affairs with greater civility and an absence of temper and petulance, it is the Region that will suffer. I do not intend to go down that road; but I must ask you to take what steps you consider appropriate on your side to ensure that Secretariat officials do likewise. For the time being, I must affirm Sir Alister's request that communications to him, and I must add to me, from the Secretariat on RNM matters be routed directly through you.*

My resulting memo of 18 December to Secretary-General Carrington on 'Sir Alister McIntyre's Letter of 19 November 1998" provided evidence to show that the RNM Chiefs had dismissively assumed that no work had been done on the Financial Services Study. The full text of my memo to the SG is as follows:

> *In his letter to Sir Shridath Ramphal, Sir Alister McIntyre accuses me of being "rather rude" and of exhibiting "discourtesy if not insolence". I doubt whether most of those who attended the 7 November Meeting would agree with such strong words and, as I have never heard such a description made of my behaviour at any time during my rather long professional career, it is appropriate to set the record straight. Of course, since the Webster Dictionary defines an insolent person as being "disrespectful of custom or <u>established authority</u>" (my emphasis), I would hope*

that no-one in the Region feels that he is so big as to take offence at attempts by others at self-defence against unwarranted attacks.

2. At issue is the reference to the Study on Financial Services in the "Note on the Regional Negotiating Machinery (RNM) Programme of Policy Studies and Training Workshops and Seminars" (attached) that was presented to the Second Special Meeting of COTED. In paragraph 2 of the Note, it is stated as follows – "The status of the study on financial services is not known". These are the only words of reference to the Study in the Note. The tone is provocatively dismissive and pregnant with innuendo, implying that those responsible for the Study were somewhat delinquent. The truth is that as early as March 1998 a draft of the Study was presented to the RNM Working Group on Global Trade and Economic Issues in Port-of-Spain, with a copy immediately after being sent to Sir Alister (and, later on, a status report). Subsequently, the Study was examined by a Special Meeting of Senior Finance Officials and other Technical Experts hosted by the Barbados Government (in April 1998); its main findings and recommendations were presented to a Meeting of Finance Officials Preparatory to the First Meeting of the Council on Finance and Planning (COFAP); and the deliberations of the Officials were reported to the COFAP Meeting in Castries (on 29 June 1998). The transparency of the process is self-evident.

3. Given the above, it is clear that a little bit of investigative effort in compiling the Note for the 7 November COTED Meeting would have easily revealed the true and very advanced "status" of the Study on Financial Services.

4. Finally, since Sir Shridath saw it fit to send a copy of Sir Alister's letter to all COTED Ministers and others, it would be appreciated if you could do the same with this Memo in any response you make to the letter of 15 December 1998.

For the next few years, preparations continued for entering into the intensive stage of the negotiation process. Because financial services are a sensitive sector and a critical input into all other areas of economic activity, special treatment was expected to be given in the negotiations. In addition, each lead author was required to produce a full-fledged negotiation brief. Maurice Odle produced a seventy-page Paper, in addition to nine (9) Annexes, entitled *'Towards a CARICOM-EU Financial Services Agreement: Liberalisation Strategies and Negotiation Options'*, dated 7 April 2003. My seventeen-page Executive Summary was structured as follows:

(i) **Structure, Performance and Competitiveness and Policy Implications**
 (a) *CARICOM Experience*
 (b) *EU Experience*
(ii) **CARICOM and EU Offensive and Defensive Strategies**
 (a) *CARICOM Approach*
 (b) *EU Approach*
(iii) **CARICOM Negotiation Options**
 (a) *WTO equivalence*
 (b) *WTO Plus*
 (c) *Equivalence with Proposed FTAA Agreement*
 (d) *Equivalence with, or Less Than, Chile's Schedule with the EU*
 (e) *Near Equivalence with CARICOM's Protocol II Arrangements*

The EPA was signed on 15 October, 2008 and the First Five-Year Review was issued on 14 July, 2015. The findings of the Review are reflected in a Joint Communiqué that was issued on 16 July, 2015 at the Third Meeting of the Joint CARIFORUM-EU Council that was held in Georgetown, Guyana. Selected aspects of the Joint Communiqué include the following:

> *The Meeting noted that CARIFORUM States had not yet been able to fully convert the market access offered by the EPA into meaningful market presence ... there was agreement that the lessons learnt so far in implementation pointed to the need to pay close attention to institutional capacity, built-in constraints of the Agreement and CARIFORUM's supply side capacity constraints in order for the full potential of the EPA to be realised". With respect to services which account for approximately 70 percent of the GDP of CARIFORUM States, whereas it was recognised that the EU was making efforts to facilitate visa applications by CARIFORUM entities, "concerns were, however, expressed that some CARIFORUM service suppliers continued to be constrained in establishing and maintaining market presence in the EU (and that) the investment and trade in services provisions of the EPA have not yet yielded all the anticipated benefits and concluded that CARIFORUM and the EU should work towards ensuring that the provisions deliver their full potential.*

The second Five-Year Review of the EPA is certainly overdue but the findings are unlikely to be much less discouraging. There are at least two general lessons to be learnt. *First*, despite certain waivers and concessions accorded to CARIFORUM investors and suppliers, the EPA was not sufficiently non-reciprocal in nature. There was not a level playing field, given the wide disparities in capacity between the CARIFORUM and EU partners. *Second,* besides allowing itself to be forced to enter EU negotiations jointly with the Dominican Republic (with whom it hitherto had very little contact), the strategy of the Caribbean entering separate negotiations with the EU, rather than jointly with its long-standing Africa and Pacific partners of the ACP grouping, probably made for reduced bargaining power.

But, rather than relying on my assessment, it would be useful to learn of the views of certain well placed players and experts. For example, the Director-General of the European Commission, Stephano Manservisi, eager to shape the post mortem narrative, quickly wrote his counterpart, the CARICOM Secretary-General, Edwin Carrington, and began by saying the following:

> *Let me start by saying that I believe that both sides, the Caribbean and the EU should be rightfully satisfied of the conclusions of the EU-Caribbean EPA. I believe that you personally and the leaders of the Caribbean region displayed a determination and vision that was catalytic for the outcome of the negotiations.*

But certain Caribbean experts were not so optimistic. For example, Professor Norman Girvan (former Secretary-General of the Association of Caribbean States – ACS) in a communication of 25 January 2008, was very sceptical of the benefits to be derived and, equally important, felt that the EPA would adversely affect the thrust and trajectory of the integration process and prospects, as follows:

> *The EPA sets up an elaborate institutional structure of governance, depicted in Box 2. At the apex will be a Joint Cariforum-EC Council, a ministerial body with the power to 'take decisions on all matters related to the Agreement', which decisions are 'binding on the Parties' which 'shall take all measures necessary to implement them'. These decisions of the Joint Council will therefore have automatic legal force over member states, buttressed by an enforcement machinery that provides for resort to trade sanctions in certain instances. This is a property of decision-making that has so far been lacking within the organs of governance of the Caribbean Community itself including the Conference of Heads of Government, its supreme authority. In effect, it endows EPA implementation with a degree*

of supra-nationality which CARICOM governance itself does not possess.

It is ironic that, with virtually no consultations or discussion on the substantive issues involved, CARICOM governments have been prepared to endow a Joint Council set up with the Dominican Republic and with Europe, with legal powers that it has been unable to agree on giving its own organs of governance after several years of inconclusive discussion! On paper, the requirement of decisions being taken by consensus will give Cariforum states a formal veto power. But clearly the EC will have the upper hand in the power relationship by virtue of its control over market access and development assistance. Any doubts about the EC's willingness to use this leverage would have been removed by its conduct during the EPA negotiations. Further CARICOM's Council for Trade and Economic Development (COTED) would seem set to suffer a considerable diminution of its role and authority as its room to manoeuvre in external trade negotiations will also be circumscribed by EPA obligations.

Norman Girvan went on to say the following:

The CARICOM agenda is for the most part absent from the EPA. The EPA development chapter (Part 1) locates the agreement within a development approach that is centred on trade liberalisation and integration with the world economy. References to development cooperation in specific sectors bear no relation to the region's sectoral development priorities. The phasing of EPA implementation is not dovetailed with CARICOM's agreed phasing of CSME implementation. Import liberalisation of goods and the opening of service sectors under the EPA are not synchronised with the Community's own national and regional development strategies. Impending CSME regimes for investment, services, harmonised taxation, incentives, intellectual property, competition, government procurement, telecommunications and the environment are not points of reference in the corresponding sections of the EPA, nor is their establishment anticipated in the text.

There is thus a very real possibility of contradictions between CSME and EPA implementation measures, both in content and in sequencing. In any such clash of agendas the odds favour the EPA; for it is legally binding, embodies supranational governance, is reinforced by the leverage of market access to Europe and is supported by EC funding – all of which are lacking in the CSME.

The most likely scenario, then, is one in which the CSME is melded into the EPA as an adjunct to the larger scheme of economic integration with Europe (and collaterally, with the Dominican Republic). Within 10-15 years the CARICOM Common External Tariff will have largely been eliminated; market integration in goods, services and investment with much larger and more economically powerful trading partners will be far advanced; and policies in key areas will have been adapted to suit. EU and possibly DR firms may be dominating the most profitable sectors. In a sense, the logic of the EPA is to replace the CARICOM Single Market and Economy with a 'Cariforum-EU Single Market and Economy'. That this logic is integral to the EPA's objective is clear from a reading of the Preamble and Part 1; and from examination of the Cotonou Agreement from which EPAs were derived [1].

However, there is a further complication that arises out of the way in which the EPA is legally structured. The Caribbean Community as a juridical entity is not a Party to the EPA. The Parties are 15 Cariforum states, the European Commission and the 27 member states of the European Union. The 15 Cariforum states will each sign in their individual capacity. The EPA reportedly distinguishes certain obligations for which Cariforum states are collectively responsible from another set of obligations for which they are individually responsible. The reason was to avoid a situation where the collectivity could be exposed to sanctions from the EC as a result of the actions of just one member.

One consequence of this will be to put CARICOM member states in competition with each other for the fulfilment of their EPA obligations and their access to EPA benefits and opportunities, in subjects related to their individual obligations. It is even possible to envisage a situation in which one (or several) CARICOM member states join with the EC in bringing a complaint against another CARICOM member or members.

To put it another way, which countries will be 'first' to negotiate mutual recognition agreements for their different classes of professionals? To streamline their customs administration in line with EPA implementation? To amend their Intellectual Property legislation and institutions to make them EPA-compliant? To adopt the required public procurement procedures? Those countries will have a built-in advantage in securing 'development cooperation' from Europe and their exporters will have an advantage in taking advantage of market access opportunities. Given the wide differences among CARICOM countries in levels of economic and social development and in the quality of institutions; the likely consequences are undermining of regional solidarity and heightened intra-regional inequalities.

For his part, Professor Havelock Brewster (ex-Guyana Ambassador to the EU and Director at both UNCTAD and IDB) was critical of the entire approach to the negotiations between CARIFORUM and the EU, as reflected expansively in the following:

- *Our international (trade/economic/political) negotiations need to be informed in advance of a clear vision, including its scope, of what it is we want to get out of these arrangements, for the short and longer term.*

- *We need to do more to involve all our stakeholders in the formulation of such a vision, and in the subsequent policy-making and negotiating processes. Good governance requires the provision of full and up to date information in all phases of the negotiating process – before, during and after. Thus greater efforts are needed in respect of public disclosure and transparency, explanation and public discussion, before policy positions are determined. It is not enough merely to provide pro forma opportunities and invitations to meetings. We know very well that there has not been a tradition of participation of the private sector, organised labour, non-governmental organisations and civil society in policy formulation and negotiation; and often, by default, there is merely token presence. Thus more pro-active, affirmative methods need to be used to ensure effective public participation.*
- *We should avoid accepting templates (such as draft agreements, working-papers, and non-papers) offered by our negotiating counterparts. The very conceptualisation structures of these templates mask substantive pre-commitments that we cannot assume are always in our interest.*
- *As a matter of principle, we should also avoid accepting financial and direct technical assistance from the very parties with whom we are negotiating.*
- *We need to do more to initiate and maintain links, exchanges and consultations with our Southern partners (other ACP groups, the group of 77, GRULAC), with a view to building up international solidarity.*
- *We need to manage the use of supportive interest groups in negotiating Partners' countries. There are immense possibilities in this strategy – pursued through the media, business groups, non-governmental organisations, trade unions, Diaspora organisations, Diaspora Parliamentarians, the EU Parliament, the Black Caucus in the US, the EU Member States themselves.*

The Commission is not as monolithic a power bloc as it may seem from the outside.
- *Negotiating propositions should always be subjected to a test of symmetry in commitments. For example:*
- *The EPA text is characterised by non-binding, declaratory, general statements on the part of the EC.*
- *Whereas CARIFORUM commitments are specific, time-bound, binding and sanctionable, e.g. its liberalisation commitments in respect of goods and services, customs administration, trade facilitation, strengthening intellectual property protection, etc.*
- *Also, there is no symmetrical, bankable assurance that liberalised access will actually result in export performance/ presence, as there is no real connecting link between the two. This is a clear lesson of the 32-year history of the ACP relationship with the European Community.*
- *Specific, time-bound commitments on the part of the EC in support of economic adjustment and transformation are generally absent.*
- *As a matter of principle, we should not undertake commitments that go beyond what is already settled or implemented on our side, and that may result in compliance with external agreements becoming the driver of internal/regional policy, e.g. financial services, other services, investment, competition, government procurement, e-commerce, Intellectual Property, free circulation of goods, the environment.*
- *Again, while the EPA text is replete with references to development cooperation in various sectors, and endorses a range of development supporting measures, it is questionable how far these are binding in terms of specific, effective actions and measures to be undertaken for which the EC can be held to account.*
- *Even in quantitative terms the projected European Development Fund allocation is far from commensurate in relation to our*

development/fiscal adjustment needs, and the "development dimension" expectations of the Agreement. At Euro 165 million over five years it amounts, on average, to Euro 2.2 million per country per year.

- *We should avoid entering into open-ended commitments with closed-end time-lines.*
- *Closer attention needs to be given to institutional commitments entered into in regard to the governance of international agreements. In particular we need to guard against pre-emption of powers that our regional institutions do not themselves possess. For example, the Joint CARIFORUM-EC Council.*
- *Member-governments need to be more abreast of the conduct and progress in the negotiations, and continuously involved in the process, aborting unacceptable propositions, where need be, or finding ways forward for difficulties as they arise. Free-riding on the part of governments and excessive reliance on regional bureaucracies deprive the negotiating process of the highest level policy direction and authority that are needed in negotiating with parties who have pre-determined agenda, and who are also much better equipped and more vigilant than we are.*
- *A clearer demarcation by the Heads of Governments of the respective responsibilities of the Caribbean Community Secretariat (CCS) and Caribbean Regional Negotiating Machinery (CRNM) is now needed. An Agreement like the Economic Partnership Agreement with the European Community (and other prospective Agreements) go far beyond trade issues, and cannot be left, in terms of technical advice, exclusively to a specialised trade negotiations sub-agency of the Community like the CRNM. For example, the development dimension of the EPA is an all-encompassing matter that involves the present and future development of the Caribbean Single Market and Economy, and regional economic, social, cultural and political development more broadly.*

- *Finally, training in trade/economic negotiations-liberally offered, financed and conducted by our negotiating counterparts or international institutions, like the WTO, the EC and the World Bank, in the Caribbean and elsewhere, needs to be re-examined in respect of their structure and content, as they are based on pre-determined concepts, theoretical assumptions and selective interpretations of historical experience that are more in the interests of the developed world. As a result, the local graduates of these training or graduate courses who become government and Community negotiators are at a clear disadvantage in terms of applying the skills they have newly acquired to the interests of developing countries.*

A final comment/perspective from the EU, no matter how biased, is warranted. The second official Five-year Review of the workings of the EPA are, at the time of writing, still not available, but a concluding paragraph in the Executive Summary of an 'Implementation Report by European Commission, 2021', entitled *'Ex-Post Evaluation of the EPA Between the EU and the CARIFORUM Member States*, states as follows:

The main obstacle in the implementation of the EPA lies in the insufficient incentive the EPA generates in the productive sectors of the CARIFORUM economies. The economic operators in the CARIFORUM States, especially micro, small and medium-size companies find it almost impossible to take advantage of the market access opportunities in the EU due to the existing trade irritants in the EU market and capacity constraints. It is essential to obtain private-sector support and political drive for the full implementation of EPA.

CHAPTER SIX

CARICOM INTEGRATION CHALLENGES (2000-2011)

The CARICOM Single Market and Economy (CSME) is essentially a work-in-progress and builds on certain integration type agreements to date, such as Agreement Relating to a Functioning Single Market in 2006; Revised Treaty of Chaguaramas (including a regulatory framework for the CSME) in 2001; Common Market (and Community) in 1973; and a Free Trade Area in 1968. By the turn of the 21st century, considerable progress had been made in establishing (less so in implementing) the trade-based framework of the Single Market, but insufficient forward movement had taken place with respect to negotiating intra-regional agreements on aspects of the stipulated regulatory framework of the Single Economy, such as with respect to capital and financial flows; a financial services agreement; along with stock exchange consolidation and tax harmonisation; and an investment code. Nevertheless, there has been progress in areas such as cross-border establishment of enterprises, including banks and insurance companies, cross-border movement of labour, and various aspects of functional cooperation. But for the Single Economy process to really succeed in a rapidly changing global economy, it was also necessary for there to be a sound macro-economic policy framework and a regional economy exhibiting sustained growth and development.

REQUIRED RESEARCH

Having effectively parted company with the RNM, I was made the Special Economic Adviser to the Secretary-General (SG) of CARICOM, Edwin Carrington, and my main assignment was to further the regional integration process, with particular reference to the development of a Single Economy. I was also made Head of the Economic Intelligence Policy Unit – EIPU. I immediately set about acquainting myself with the literature and commenting on issues of relevance to the Region.

In this regard, a number of Economists, a few of whom I have already referenced, had made significant contributions to the issues of regional economic transformation and integration. Here, I will simply refer to certain aspects of my contribution to knowledge in the subject area. One of the Papers I wrote, delivered on 17 May 2000 at the UG Institute of Development Studies, was on *'CARICOM and the Interface of Regionalism and Globalisation: Intractable Challenges and Limited Opportunities'*. The Paper "attempted to show that, from the Caribbean perspective, there is an inherent high voltage tension at the level of contact between the regional integration set-up and the globalisation process". The Paper's full conclusion is as follows:

> *The whole is usually greater than the sum of its parts, since social phenomena tend to synergistically reinforce one another. The combination of the global trade measures, investment measures and finance measures, therefore, make for a formidable global economic architecture. The salient point about today's globalisation process which distinguishes it from the internationalisation tendencies of the past is its rules based nature. With respect to global trade, in particular, the system is mandatory and countries are locked into a process in which there is no easy possibility of "rollback" of measures that have already been agreed-on, :standstill is expected with respect to identified existing protectionist measures, and "progressive liberalisation" in the*

future is a commitment made by all WTO members. In a sense, globalisation has, to a great extent, appropriated regional and national policymaking authority and is encroaching considerably on the traditional sovereignty of States.

What this Paper has attempted to show is that, from the Caribbean perspective, there is an inherent high voltage TENSION at the level of contact between the regional integration set-up and the globalisation process. The TENSION occurs both at the level of the regional grouping as a whole and with respect to the welfare of particular countries. It also affects every major sector – commodities, manufacturing and services. The problem relates not only to the issue of removal of preference (which, before the end of the Cold War it was apparently legitimate for small countries to enjoy) but, also, to the very structure of the global system and its capacity to distribute benefits equitably.

There is a sense of urgency and almost impending crisis because the Caribbean region is at the very cutting edge of both of the very fast evolving regionalisation and globalisation processes. The FTAA is due to come into being in the year 2005, reciprocal (as against preferential) trade relations between the ACP and the EU in the year 2007 and, in the intervening period, a host of free trade arrangements with groupings and individual countries in Latin America amounting to what one author has described as "a series of concentric relationships and groupings" (C.Y. Thomas, 1999).

At the same time, the Caribbean, already a very globalised economy with exports of goods and services as a percentage of GDP exceeding 55 per cent on average (unweighted) for 11 of the CARICOM countries in 1998 (CDB, 2000), finds itself involved in WTO negotiations for further liberalisation and more extensive and intensive global insertion. Interacting with this constellation of regional and global integration arrangements is our own Caribbean process of economic deepening towards a Single Market and Economy.

One major problem is that the new dispensation of global governance does not make for any explicit recognition of small economies as a special genre, except perhaps in the case of the FTAA. There is a "one size fits all policy", particularly at the WTO where, in addition to measures such as TRIMs and TRIPs not being conducive to the transformation prospects of developing countries, the transition period post-January 1995 (the date of accession of the Uruguay Round arrangements) is typically only five years, with an extension of three years for the least developed countries.

This adjustment period is much too short for developing countries to be able to arrive at competitive parity with the developed countries who, over a period of 50 years, had eight post-GATT 1947 rounds of restructuring negotiations to arrive at their present position. Far from there being a levelling of the playing field, there is, as I have so aptly coined and described on a previous occasion (M. Odle, 1999) a "persistently uneven playing surface" (PUPS). The present international set-up does not make for "catch-up" or "convergence" of economies over time; there is likely to be a continuation of the process of increasing disparities (P. Bairoch and R. Kozul-Wright, 1996).

Opting out of the evolving global arrangements is not a viable option as it would probably lead to further marginalisation and miniaturisation for small economies. Accordingly, the Caribbean is in the forefront of the call for "Review, Repair and Reform" (RNM, 1999). The objective is 'Globalisation with a Human Face'. The process of economic globalisation may be irreversible but the rules governing it are not.

Finally, the opportunities being opened up by the global liberalisation process are probably very limited when compared with the challenges that have to be overcome and the repositioning that has to take place for effective "contending with destiny in the 21st century" (K. Hall and D. Benn, 2000). With respect to trade, we have already mentioned that access to a country does not necessarily mean effective access to a market. Even with effective market access, the Caribbean, like many other developing countries, suffers from serious structural supply-side weaknesses.

A second Paper of mine was delivered on 19-21 June 2007 at a World Bank-sponsored 'Conference on the Caribbean – A 20/20 Vision' in Washington D.C., entitled *'International Competitiveness of Caribbean Economies'*. The Paper argued that "although the World Economic Forum's nine indices (re institutions, infrastructure, macro-economy, health and primary education, higher education and training, market efficiency, technological readiness, business sophistication and innovation) and World Bank Indicators (including starting a business, licensing, employing workers, registering property, accessing credit, protecting investors, paying taxes, trading across borders, enforcing contracts, and closing a business) constitute useful devices for assessing competitiveness potential and for informing policy making, they are not necessarily totally appropriate, or the weighting given appropriate for all countries. One size does not fit all. The indices and indicators also do not constitute an exhaustive list. In the Caribbean, there are a number of location factors which can have a significant impact on the "competitive process". The Paper concluded as follows:

> *The Caribbean economies are at a critical conjuncture in which the forces of globalisation are requiring a Darwinian instinct for survival. The rules of the competitiveness game require a paradigm shift and sea change in attitude on the part of all stakeholders. True competitiveness is required for sustainable growth. Competitiveness is not a static but dynamic process in which countries are continuously gaining and losing ground. Now a word about what is required of each of the stakeholders.*
>
> *The private sector and its national and regional representative institutions, industry associations, and other support bodies, need*

to be much more pro-active than they have hitherto been. In this regard, the Caribbean Business Council, whose establishment the Heads of Government approved over a year ago and which is yet to get off the ground, needs to have as one of its functions that of a Competitiveness Promotion Council since the currently conceived Regional Competition Commission is essentially a regulatory body.

With respect to the individual firms, there is a need for nimbleness and flexibility. Creativity is at a premium in terms of overcoming challenges and seizing opportunities. What may be required is for a firm to continuously re-invent itself, to have a capacity to effectively adopt and adapt imported technology, including information technology, and seamlessly incorporate countless product and process innovations. The aim is to be a 'world class' company.

The Government also, has its work cut out for it. Apart from negotiating favourable trade and investment agreements with Third Parties and providing an appropriate macro and micro-economic policy framework in a conducive business environment, technical and other assistance should be provided to enterprises in need, in keeping with the functions of an entrepreneurial oriented government and in the best traditions of public-private sector partnership. This is not necessarily the same as "picking winners".

Labour also has a critical role to play and high levels of on-the-job training are required. At the regional level, the integration process can derive greatly increased benefits when the movement of artisan labour is freed up, given the importance of the construction sector in building tourism capacity, inter alia. While labour productivity is one of the pillars on which is built international competitiveness, fair wages and reasonable working conditions should be an objective, although increasing competition and the urge to engage in mergers and acquisitions tend to threaten security of employment. In this regard, the question should be asked: International competitiveness, for whose benefit? The Caribbean's rank in the United Nations Human Development Index is not too favourable, and so the Region needs to be interested in supporting the call made in some quarters that, internationally, the call should be for "compassionate rather than cutthroat competitiveness".

Finally, civil society is integrally involved and the role of the universities, business schools and technical institutions is pivotal from the point of view of teaching and training in areas of relevance to a rapidly evolving technological environment as, also, research and development (R&D). Also, there is need to reduce the disconnect between R&D undertaken by the tertiary institutions and implementation and commercialisation by the private sector. The Caribbean Research Competitiveness Funding Agency that has been proposed by the University of the West Indies should help to bridge this divide.

The future is indeed partly in our own hand.

Competitiveness is one of the important factors in determining resilience and sustainability. So, also, is the regulation, supervision and management of financial institutions. Internationally financial crises have always found the Caribbean wanting, in terms of both preparedness and effectiveness of response, as has been my experience since joining the CARICOM Secretariat in 1997, the year of the Asian Meltdown by the Asian Miracle Economies that initiated the international financial crisis. I therefore produced, early 1999, a Paper entitled *'A Note on the Potential Impact and Implications of the International Financial Situation: Ten (10) Major Policy Lessons for CARICOM Developing Countries'*. For each of the ten policy areas that I have identified, the implications for the Caribbean were as follows:

(1) Foreign Currency Borrowing Needs to be Carefully Monitored, if not Controlled

While the Caribbean cannot be said to be 'suffering' from a surfeit of inflows of foreign short term funds, recent international experience offers up a number of policy measures that would need to be considered to either prevent or counter adverse consequences. Although the capital deficit Caribbean Region would want to attract foreign loans, the purposes for which they are used should at least be carefully monitored. As a strategy for approaching the international capital market, the Region should also explore the possibility of 'collective guarantees' as a way of reducing the costs of borrowing (even though it is questionable whether there should be any government guarantees at all of private debt).

(2) Prudential Regulation and Supervision Require Strengthening

The financial crisis in Trinidad in the 1990s and the crisis in Jamaica of the last three years indicate that the Region is not immune to an Asian type of financial meltdown. While the introduction of Financial Institution Acts in the 1990s in many CARICOM countries has helped to remove the regulatory arbitrage that existed between banks and near banks and to institute other reforms, in many cases (e.g. Guyana) it cannot be said that implementation of all of the 25 Basle Principles has taken place. In addition, rating agencies and credit bureaus are virtually non-existent in the Region. The Jamaica experience showed not only that banks with a high proportion of non-performing loans were allowed to continue for some time without the true situation being revealed but, also, that certain firms and individuals were able to acquire loans from many financial institutions without any of the latter knowing the true extent of their indebtedness and leverage behaviour. The Jamaica experience also shows the need for a more effective Supervisor of Insurance system (which does not exist at all in the case of Guyana) and the contamination dangers associated with financial conglomerates and the blurring of the term structure distinction between banks and insurance companies. This shows the need for adequate information disclosure.

(3) Greater Transparency is Required in the Guarantee Relationship Between the State and the Liabilities cum Assets of Financial Firms

The moral of the story is that financial systems need a careful balancing between the encouraging of risk taking and the guaranteeing of acceptable minimum social outcomes. The problem is rather systemic as the current crisis in Jamaica, for example, bears a considerable degree of similarity to the Asian crisis in terms of moral hazard and the behaviour of the domestic banks. "Some of those delinquent borrowers are themselves connected parties to the bank "(The Gleaner, 13 July 1998) and the financial institutions took excessively risky positions in the expectation that in a crisis the Government of Jamaica would bail them out (The Gleaner, 16 July 1998).

The issue seems to be not whether governments should provide a safety net but what form that assistance should take. Trinidad and Tobago had already introduced deposit insurance following their financial crisis of the mid-1950s. Jamaica has now made a decision to follow suit with a guarantee involving less than full recovery of deposits. This partial approach is justified, since full deposit insurance many cause the exercising of even greater riskiness in portfolio selection. "Bank owners bear only a portion of the downside risk but stand to gain, through higher profits, a large share of the upside risk". (M. Brownbridge, 1998). This "narrow" approach to deposit insurance should also logically rule out the guaranteeing of international bank loans to private borrowers; the trade-off is probably a lower supply of such loans or a higher rate of interest. Governments would also need to be supplied with better and more timely information on the operation of the financial institutions since, as the Jamaican experience shows, the latter tend to seek assistance only when there is considerable deterioration in their situation and after the managers/entrepreneurs have already taken action to minimise any personal disadvantage (G. Bonnick, 1998).

(4) Permissive Portfolio Investment Policy Requires Compensatory Defence Mechanisms

Portfolio investment is not yet an important phenomenon in the Caribbean financial system. However, it is not too early to start thinking as to what policies should be employed to deal with this issue. Malaysia has reimposed capital controls, although many commentators are of the view that this strategy does not represent a viable long term option. We have also alluded to the proposal of a tax on capital outflows (and inflows). What perhaps is even more important and constitutes the only defence is for a country to have its macro-fundamentals right, particularly its foreign exchange rate and reserves policies.

(5) A Fixed/Pegged Exchange Rate Policy Needs to be Backed by Adequate Reserves

CARICOM countries' dependence on foreign commercial loans is not such as to make a significant increase in reserves a sine qua non for any of the existing foreign exchange rate regimes – fixed rate as in the case of Barbados, flexible (within a notional band, as in the case of Guyana, Jamaica and Trinidad and Tobago) and currency board, as in the case of the OECS territories. The

Asian experience is not necessarily a pointer to the Caribbean countries to change their foreign exchange regimes, since there are advantages and disadvantages with each system, although single market convergence policies in the Region and the memories of the volatile 1980s would tend to recommend a fixed rate regime by all Member States.

Higher reserves usually involve a social cost, since the loss incurred from foregoing use of the foreign exchange resources, tends to be greater than the interest earned on the instruments in which the reserves are held. Also, while international borrowing can lead to an increase in the level of reserves, it can involve offering a higher interest rate than that earned on reserves.

Nevertheless, the global financial crisis suggests the need for greater prudence and caution. Caribbean Governments should err on the side of excessive reserves, especially the pegged exchange rate regimes, since a regional policy of pooling of reserves is probably not politically feasible given the past experiences with their Multilateral Clearing Facility. A flexible or crawling peg regime, with movement within a certain band, would probably require less of an increase in reserves. At the same time, it would be a pity if countries are forced to use more of their export earnings to accumulate reserves when these could be used to finance imports of new plant and equipment (M. Feldstein, 1998). An IMF with a real lender of last resort function would effectively reduce the required rate of increase of reserves.

(6) A High Interest Rate Regime, Even if Necessary, is not Always Sufficient to Stabilise the Exchange Rate

In recent years in the Caribbean, despite the absence of significant inflation, short-term rates were near double digit in some countries and well above 10% in others, with a figure approaching 30% in Jamaica. Even such high rates failed to produce perfect currency stability in all countries. One lesson that certain Caribbean countries (the non-currency board ones) could learn from the current global financial crisis is that, if a real attack on their currencies occurs, measures other than merely increasing the interest rates may have to be mainly relied upon.

(7) Anti-Contagion Policies Need to Include Some Counter Cyclical Objectives

The Caribbean Governments would therefore be concerned to know how they could be spared such boom and bust economies and stop-go measures in dealing with spill over effects from the current international situation (or any future global crisis). Already certain exports from the Region have been badly affected. For example, the estimated shortfall in petroleum earnings in Trinidad and Tobago in 1998 is equivalent to 4.8% of GDP, owing to prices falling by nearly 50% to below $10 per barrel, (with somewhat smaller declines in methanol, ammonia and urea petrochemical prices) and equally acute in the case of Guyana "whose export earnings from plywood in the first three months of 1998 were down by 60 percent compared with the same period in 1997, and whose earnings for the whole year are expected to fall by nearly a half" (UNCTAD, 1998, op. cit.). Prices for bauxite exports from Guyana and Jamaica have also remained in a slump. In the manufacturing sector, the massive devaluations of the Asian countries, along with their determination to export themselves out of a recession, is likely to make Caribbean products relatively less competitive and less foreign exchange earnings. In the services sector, as a result of the decline in world demand and the secondary impact of the crisis on Europe and North America, there may be reduced tourist arrivals, perhaps with a lag, and international bank loans are expected to be in shorter supply and higher priced, given the crisis of confidence in the market.

Despite their structural dependence, the Caribbean economies cannot but strive to attain a 'steady path' of economic growth and development, since the alternative has dire social consequences. This would require policies involving minimal fiscal deficits, non-excessive foreign borrowing by either the public or private sector, more than adequate foreign exchange reserves, increasing diversification in the real sector, and increasing investment (and saving) rates, inter alia. One measure whose role in the package of policy measures should probably be minimised wherever possible is the reliance on very high interest rates, owing to its contractionary effects.

(8) Liberalisation and Insertion into the Global Economy Requires a Rather Cautious Approach

Now, how relevant is all of this to the Caribbean. For one thing, the Caribbean had long ago reached a much more advanced stage of financial liberalisation, from a legislative/regulatory point of view, than Asia. The management of the financial institutions was also conducted on a somewhat more conservative basis than those in Asia up to the time of the beginning of the crisis. However, a clear implication for Caribbean decision-makers is "the need for a liberal/conservative mixed type of strategy" with respect to the financial services sector and the WTO negotiating process. (Bourne, Carmichael, Clarke and Odle, 1998). There may also be implications for the WTO liberalisation process with respect to the real sector, despite the latter's mandatory nature. In this regard, maximum use should be made of transition periods and exceptions and exemptions, not to lull producers into greater complacency, but to give them time to prepare for an increasingly unforgiving world. The real issue is one of pace of insertion into the global economy. Festina Lente (hasten slowly) should be the watchword.

(9) Selective Adoption and Adaptation, Rather Than Wholesale Replication, of the Asian Model is Appropriate

What then is left of the Asian development model that is useful to developing countries like those in the Caribbean? Has the Asian model become an anachronism? While there are not-insignificant policy differences between the Asian countries themselves, it can be said that a positivist role of the State is still essential for overcoming market failures. This role of the State is not one of engaging in production activities itself, but of offering various types of support and stimulants to the producer enterprises and removing unnecessary restrictions and bureaucratic hindrances. In addition, emphasis on appropriate macro-economic policies, the provision of adequate infrastructure and a highly trained labour force, inter alia, would tend to constitute necessary conditions for a dynamic entrepreneurial system. What is probably unnecessary, however, are constraints on true political freedom and the capacity of labour to organise. Of course, no affected Asian economy can be said to be very small (Korea is the world's eleventh largest) and so the model is not entirely relevant because of some of the special inherent constraints that are familiar to the small Caribbean countries.

(10) Developing Countries Need to Struggle for IMF Policy Reform to Complement National Policy-Making

Third, developing countries, including those in the Caribbean, need to collectively struggle for IMF lending practices that embody more of a human face. For example, the IMF sanctioned remedial strategies for the affected developing countries include the raising of already high interest rates, whereas the solution adopted by the major developed countries (USA, Japan and Western Europe) for countering deflation associated with the very same international crisis involved a reduction of already low interest rates. There is what I would choose to describe as a *persistently uneven playing surface (PUPS)*.

INTRA-CARICOM NEGOTIATIONS DYNAMICS

The task of successfully negotiating certain CARICOM Single Economy instruments was a challenging one, from an operational point of view, with possible obstacles or delays at each stage of the process. *First*, the Conference of Heads of Government must signal that the timing is appropriate for undertaking such an exercise. *Second*, the research has to be undertaken and appropriate Articles, clauses and other provisions formulated in a Draft Instrument. Then, an intra-regional Committee of senior officials have to agree on the contents of the Draft. This stage of the project is quite problematic for a number of reasons. Membership of the Committee tends to be open-ended and size can vary considerably. A country representative might join the Committee rather late in the negotiation process and hold up progress by wishing to be informed as to what preceded his/her entry. In addition, a country may change its representative in the middle of the negotiation process and the latter may wish to question every Article or clause that had already enjoyed consensus. Moreover, when rotation takes place, the country representatives invariably do not brief each other on what took place at the previous Meeting. There is, also, the psychological or human element, in that it is easier to say "No", rather than "Yes", since there is less explaining to do to one's boss or the line Minister back home. *Third*, a Meeting of Senior Officials in the Ministry of Finance (or an alternative Economics Ministry) is required to provisionally approve the Draft Agreement. *Fourth*, if approved, the Draft is later discussed and possibly given the go-ahead by a Meeting of the Council for Finance and Planning (COFAP) for its consideration by the next Conference of Heads of Government of the Caribbean Community.

In the case of the proposed CARICOM Investment CODE (CIC), a Paper had been presented to COFAP in 2001 and there had been no basic objection to the approach that I and my team at the Secretariat were taking, as the basis for formulation of a Draft Caribbean Investment Code. Several meeting sessions were then had with Senior Finance Officials to fine-tune the Draft.

Proposed CARICOM Investment Code (Underlying Principles)

In light of the provisions contained in the Revised Treaty for a CARICOM Investment Policy and later decisions of the relevant Community decision-making body, the Community is in the process of formulating a CARICOM Investment Code. The preparatory diagnostic work for the formulation of this Code is currently underway. However, preliminary discussions on the issue have highlighted the following:

The instrument should be, in most part, binding on all Member States.

(i) The instrument should apply to both intra-CARICOM investment and flows of extra-regional origin either in a holistic instrument or two parallel instruments;

(ii) Policy and related legislation, regulations and administrative practices should be transparent and explicit;

(iii) The harmonised investment policy should be promotional in nature and as all-encompassing as possible, although national concerns about sensitive areas should be respected through special provisions for certain sectors such as financial services;

(iv) A negative list approach should be adopted with the number of reserved sectors and industries reduced to an absolute minimum;

(v) There could be differential treatment for the less developed CARICOM States by way of exceptions or transitional periods;

(vi) National treatment and Most-Favoured Nation treatment will be observed, wherever possible;

(vii) Transfers of profits, dividends and interest will be unimpeded, except possibly during balance of payments crises;

(viii) The instrument should be WTO-compatible and, wherever possible, WTO-plus in approach;

(ix) The instrument should build on current FTAA negotiations in the area of investment, services intellectual property and competition policy areas.

Source: Based on a Paper presented to the COFAP, January 2001

But alas, as the saying goes, "t'is many a slip twixt the cup and the lip". To my surprise, a Draft of the CIC, which I was about to present to a July 2010 Conference of Heads of Government, was prevented (by the then Attorney-General of Barbados – Mia Mottley) from moving forward for want of sufficient country examination. It seemed as though the hybrid approach taken in the one composite document, with different conditions/clauses pertaining to intra-CARICOM Investment, on the one hand, and third party countries, on the other (where necessary) was too novel an approach. I resigned a few months after the Conference and, a dozen years later, a CIC is still to see the light of day.

The problem seemed to be a misunderstanding with respect to strategy. Ever since I presented a Paper on 23 June 2004 (at a Workshop in Trinidad and Tobago on the formation of a Regional Association of Caribbean Investment Promotion Agencies) entitled *'Strategies, Structures and Synergies Relating to a Caribbean Association of Investment Promotion Agencies (CAIPA)'* and subsequent interactions at regional fora, I was under the impression that the Caribbean Governments were interested in having a very attractive foreign investment regime, partly in order to compensate for the region's extremely small market size, weak infrastructure and limited skills, *inter alia*. However, International Institute for Sustainable Development (IISD) consultants (Mahnaz Malik and Nathalie Bernasconi-Osterwalder) that the RNM hired, at a rather late stage, to review the Draft Code, saw it fit, in September 2009, to make a number of recommendations, including a "positive list" approach, rather than the Draft Code's "negative list" approach. The eight major recommendations of the consultants are reflected in their conclusion, below:

(i) *Assess the costs and benefits of unilaterally extending the liberalisation and protection benefits in the agreement to extra-CARICOM investors without reciprocity and review Article 2 on scope and Article 6 on national treatment accordingly. The narrowing of the definitions of investment and investor in Article 1 could also be considered.*

(ii) *Clarify the relationship of the draft code with existing and future treaties, in particular by putting limits on the MFN obligation under Articles 7 (MFN), 4 and 5 (Relationship with other agreements).*

(iii) *If CARICOM Member States conclude that they want to extend the scope of application of the code to extra-CARICOM investors, it will be useful to consider the use of a positive list approach to market access for investments as an alternative to the approach used in the draft code. This would implicate a review of Articles 2 (Scope of the Agreement), 6 (National Treatment) and 14 (Reservations).*

(iv) *Improve the formulation of the substantive protections by introducing narrower, precise and focused language preserving regulatory space in the substantive obligations set out in Part 2 (Articles 6, 7, 8, 9 and 12).*

(v) *Consider expanding the range of public interest issues and remove the reference to a "disguised restriction on investment" in Article 15. In addition, consider including an explicit right for states to regulate in the public interest.*

(vi) *Reformulate the investor-state dispute resolution clause by excluding framework provisions (Articles 16-21) from its scope.*

(vii) *Clarify the relationship between the right to appear before the Caribbean Court of Justice and the access to international arbitration under the draft code for CARICOM investors.*

(viii) *Exclude more clearly the rights of extra-CARICOM investors to pursue international arbitration under the treaty by redrafting Article 23(3). This article is currently unclear.*

The CARICOM Financial Services Agreement (CFSA) suffered a nearly similar fate.as the CIC. Having gone through the extended process described above, the stage had been reached where, at a COFAP Meeting, only one Government still refused to commit itself to signing the Draft (already considerably watered down in an attempt to reach consensus) which was to be presented at the next Conference of Heads of Government. I pleaded with the Secretary-General that the Draft Agreement, which had found favour with the Committee of Central Bank Governors, was too important to fail, and that Jamaica, somewhat hesitant, could subsequently join at a time of its choosing; all to no avail. Consensus meant unanimity and was sacred in the Region. In any event, at the last moment, Prime Minister Ralph Gonsalves, of St Vincent and the Grenadines, normally a true integrationist, stated that he too was unwilling to sign unless the Caribbean Development Fund (CDF) approved his request for funding for his airport that was under construction. I was at that time a Member of the CDF Board, which was not prepared to deviate from its operational principles, despite the enormous political pressure it tended to find itself in (and which resulted in its Chairman, Shelton Nichols, having to resign). This position of the Prime Minister constituted a rather perverse expansion of the concept of 'single undertaking' – "nothing is agreed until everything is agreed". As with the CIC, a CFSA is still to see the light of day. CARICOM seems to find it easier to sign Agreements with Third Parties (developed countries) than proposed draft Agreements among themselves).

Negotiation of stock market consolidation did not fare much better. The Less Developed Countries (LDCs) of CARICOM that constituted the Organisation of Eastern Caribbean States (OECS) were part of a single stock exchange system but their invitation to the More Developed Countries (MDCs) to merge with them to form a consolidated regional system, after much effort, failed, with the MDCs preferring to continue with their system of cross-listing of companies registered in their respective jurisdictions.

In addition, the attempt at promoting convertibility among the currencies of the various Member States and the process at forging a Single Currency in the Region were not successful, partly because of

Chairman, Prime Minister Dr Ralph Gonsalves, visits the CARICOM Secretariat in March 2007. From left: H.E. Edwin W. Carrington, Secretary-General, CARICOM, Ambassador Colin Granderson, Dr The Hon. Ralph Gonsalves, Ambassador Lolita Applewhaite, Dr Edward Greene, Neville Bissember, Assistant General Counsel, and Dr Maurice Odle, Economic Adviser to the Secretary-General.

economic instability and related failure to satisfy stipulated convergence criteria and a lack of political will (staying power). The reasons for the failure of the Caribbean to emulate the EU's successful EURO introduction experience is reflected in the following extract from a Paper of mine entitled *'The Euro as a Model for Establishing a Caribbean Currency Unit?'*, presented at the Caribbean Association of Industry and Commerce (CAIC) sponsored Conference on 'Caribbean Public and Private Financial Sector Collaboration on the Impact of the Euro on Regional Trade and Monetary Policy' Trinidad, 8 October 1999. My views, contained therein, include the following:

(i) *Governments in the Caribbean need to have a certain amount of political will to be able to stay the rather painful stability course of tight monetary and fiscal policy (For most of the 1990s, the EU average rate of unemployment was around 10 per cent, a very high figure, historically speaking). The opposition parties would need to be fully on board, as also the population at large, otherwise the venture can be torpedoed.*

(ii) *The national monetary authorities in the Caribbean need to have the required institutional will to manage and operationalise the process, even though this would involve a process of rapid diminution of the national capacity for independent macro-economic policy making. At the May 30, 1994 Meeting of CARICOM Central Bank Governors, it was announced that "the time was not appropriate for the establishment of a regional monetary union", ostensibly because of global instability and, also, switch by Trinidad and Tobago a year earlier from a fixed to a floating exchange rate regime. However, no new timetable was set and the process now appears to be an open-ended gradual approach.*

(iii) *Because of the dependent nature of the Caribbean economies in which the average of exports plus imports as a per cent of GDP is around 75 per cent (as against an EU figure of around 26 per cent – about the same as for the USA and Japan) there is likely to be slippage (especially as a result of changing/falling commodity prices) with respect to the policy convergence targets and so a greater degree of flexibility may be required in order to move to the next stage of monetary union. For the floating rate regimes, in particular, export earnings critically affect not only the import cover, and the debt service ratio criteria but, also, the ability to remain within the stipulated floating exchange rate range. There may very well be need to widen this range or for countries to be able to exercise waivers in order to be able to proceed to the next stage.*

(iv) *The level of preparation the EU has shown to be required in finally arriving at a common currency suggests that the corresponding CARICOM Year 2000 target can in no way be attained. Stability harmonisation issues relating to such additional variables as the rate of inflation and the level of interest rates are still to be seriously addressed, as is the setting up of a Caribbean Central Bank (that includes both the OECS and non-OECS countries). In a sense, therefore, policy convergence involves both primary eligibility criteria and secondary eligibility criteria.*

(v) *The failure of the UK (and certain others) to immediately join the Euro zone suggests that there is nothing inherently unworkable with a multi-tier strategy which permits those CARICOM States that qualify to begin the common currency regime and invite those who later qualify to subsequently join the process.*

But even this strategy has an element of uncertainty, since destabilisation resulting from new reciprocal regional and global trade arrangements (involving loss of preferential market access) will for a long time threaten to derail the process. Timing is key.

(vi) *The 15 per cent slide in the value of the Euro over the first six months of 1999 (due in part to the Kosovo problem and conflicting policy speeches by European Ministers) is further proof of the need to ensure that a common currency introduction does not coincide with unsettling events. Perhaps the new rate should be slightly lower than the expected market rate, on introduction.*

(vii) *A massive re-tooling and re-education exercise would be required before the actual first step in the introduction of the common Caribbean currency (which we may call the "Carib" dollar) could be taken. For example, the Deutsche Borse, which runs the Frankfurt Stock Exchange, spent six months fine tuning its trading and settlements system for the Euro; and the Deutsche Bank, in order to prevent foul-ups in its commercial banking system, conducted 59 trial runs, linking its computers with clearing systems around Europe. Even in the UK, which decided along with Denmark, Greece and Sweden not to immediately join the Euro arrangement, the government in 1997 established a Business Advisory Group which brought together a number of business organisations plus the TUC and Consumers Association for discussion of detailed practical issues. A Euro Preparations Unit was set up in the Treasury to provide support to business (particularly via press and radio ads and direct mailing to the country's 1.6 million SMEs) and public authority preparations. In addition, Government departments have been examining the likely impact of the Euro on their internal systems and operations.*

(viii) *The introduction of a common currency is not only a technical issue but, also, a public relations exercise which requires popular support for its ultimate success. For example, there will be a considerable administrative and accounting burden on the many thousands of retail businesses who have to alter their machines and the prices of all their myriad items and, also, on the consumers and wage earners who have to ensure that adjustments do not make them worse off.*

(ix) *As in the EU, there would need to be a transitional period with the introduction of the Carib as an accounting system that parallels the existing national currency accounting systems and, later on, the definitive introduction of the replacement physical Carib cash and coins. This is designed to ensure a hitch free process.*

(x) *While a common currency is desirable, it has to be borne in mind that the expected benefits would be conditioned by the peculiar nature of the CARICOM economies. Theoretically, the Carib would represent and signal -*

(a) a stable regional economic policy environment;
(b) a stable exchange rate regime, thus making it easier for regional companies to invest across borders; and
(c) lower transactions costs.

However, transactions costs in the Caribbean are not very great because dollarization of intra-regional trade exists and other deals are normally settled in US dollars. Second, the value of intra-regional trade is only about 15 per cent of total trade; intra-regional investment is even more limited than trade; intra-regional portfolio flows and bank loans are minimal; and labour mobility is confined to only skilled workers. The net gains would be less than with the Euro, the latter's benefits when fully operational being estimated to be 0.25% to 0.5% of EU GDP based on the EU Commission's calculations.

(xi) *Third, while the European Monetary System contained an implicit element of reserves pooling, no such thing exists in the Caribbean despite the fact that the Report of Governors of the Central Banks in 1992 had stated, based on capital flight of earlier years, that "a common currency for the Caribbean, though it might in principle be adjustable, should be held fixed for the first several years of its existence and that monetary and fiscal policy should be so managed to serve this goal". The Governors proposed a Stabilisation Fund, similar to the failed CARICOM Multilateral Clearance Facility of the 1980s. A fixed rate regime needs higher reserves than a floating rate system. Moreover, the volatility of short-term flows and export earnings in a rapidly globalising economy and the related recent*

> *experience of Asian fixed exchange rate economies should act as a warning. According to the 1999 UNCTAD Report on Trade and Development, whereas reserves in the developing countries in the 1980s were on average about 3.5 months of imports, in 1998 they were 5.3 months and for the emerging market economies 5.5 months. The present CARICOM convergence goal is 3 months import cover.*

A common currency in the Caribbean is neither a dream nor a reality. A common currency does not appear overnight. It is part of a long process and a long haul. Perhaps the time-table that was set for the Caribbean's introduction of a common currency, i.e. seven years (1993-2000) was probably too short. For example, the European Monetary System was set up in 1979 with the ECU as its pivot and the accounting aspect of the Euro was only introduced in 1999. All this time was required, despite the considerable organisational capacity and high degree of trade, investment and financial integration in Europe. But the Caribbean needs to keep the faith, since we are chartering virtually new territory. The Eastern Caribbean Central Bank (ECCB) experience is only partially relevant since it derived from a Currency Board arrangement and a single imperial currency. The CFA Franc Zone, made up of the West African Monetary Union (WAMU) and the Central African Monetary Area (CAMA) had similar origins, with both currencies pegged to the French Franc and convertible into each other at par. The Eastern Caribbean and African countries therefore had no prior national currencies, thereby reducing the degree of sovereignty that had to be relinquished.

Despite the abovementioned disappointments, considerable progress had been made in developing a regional financial architecture, and related institutions and practices, by the time of my resignation from the

CARICOM Secretariat in April 2011. I was involved at various levels in many aspects of the following four major areas:

1. Development Finance and Resource Pooling
Institutions established included the Caribbean Development Bank (CDB); the Caribbean Development Fund (CDF); Sub-Regional Stock Exchange Systems; and the Caribbean Association of Investment Promotion Agencies (CAIPA).

2. Financial Standards – Support and Facilitation
Institutions established included the Regional Credit Rating Agency (RCRA); the Regional Credit Bureau (RCRB); the Caribbean Financial Action Task Force (CFATF); and the Caribbean Centre for Money and Finance.

3. Financial Industry Associations
Institutions established included the Caribbean Confederation of Credit Unions (CCCU).

4. Regulatory Financial Organisations
Institutions established included the Committee of Central Bank Governors (CCBG); Eastern Caribbean Central Banks (ECCB); Caribbean Group of Bank Supervisors (CGBS); Caribbean Association of Insurance Regulators (CAIR); Caribbean Association of Pension Supervisors (CAPS); Caribbean Group of Securities Regulators (CGSR); Regional Competitions Commission (RCC) and CARICOM College of Regulators (CCR).

While the above reflects an impressive array of institutions, even in this regard there were a number of hiccups. For example, the Conference of Heads of Government failed to reach agreement in 2003 concerning the establishment of a Regional Stabilisation Fund and a Caribbean Investment Fund was wound-up in early 2009 after seven years in existence. In addition, a Petroleum Fund that was set up in 2005 also ceased operations in 2009. This latter development was a significant blow to the concept of equitable sharing of the benefits of economic integration. One petroleum producing Caribbean Member State, Trinidad and Tobago, was enjoying persistent trade surpluses in manufactured goods with the rest of the Region, owing to its low energy costs and so Prime Minister Manning agreed to establish a compensatory fund that other Member States (particularly the LDCs) would access for developmental purposes. The incoming, and less integration minded, Kamla Persad-Bissessar administration immediately disbanded the Fund, declaring that Trinidad and Tobago was "not an ATM machine". I was in charge of evaluating projects, for which disbursements were sought, over the 2005-2009 period that the Fund was in existence, and the total (in US$m.) and its percentage for successful recipients were as follows: Antigua and Barbuda 23.26(9.74); Belize 10.00(4.18); Dominica 16.89(7.07); Grenada 35.95(15.04); Guyana 32.90(13.77); Jamaica 3.16(1.32); Haiti 12.54(5.25); Montserrat 16.30(6.82); Saint Kitts and Nevis 3.00(1.25); Saint Lucia 3.89(1.62); St Vincent and the Grenadines 5.65(2.36); Organisation of Eastern Caribbean States 16.20(6.78); LIAT Airline Authority 50.00(20.92); CARICOM's Strategic Plan for Regional Development 0.30(0.12). The cessation of the Petroleum Fund was particularly unfortunate, since it favoured the LDCs and, while in existence, its total disbursements were nearly equal to that of the Caribbean Development Bank (CDB) and the Caribbean Development Fund (CDF) combined.

    The efforts at financial integration, an important part of my remit, were partly designed to assist the process of macro-economic transformation and sustainable development. Because of the extreme lack of diversity and open (export/import) nature in most CARICOM economies, there was a considerable amount of vulnerability to shocks in the global economy and a lack of resilience conducive to speedy recovery. This adverse economic situation in the Region was further amplified by the frequency of increasingly catastrophic hurricanes, given

With UWI Professor Andrew Downes, T&T Director of Trade Bernard Sylvester and T&T Director of Industry, Dr. Punette, at a Working Session of the Strategic Plan for Regional Economic Development.

the geographic location of Member States. Moreover, CARICOM did not find favour with the International Financial Institutions (IFIs) in their request for loans under preferred versus market conditions to deal with this endemic situation, because of their relatively high income (except for two countries, Guyana and Haiti). This vulnerability meant that the Caribbean could not escape the transmission effects of the international financial crisis that originated in the USA in late 2008. The Trinidad headquartered conglomerate, CL Financial Group (CLICO) had invested in too much real estate assets in the USA, particularly Florida and, when prices collapsed, there was a ripple effect throughout the Caribbean region (because many of their financial institutions had interest in CLICO). This gave me the opportunity to successfully campaign for region-wide introduction of deposit insurance, since it previously existed in only four Member States – The Bahamas, Barbados, Jamaica and Trinidad and Tobago. Certain regulatory weaknesses still remain.

At a Heads of Government Conference in July 2019, there was a "call for new methodologies for small island developing states in determining graduation to middle income and high income status, including consideration of our vulnerabilities". The issue is also regional in scope and pertains to the lack of sufficient progress with respect to the Single Economy itself. Also, at a previous Heads of Government Conference in July 2018, a call was made "to create enabling support measures for.an Investment Policy and Investment Code, an Incentives Regime, and an Integrated Capital Market, beginning with model Securities Legislation". They mandated the Council for Finance and Planning (COFAP) to finalise these instruments over the course of the year and to be completed by July 2019. The deadline has passed.

In the final analysis, the various intra-regional agreements, institutions, mechanisms and instruments are designed to accelerate the process of Caribbean development and economic transformation. In this regard, the private sector has a critical role to play and so I organised in Barbados, in 2009, a very large conference, called *'Caribbean Connect'* (reminiscent of the one I organised in South Africa ten years earlier – 'Africa Connect') featuring dozens of regional champions of industry, labour leaders, Ministers with economic portfolios, senior government officials and other stakeholders. The net- working and deal making was considerable and the Conference, described by Prime Minister Arthur as the best he had ever experienced, might have contributed to the recovery from the global financial crisis.

Not so successful was the use that was made of a 2010 Study entitled *'A Strategic Plan for Regional Development within CARICOM: A Regional Public Goods Approach, 2011-2016'* that was conceived by a team of the best economists in the Caribbean Region and the process co-chaired by yours truly. This regional plan was designed to complement the various national plans by collectively utilising regional development institutions and funds and management skills in critical sectoral areas. Unfortunately, when the plan was completed, certain colleagues in the Secretariat conspired to prevent its implementation, on the grounds that it was too economics centred and lacked a sufficient social dimension. I was extremely disappointed and felt that my further employment in the CARICOM Secretariat would serve no useful purpose.

INADEQUATE MARKETING

I had been coming around to a resignation point of view for some time. A major concern of mine was the lack of support for a quinquennial publication that I had conceived and of which I was the Lead Author, called *'Caribbean Trade and Investment Report' (CTIR)*. When the Secretary-General, Edwin Carrington, during the course of an assembly of staff, heard from me that such a Study was in train in year 2000, his first remark was to quizzically, nay angrily, enquire "who knows of such a planned Study". (As will be shown below, the Secretary-General had, three years earlier, been given a document, entitled *'A Proposed Publications Programme for the CARICOM Secretariat'*, in which future publication of a CTIR was mentioned). No one in the audience owned up to knowledge of such an undertaking, even though at least three of those present were participating as researchers. A case of bureaucratic intimidation. He then proceeded to say that, if he does not know of something, then it does not exist. The Secretary-General further added that one of his predecessors, William Demas, had once told his staff members that the CARICOM Secretariat was not a research institute. My feeling at the time was that the words of Demas, an avid researcher himself, were being taken out of context.

Despite the lack of support, bordering on hostility, I persisted and CTIR, 2000 was prepared entirely by a team that I led of staff members (including Enid Bissember, David Lord and Evelyn Wayne) and subsequently published by Jamaica-based Ian Randle Press with the sub-title *'Dynamic Interface of Regionalism and Globalisation'* (pp.325), Five years later, CTIR 2005 had the sub-theme *'Corporate Integration and Cross-Border Development'* (pp.504); and the sub-theme of 2010 was *'Strategies for Recovery, Renewal and Reform'* (pp.331). For most of this ten-year period, Owen Arthur, the Head of Government with portfolio responsibility for economic integration, was an enthusiastic supporter and urged that CTIR should become an annual publication, but the Secretariat did not see it fit to provide required resources; in fact, no financial resources were made available by the CARICOM Secretariat for the three Studies.

For CTIR 2005, I was able to secure funding from the Swiss Agency for Development and Cooperation (SADC) through the facilitative efforts of Theo Gittens, an official in the United Nations Development Programme (UNDP); but because the Deputy Secretary-General, Lolita Applewhaite, diverted some of the Swiss ear-marked resources to the general Secretariat budget, I had to persuade the President of the CDB to make up for the shortfall.

For CTIR 2010, I was able to secure funding from CDB, the European Commission, the Inter-American Development Bank (IDB) and the Organisation of American States (OAS). Sensing it would be my last CTIR venture, I stated, in my Remarks at the Launching of CTIR 2010, that "it is hoped that the time will come when the CARICOM Secretariat will be able to make the CTIR an annual publication". However, meaningful resources of both a human and financial nature are required to be devoted to this exercise. Since my resignation at the end of 2010, there has been no further publication of CTIR, whether annually or quinquennially, despite the fact that every regional (and global) organisation has one or more flagship publications. Excerpt from the substantive Notes, on which my CTIR 2010 launching remarks were made, are as follows:

1. *CTIR 2010 is the third in the series of quinquennial benchmark reports on the workings of both the regional integration process and other major issues relating to the CARICOM development paradigm and the changing global context.*
2. *The title 'Trade and Investment' is therefore something of a misnomer, as can be gauged if one were to look at the titles of the three Sections of the Report and the titles of the ten constituent Chapters.*
3. *The analysis in the various Chapters attempts to not only review lessons learnt from past experiences, particularly within*

the last five years, but also future strategic options and policy implications.

4. The Report is oriented to the needs of regional policy makers, academic researchers, business interests, civic society and the general public.

5. The report is intended to fill an important gap since there are not many home grown publications dealing with regional issues. Moreover, international and hemispheric publications typically devote little space to the CARICOM experience. When the foreign publications are expansive on regional issues, they tend to show little concern or sympathy for the peculiar problems of small countries.

6. On the Caribbean Community's part, a lot of the regional data and information on which decisions are taken are not readily available and so it is hoped that the CTIR publication fills this other void. Nevertheless, available data sets are still in many respects structurally inadequate and not sufficiently up-to-date for analysing and monitoring the regional integration progress and general economic performance. The national statistical departments need to undergo a serious retooling exercise.

7. It is hoped that the time will soon come when the CARICOM Secretariat will be able to make the CTIR an annual publication. However, adequate resources of both a human and financial nature are required to be devoted to this exercise.

The lack of support I received for the CTIR from the top echelons of the Secretariat relates to a much wider information and publication issue and mind-set. For example, there was for decades, and still is, no system of declassification of documents relating to bi-annual Conferences of the Heads of Government or the regular Meetings of the various Ministerial Councils (of Trade and Economic Development; Human and Social Development; Foreign and Community Relations; and

Finance and Planning). Moreover, the Communiqués issued, following press briefings, at the end of Conferences of the Heads of Government tend to be much too terse

Within two months of my employment at the CARICOM Secretariat, I became involved with the issue of a publication policy. It all began on 28 July 1997, when I wrote a memo to the Secretary-General on the subject of "A Proposed Publications Programme for the CARICOM Secretariat". The memo reads as follows:

> *Since April, I have read a number of consultants' reports (and, also, in-house papers by Secretariat staff members). However, in certain cases, staff members in one Directorate did not even seem to be aware of the consultants' reports contracted by another. Some of the Reports are sufficiently interesting, and of a high enough quality, as to warrant publication. In any event, there should be a listing of all such consultants' reports, under appropriate subject headings.*
>
> *Now that the RNM is about to undertake a series of studies and policy papers, I feel that this is an appropriate point to embark on a programme of selective publication of CARICOM sponsored manuscripts. The attached is an elaboration of this proposal.*

The structure of the proposed programme and the justification therefore are reflected in the following excerpts:

> *In recent times a number of very interesting reports have been produced (at not inconsiderable cost) and some of these merit exposure to a wider audience than the trade and industry officials who traditionally attend Council and other CARICOM Meetings. Both the business and academic community could certainly benefit from the information and knowledge contained in these unpublished documents and the general public would not only acquire a better and more transparent understanding of the basis*

for regional decision-making but, also, would begin to view the CARICOM Secretariat as a think-tank, rather than as a mere bureaucracy. At the moment, there is not even a proper listing of these reports in the Secretariat).

Of course, a publications programme must be based on a clear publications policy featuring priority themes and an appropriate analytical thrust. In particular, the publications would need to be policy oriented, rather than academic in nature, and user-friendly for decision-makers and practitioners. Very careful formulation of the terms of reference of each study would therefore be necessary. In addition, in order to maintain objectivity, the consultants' reports would need to be revised and carefully edited to reflect the considered judgment of the Secretariat, rather than solely that of whichever consultant/expert happens to have conducted the research work. In one or two cases, certain sensitive material may need to be sanitised out of the report, prior to publication. Above all, selectivity (with respect to which report to publish) would need to be exercised in order to ensure quality and excellence. This is particularly necessary in the early stages of a programme when credibility and reputation are at a premium.

The publications programme could probably include three different (and distinct) series. One could probably encompass Global, Regional and Plurilateral Integration (GRIP) manuscripts.

Since there are likely to be vast differences between the Studies, on the one hand, and the Policy Papers, on the other, in terms of depth, breadth and orientation, there may be justification in dividing the GRIP publications into two series: Sub-Series A to include the Studies and Sub-Series B to include the Policy Papers.

A second Publication Series could revolve around the subject areas and themes of Trade, Investment and Economic Development (TIED). The TIED Series could consist mainly of

Technical Studies *that are both substantive and interesting as, for example, the Diagnostic Studies on the Enabling Environment for Investment in Various CARICOM Counties. (In the case where a Government does not, because of the sensitive nature of the material, want a particular country study to be published, it may be possible to combine it with other country studies in the form of an overview). The Papers delivered at important CARICOM workshops could also be published as technical studies. A Sub-Series of* ***Working Papers*** *could also be introduced to take account of instances where a manuscript does not quite reach the analytical and informational depth of a technical study but, nevertheless, is sufficiently interesting to warrant publication. (Young CARICOM members of staff could be invited to make contributions, with the incentive of the work appearing under their own name, to this Sub-Series). It is, in addition, possible to envisage another Sub-Series in the form of an annual publication entitled* ***Caribbean Trade and Investment Report.*** *ECLAC (Port-of-Spain) may be interested in collaborating in this latter venture and each year's report could highlight a particular theme or issue. Current ECLAC (Santiago) reports tend not to include sufficient information on CARICOM countries.*

A third Publication Series, on "Community Developments" already exists in the popularised and journalistic form of ***CARICOM Perspective*** *and* ***CARICOM View****. The general "man-in-the-street" outreach medium could be usefully complemented with the sorts of publications mentioned above.*

Finally, a publications programme like the one described above would require a considerable amount of back-up support. Someone would need to, in addition to his or her normal duties, perform the functions of a Publications Manager, including the task of coordinating the research outputs of the relevant Directorates and Units of the CARICOM Secretariat. There would also be need for someone to perform the functions of a Chief

Technical Editor. In addition, the research skills in the Secretariat would need to be strengthened and the statistical bases and information collection systems streamlined and made more effective.

Soon thereafter, I wrote the Directors and the Programme Managers of the four Directorates in the CARICOM Secretariat requesting a list of studies, reports and other analytical papers that might have been produced in-house or by consultants, that they were aware of, but I got no response from anyone. I therefore decided that I would focus my energies on producing a first Caribbean Trade and Investment Report, which was duly published in 2000. The Report was well received within the Region, but it did not generate excitement within the Secretariat.

Late the next year, 19 September 2001 to be exact, the Director of Information and Communication, Jacqueline Wiltshire-Forde, wrote a memo to Directors, Advisors, Programme Managers and Deputy Programme Managers, copied to Members of Executive Management Committee (EMC) requesting information on what newsletters and other public relations mechanisms currently existed in the Secretariat and their "scope, targets and objectives". In a pointed response some months later, on 15 February 2002, the Deputy Secretary-General (DSG) Carla Barnett wrote all stakeholders informing them that EMC had established an Ad Hoc Editorial Committee *"to facilitate central awareness and harmonisation of messages with respect to CARICOM Secretariat publications (and need) to inform the Chairman of the Editorial Committee, as early as possible, of any communication products emanating from your Directorate/Programme".*

A few days later, I wrote the DSG indicating that the proposed Editorial Committee might be appropriate for evaluating newsletters, but its composition was not appropriate for the purpose of giving intellectual direction with respect to regional integration policy research. My memo of 25 February, 2002 read as follows:

I refer to your memo of 15 February 2002 which indicated that the EMC had recently approved the establishment of an Ad Hoc Editorial Committee to deal with CARICOM Secretariat publications. The Committee's formation seems to have been occasioned by an explosion of CARICOM Secretariat Newsletters and its composition reflects a need for promoting "harmonisation of messages". As you indicated, the Committee consists of the Director of Information and Communication as Chairperson, along with the Programme Manager and Deputy Programme Managers of Information and Communication; Deputy Programme Manager, Conference Services; Public Relations Officer in the Office of the Secretary-General and Administrative Officers attached to Directorates.

2. As you are aware, the work programme of the Economic Intelligence and Policy Unit (EIPU) includes the publication of technical and working papers for the benefit of CARICOM decision-makers (in both the public and private sectors) and civil society. The Caribbean Trade and Investment Report 2000 is our flagship technical paper. It is our intention, also, to develop a Policy Studies Series involving the publication of Working Papers from time to time. This would require the services of an Editorial Committee. Unfortunately, the composition of the Ad Hoc Editorial Committee that the EMC recently established does not seem to be one that can make for giving of intellectual guidance to analytical publications. The EIPU would need a more high level editorial committee which should be both representative of the structure of the Secretariat and functionally reflective of the integration policy remit. In addition, the members should have a genuine interest in research issues, a willingness to exercise their independent critical powers, and a capacity for good judgement. In this regard, specific staff members who could be invited to become members of such a High Level Editorial Committee could include the following: Byron Blake, Eddie Greene, Duke Pollard, Jacqueline Wiltshire-Forde, Philomen Harrison, Marcelino Avila, Valerie Alleyne-Odle and David Lord. I would suggest the appointment of Amos Peters (SPO, EIPU) as the Editorial Assistant and Secretary to the Board.

3. I shall be grateful for your views on the matter.

The DSG replied to me on March 2 indicating that technical policy studies would indeed need a higher level Editorial Committee, but that higher level staff may not be able to devote enough time to the editorial exercise, with the resulting need also for external readers/editors:

I received your memorandum of 25 February on the above. Indeed, you are correct, the Ad Hoc Editorial Committee was established by EMC to coordinate the "message" and exert quality control over the public education/public relations publications which the Secretariat currently publishes or is planning to publish. These include the magazines, web pages, press releases, newsletters, calendars, etc. which we use to disseminate information to general or specific audiences at this time.

The Caribbean Trade and Investment Report and the possible Policy Studies Series which you mention are indeed publications of a different nature, which require the additional element of subject-specific technical editing. You have suggested that the answer to this specific need is the establishment of a "High Level Editorial Committee". The question I would ask is whether the persons you have suggested would have the time required to systematically devote to this endeavour so as to allow the journal to meet publication deadlines. Perhaps the route of external readers combined with a smaller internal committee, or an editor and internal readers, or some reasonable and workable combination of internal and external editorial effort should be explored.

I would also like to suggest that it is imperative to have the decisions on size, format and content of journals taken by persons not involved in the writing or technical editing of the articles so as to keep the finished product within reasonable and agreed limits on length and cost. This will also help us to ensure that the more technical publications contribute as well to our public education/ public relations efforts.

All this, of course, is an academic discussion until EMC has received a proposal to make the CTIR, or any other journal, a regular and sustainable publication. We still await your proposal in this regard.

The DSG had, in a 2 March 2002 memo, indicated that she had received a courtesy call the previous week from Dr Compton Bourne, the President of the Caribbean Development Bank, who had indicated that the Bank was willing to collaborate with the CARICOM Secretariat in preparing technical publications. I followed up with a long letter to Dr Bourne, dated 11 April, 2002 in which a CTIR was proposed, *inter alia*, and ideas detailed on form of collaboration; type of content; scheduling and reporting; mode of financing; quality control; structure of the research team; production flow; and launching of the finished product. A Director of the Bank, Alan Slusher, wrote to me a follow up letter, dated 28 April 2002, exploring further the substance and logistics of the proposed collaboration and I reported to SG Carrington on the developments in a memo dated 5 December 2002.

The Editorial Committee idea was never developed and implemented by EMC and a publications programme never really got off the ground, partly because the DSG resigned her position at the Secretariat not so long after, and partly because certain EMC elements, imbued with a certain bureaucratic culture, were not very enthusiastic to the idea. Publications wise, I continued to focus on CTIR and preparing personal articles and papers for national, regional and international fora, *inter alia*.

The lack of publicly disseminated information on the past and current achievements of CARICOM, and the paucity of everyday commentary in the mainstream media on regional integration related activities, have contributed to a generally perceived view that CARICOM is a dormant institution, rather than the live and vibrant (though challenged) institution it really is. In addition, the bane of confidentiality and the continuous failure to declassify reports and proceedings of important regional meetings, along with the reluctance/inability to develop a meaningful publications programme, limit information that should be available to decision makers, university scholars and other stakeholders (in both the public and private sector) and prevent the emergence of the next generation of committed regionalists. There was inadequate marketing of the integration phenomenon.

CRITICAL ANALYSIS OF INTEGRATION EXPERIENCE

The Caribbean has, for decades, been involved in the optimistic and daunting process of trying to emulate certain aspects of the European Union integration experience. One reason for falling short, it is said, is the very small size of the economies in the Region, and the relatively puny size of even the largest of the domestic firms, plus the related disadvantages in trying to achieve the required level of international competitiveness. However, small size is only one of several limiting factors, since a not insignificant level of progress has been made in pursuit of the regional integration objective, as reflected in the following 7 June, 2008 memo from me, in reply to the Paper *"Nano-Firms, Regional Integration and International Competitiveness"* (D. Benn and K. Hall, 2006) of the then Caribbean Chief Executive Officer (CEO) of the RNM, Richard Bernal, on the role of the CSME in compensating for small size and in furthering economic transformation:

The paper is interesting and persuasive in its argumentation. I however only wish to comment on the second half of the paper and the role of the CSME in compensating for small size and in furthering economic transformation.

First, the overall impression is given that besides (the preoccupation with) trade in goods, nothing much has been achieved in the regional integration process to date. However, since 2001, there has been free intra-CARICOM trade in services; free establishment/entry in small scale sectors that had previously been reserved for domestic investors; free movement of capital; free movement of labour for an increasing number of categories of skills; and free access to land for commercial purposes. (Freeing-up of the factors of production is critical to success).

Second, capital market integration, even when complete, cannot have a very significant impact if the capital market in the individual countries remains underdeveloped. At the moment, only a minority of enterprises choose to go public and offer their shares because of family firm traditions of retaining control at all costs. Note also that, although there are only 13 cross-listed securities on the stock exchanges in the Region, they account for well over 50% of the total market capitalisation.

Third, this same family firm ethic acts as barrier to new ideas and innovative practices and makes for limited entrepreneurial development. Competitiveness is both a culture/practice and efficiency condition that warrants continuous struggle. The failure to take advantage of the preferential market access that we enjoyed for decades is a clear sign of a lack of supply capacity (and not simply a product of complacency).

Fourth, while size matters and mergers and acquisitions (M&I) can help to mitigate the nano condition, it should be remembered that lack of adequate capital formation is a major weakness in the Caribbean and the M&I phenomenon, by itself, does not add to the regional stock. What is equally important are continuous rounds of greenfield investment, embodying the latest technology and innovation, following the M&I. Moreover, many of the large

Caribbean firms are really conglomerates and doubling of a firm's size does not necessarily imply a doubling of its core strength.

But the critics are many and important actors, such as Heads of Government, academics, media commentators and civil society have for some time been expressing concern at the slow progress in the integration process, despite the valiant efforts of former Prime Minister of Barbados, for whom I wrote a short tribute in the Guyana *Stabroek News* on his passing -

Owen Arthur's Passing: Condolences

The passing of former Prime Minister of Barbados, Owen Arthur, is a great loss to Caribbean intellectual thought, practice and leadership. I co-authored with him in 1985 a UWI published book, entitled: 'Commercialisation of Technology and Dependence in the Caribbean', and witnessed at first hand his seamless transition from political-economy steeped academia to political activism and ultimate political power. His assumption of the position of Prime Minister in 1994 and assignment by his peers, until his demitting office in 2008, as "Lead Head of Government" for furthering of the Caribbean Single Market and Economy process, resulted in very significant acceleration in regional economic integration.

This acceleration coincided with my stint as Special Economic Adviser to the then Secretary-General of CARICOM, with specific responsibility for deepening the Single Economy process, and I can therefore attest that Owen Arthur had a real understanding of the intricacies and requirements of true economic integration and it was a revelation to observe the drive and energy with which he sought to educate his colleagues on the issue at their various Heads of Government Conferences. When Prime Minister Owen Arthur spoke, everyone listened. It is therefore not surprising that, with the ending of his three term leadership in 2008, the economic

Prime Minister Owen Arthur, an indefatigable regionalist

integration process began to lose momentum and to experience a virtual "pause".

Sincere condolences to his wife Julie and the extended family, Owen joins a very selective group in the pantheon of truly great West Indian leaders.

Maurice Odle

In celebration of the 40th anniversary of the Treaty of Chaguaramas setting up the Caribbean Community, I was asked to write a critical review which appeared in the CLR James Journal, Volume 22, Numbers 1-2, Fall 2016 under the title, *'Caribbean Integration: Is the Glass Half Full or Half Empty?'* Since most of the views expressed therein are still pertinent, I see it fit to reproduce below the article, despite its rather critical nature, in its entirety:

The Grand Design: *The Caribbean Integration process is at a crossroad. Having recovered from the 1957-60 failed political Federation experiment, brave decisions were made to establish the following: a Free Trade Area in 1968; a Common Market in 1973 (at a Heads of Government Meeting in Chaguaramas,*

The signing the Treaty of Chaguaramas on 4 July 1973: Prime Ministers (L-R) Errol Barrow, Forbes Burnham, Eric Williams and Michael Manley

Trinidad and Tobago); a programme of work in 1989 in pursuit of the creation by 1993 of a Single Market and Economy (CSME) arising out of a Meeting at Grand Anse (Grenada); a 'Revised Treaty of Chaguaramas Establishing the Caribbean Community, including the Single Market and Economy' (CSME) in Nassau, The Bahamas in 2001 and an Agreement (though thirteen years late) relating to a "functioning" Single Market in 2006. The Revised Treaty spoke of achieving "sustained economic development based on international competitiveness, coordinated economic and foreign policies, functional cooperation and enhanced trade and economic relations with Third States". Cooperation in security (defence) matters was later added to these objectives.

An important pillar of the Revised Treaty's strategy of sustained economic development was, as is stated in Article 52, that of "production integration" via both intra and inter-sectoral processes. In paragraph 8, with particular reference to manufacturing, it is stated that:

> *For the purposes of this Article, production integration includes (a) the direct organisation of production in more*

than one Member State by a single economic enterprise (b) complementary production involving collaboration among several economic enterprises operating in one or more Member States to produce and use required inputs in the production chain; and (c) cooperation among economic enterprises in areas such as purchasing, marketing and research and development.

The Revised Treaty also posited a deep form of integration for the other sectors. Article 51, paragraph 2(a) spoke about "cross-border employment of natural resources" and, with respect to agriculture, Article 57, paragraph 1(c) stated that a goal was "the establishment of linkages among the Member States with complementary natural resources, industries, agricultural skills and technical abilities. Close attention was also paid to services. For example, for transport, the objective was to "promote cooperation among operators of air transport and supplies, the management of inventories, inter-line and inter-modal operations, code sharing, reservations, insurance, leasing and similar operations". Concerning finance, Article 44, paragraph 1(d) pointed to the adoption of appropriate measures "for the establishment of an integrated capital market in the Caribbean Community".

Although the Revised Treaty spoke eloquently about production integration, the implementation did not match the strategy and depth espoused by Havelock Brewster and Clive Thomas in their seminal 1967 work on 'The Dynamics of West Indian Economic Integration'. That Study elaborated and championed a process of production integration (albeit state led, rather than wholly reliant on market forces) in which key basic materials sectors and basic needs goods and services activities, catering to the requirements of the entire Caribbean Region, would be allocated among Member States, according to factor endowment and a guided process of cross-border trade, investment and finance.

Limited Economic Benefits: *Economic integration is supposed to confer benefits as a result of economies of scale, scope, space and synergy. Intra-regional trade (free among Member States and operating behind a common external tariff) has never been more than 18 percent of the Caribbean trade with the world as whole. This compares with a figure of 65 percent for intra-European Union trade, as a percentage of European trade with the world as a whole.*

With respect to intra-regional investment in the Caribbean, the figure is estimated to be no more than 15 percent of total world investment flows into the Region. The figure for intra-European Union investment flows is around 60 percent of total world investment flows into Europe. The disparities are partly as a result of the economies of Europe being much more complementary than those in the Caribbean. Moreover, the very significant proportion that foreign investment is of total regional capital formation in the Caribbean has not necessarily facilitated the economic integration process. For example, the phenomenon of foreign (mainly North American) ownership probably prevented from coming into fruition the proposal made decades ago for the smelting of Jamaican and Guyanese bauxite into aluminium in Trinidad using some of the latter's surplus energy; a classic case of corporate integration versus regional integration. However, regional capital could be equally risk averse. The more recent and much vaunted plan for surplus Trinidad capital to be invested in the vast state-owned lands in Guyana, so as to feed the Caribbean, has not yet gotten off the ground. Integration perhaps has proceeded the furthest in the financial sector, as the cross-border investment experience of CL Financial (via CLICO) had indicated, despite the subsequent near terminal developments.

Further examples of financial integration are that the RBC Financial, Scotia Bank, and First Caribbean International Bank operate in 20, 21, and 18 Caribbean countries/jurisdictions, respectively, and Republic Bank, headquartered in Trinidad and Tobago, is the largest commercial bank in Guyana. In the insurance sector, Sagicor Financial Corporation, a Barbados based entity, operates in no less than 22 Caribbean locations. There is also a considerable amount of cross-border listing of securities, although the Caribbean countries are yet to agree on the merging of their national stock exchanges into a single Regional Stock Exchange.

In many cases, on-going cross-border investment (via a greenfield or merger operation) the subsidiary firm tends to behave like a 'stand-alone' entity vis-à-vis the parent. This is because the reason for going cross-border was either 'market seeking' or 'resource seeking' in nature, rather than 'efficient seeking', whereby an attempt is made to qualitatively pool attributes such as materials, capital, technology, knowhow and marketing skills, inter alia.

Unfortunately, no serious attempt has ever been made by Caribbean scholars to develop indices to quantify the gains made from the regional economic integration process.

Selected Economic Policy and Operational Failures: *Perceived failures relate to a number of areas. Barriers to intra-regional trade in agricultural goods are posed by sanitary and phyto-sanitary concerns and trade in manufactured goods is bedevilled by the contentious issue of Trinidad and Tobago export firms benefitting from subsidised cheap energy. Equally contentious is trade in labour services ("Free Movement of Skilled Nationals") due to either unwillingness to admit of certain types of skilled labour or reluctance to accord "contingent rights" (such as equal access to state-owned educational and health services) to spouses* *and children of non-nationals – a "national treatment" issue. (The problems related to cross-border right-to-work are compounded by not infrequent episodes concerning denial of entry, such as Jamaicans travelling to Trinidad and Tobago and Guyanese visiting Barbados, and certain Member States require Haitian visitors to first secure a visa). The Single Market has made considerable progress, but it is still a work in progress.*

The Single Economy project has made far less progress than the Single Market. Although strenuous efforts from early 1990s were made to effect macro-economic convergence among Member States, so as to effect a Currency Union, the Single Currency project was abandoned in the early 2000s, owing to seemingly unbridgeable policy divergence.

With respect to Intra-regional investment, after over a decade of consultation and negotiation of a Draft CARICOM Investment Code, the exercise was virtually abandoned in 2010. In the area of intra-regional finance, the same fate has befallen the Draft CARICOM Financial Services Agreement, partly because of the striving for absolute unanimity.

Similarly, CARICOM failed to agree, after over a year-and-a-half of deliberation, following the tourism fallout from the 2001 terrorism event in the USA, to set up a Regional Stabilisation Fund that could have partially cushioned Member States from the worse effects that, later on, Wall Street financial recklessness initiated in 2008. Even more damning is the reluctance of the Prime Minister (Kamla Persad-Bissessar) of Trinidad and Tobago in 2011 to further finance the compensatory Petroleum Fund, whose country's previous Prime Minister (Patrick Manning) had introduced a few years earlier in recognition of the skewed nature of the benefits accruing from an integration process in which energy endowed and low cost manufacturing Trinidad and Tobago was amassing very significant trade surpluses with its other regional partners. Moreover, the CARICOM Development Fund, which was set up by the Governments in 2008, is too poorly endowed to be able to effectively offset existing economic polarisation tendencies deriving from the workings of the integration process.

Functional Cooperation as a Soft Option: Failure on the economic front has led some officials to believe that such a shortfall could be compensated for by accelerated social and other gains via functional cooperation (as distinct from economic integration, per se). For example, educational gains have been made with the Caribbean Examination Council (CXC) system being a worthwhile mechanism for providing linkages with and standardising inputs into the University of the West Indies (UWI) and other tertiary systems in the Region.

Strides have also been made in functional cooperation with respect to health, as evidenced by the formation of the Pan-Caribbean Partnership (PANCAP) against HIV/AIDS, but it can be questioned whether a complex regional apparatus is required for cooperative progress to be made, in keeping with the "proportionality principle" that the regional bureaucracy should not be employed in areas in which the national States are eminently qualified to act. In addition, collective natural disaster re-insurance arrangements (via a Caribbean Catastrophe Risk Insurance Facility – CCRIF) have managed to secure a 30 percent reduction of premiums that would have obtained if Member States had decided to go it alone.

However, functional cooperation failures tend to exist in the transportation framework area. Although Air Jamaica has been absorbed by Caribbean Airlines, contention persists with respect to the even-handedness of the airline's regional pricing and network operational practices and, moreover, only few Member States have made financial and logistical commitment to the other regional carrier – LIAT. Regional maritime transportation *arrangements (including a proposed fast ferry) also seem to remain stillborn.*

A most glaring shortcoming exists in the legal area. Only three countries (Barbados, Belize and Guyana) so far have subscribed to both the original and appellate jurisdictions of the US$100 million capitalised Caribbean Court of Justice, preferring to continue using the last resort facility of the United Kingdom's Privy Council.

Coordination of relations with Third States also leaves much to be desired, with the focus being the soliciting of financial aid, rather than the promotion of inward investment. The most glaring example is the Region's lack of full implementation of the ruling made decades ago by the United Nations that Taiwan is a "province of China". Certain of the smaller CARICOM Member States continue to recognise Taiwan because of the aid they receive, paying little attention to the resulting difficulty in forging a coherent regional foreign policy for dealing with an emerging economic super power, mainland China. In addition, there is a lack of consensus reflected in the membership in the Venezuelan led Bolivarian Alliance of the Peoples of the Americas (ALBA) and, also, with respect to participation in the Venezuela sponsored Petro-caribe arrangement, since the Bahamas, Barbados and Trinidad and Tobago exempted themselves.

The regional security apparatus, although experiencing strengthening in certain areas, also requires better cooperation and coordination. The much mooted Trinidad and Tobago led umbrella radar system (and related air and sea patrol) for the Eastern Caribbean is yet to materialise and the drug and associated gun menace continues to burgeon, with crime tightening by police in one country possibly resulting in ballooning crime in another neighbouring country. The problem is equally one of lack of resources and lack of regional political will.

Lack of Political Will: *The CARICOM Single Market regime is still not fully implemented, primarily because of a lack of political will on the part of CARICOM Heads of Government (and their loyal Ministers and senior officials). Agreements reached at a regional level are frequently held up, either because of no ratification in the national Parliaments, slowness in making changes in the national legislation or no instituting of implementing national regulations. There is a persistent implementation deficit.*

The attempt to forge a CARICOM Single Economy regime (in which the Bahamas and Haiti were never part of the process) is in even more dire straits in that a decision was abruptly made by the Heads of Government (but which had long been telegraphed by the lukewarm nature of senior government negotiating officials) in 2011 to effect a "pause" (particularly with respect to the Single Currency endeavour) presumably in light of the lingering effects of the global financial and economic crisis. Contrast this second-best decision with that made at the same time by the European Union (EU) who were similarly impacted by the Wall Street originated crisis, not to retreat from the integration objective and to work towards a fiscal union, a banking union, and a strengthened European Central Bank 'lender of last resort facility'.

The leaders of the Caribbean countries seem reluctant to relinquish too much power and are comforted by the rather gratuitous declaration in the Treaty of Chaguaramas that they are a "community of sovereign states". So much so, that the recently elected Jamaican Government is stridently proclaiming a lack of benefits accruing to their country (and a polarisation that benefits Trinidad and Tobago) from the integration process; and a 'Brexit' type referendum could result (similar to that called by the Conservative Government in Britain over membership in the EU).

The lack of political will was made more evident within the last decade by the departure from the regional inter-governmental scene of two integration champions (Owen Arthur, on the economic side, and Percival Patterson, on the political side) who were truly imbued with the pioneering legacy of the immediate post-colonial Founding Fathers – Errol Barrow of Barbados, Vere Bird of Antigua and Barbuda, Forbes Burnham of Guyana and Eric Williams of Trinidad and Tobago. The current leaders, however, generally lack the same sense of urgency, passion and intellectual commitment to the notion of a "Caribbean Community for All". In this resulting leadership vacuum, there is also need for a CARICOM Secretary-General to act more like a pro-active General and less like a glorified Secretary.

Whither CARICOM: *The Caribbean integration process is in crisis and decision making is at a crossroad. There is a lively debate in certain quarters as to whether the way forward at this particular conjuncture is one of deepening or widening i.e. whether greater efforts should be devoted to achieving higher levels of macro-economic coordination and production integration (with emphasis on food security, energy security and various other intra-regional linkages that are analysed in a "regional public goods" framework in the somewhat neglected 'Strategic Plan for Regional Development' or whether the main emphasis should be on increasing CARICOM membership to include the Dominican Republic and the French and Dutch Caribbean territories.*

The global financial and economic crisis has exposed the extreme vulnerability, lack of resilience and undiversified state of CARICOM economies, many of which continue to stagnate. When combined with high levels of indebtedness and rapidly disappearing preferential market access to its traditional external trading partners, there is a clear need for CARICOM to forge a new development strategy.

Moreover, in the present era, open regionalism can be in conflict with the sometimes competing paradigm of neo-liberal globalisation. One example of the regionalism versus globalisation dilemma is the WTO's Trade Related Investment Measures (TRIMs) regime and the inhibiting effect on the ability of the Caribbean region to maximise local/regional content in the production process. Negotiating multilateral arrangements with a single voice also does not produce the expected results. The benefits derived from the 2008 Economic Partnership Agreement (EPA) with Europe have so far been very disappointing, partly because of the inherently unequal/unlevel nature of the playing field.

The Caribbean integration process has lost momentum (less so for the smaller countries comprising the sub-grouping called the Organisation of Eastern Caribbean States – OECS) and is increasingly failing to capture the imagination of the Caribbean population for all the reasons mentioned above. One need is to more effectively involve the private sector and, also, the labour movement and civil society in the consultation and decision making process; this would facilitate the seizure of region wide economic and social opportunities. There is also need to resurrect the Assembly of Caribbean Community Parliamentarians as well as the consultation process involving the Opposition Party leaders, in keeping with higher levels of inclusive governance. Just as important, regional integration activities need to be more transparent and studies, working papers and background documents ought to be made less confidential for the purpose of better informing and gaining better 'buy-in' of the public; in addition, high school and university teachers and researchers would be better able to service courses on regional integration and so coax out a new generation of regionalists.

The CARICOM movement has failed to live up to the intellectually transformative traditions of Brewster and Thomas and like-minded scholars and has lost sight of the political vision of the Founding Fathers. The glass is half empty as far as economic integration (with Single Economy in full retreat) is concerned, and only half full, with relation to functional cooperation efforts.

CHAPTER SEVEN

COALITION BLUES: GUYANA (2015-2020)

RE-ENTRY INTO POLITICAL ACTIVISM

On my departure from CARICOM in April 2011, it was my intention to take it relatively easy and to avoid any intensive intellectual pursuit that would lead to significant effort and related stress. It so happened that, at that time, a rented property that I owned in Georgetown was vacant and I, accordingly, took the opportunity to devote time and energy to organising and arranging the rehabilitating and retrofitting of same. It was a rather relaxing and satisfying exercise. But, then, interesting things began to happen at a political and professional level that left me with an indelible impression.

Following Walter Rodney's assassination in 1980 and my acceptance of a United Nations job in New York soon thereafter, my involvement with the WPA had gradually come to an end. (My last significant act was when I had audience in 1981 with US Attorney-General Ramsey Clark concerning the assassination). However this changed when, three or four years after my return to Guyana, I was approached by two WPA executive members, Desmond Trotman and Sheila Holder, with a request that I resume executive membership and to make as much of a financial contribution to the Party as circumstances would permit.

In Guyana, the ruling Indian-based PPP had regained office in 1992 (*via* a free and fair election) under Cheddi Jagan, who died in 1997 and was succeeded by his wife, who gave up office to one Bharrat Jagdeo in

1999 owing to ill health. At this time, the leader of the largest minority Party, PNC's Desmond Hoyte, who had lost the election in 1992, had become disillusioned about his primarily African supported PNC ever returning to power, given the ethnic nature of voting patterns, and proposed "power sharing," as a means of mitigating partisan rule. His successor, Robert Corbin, had announced a similar stance in Parliament in 2002. But, in 2003, the then President, Bharrat Jagdeo, rejected the power sharing idea, adding that the PNC was trying to gain power "through the back-door" and that "trust" must first be earned between the two leading Parties.

At the 2006 national elections, the PNC did badly and the PPP increased its majority in Parliament. Fearing that the PPP, which was increasingly being described in the media as an "elected dictatorship", would become a permanent majority, the PNC began to engage with the WPA in coalition talks. For the WPA to acquiesce, required a great deal of soul searching, since it was generally felt that PNC leaders were involved in the well-organised 1980 assassination of Walter Rodney. But recognition of the need to further the interests of the country, as a whole, rather than any one political Party, carried the day.

When national election loser, Robert Corbin, relinquished leadership of the PNC, he was succeeded by one David Granger, ex-army Brigadier, in a hotly contested and controversial election that many thought Carl Greenidge had really won. Granger was subsequently persuaded, with some effort, as to the wisdom (for purposes of ultimately gaining political power and cultivating inclusiveness) in the formation of A Partnership for National Unity (APNU) involving the PNC and a number of smaller Parties, including the WPA. As an executive member, I happened to be the WPA representative at an APNU press conference that was convened soon after its formation and my views were prominently displayed in the media, much to the consternation of my wife, Valerie, who was a senior staff member of the CARICOM Secretariat. Then, the Secretary-General at the time, Irwin LaRocque, (apparently bending backwards to isolate the Secretariat from partisan politics) surprisingly ruled that my wife, Valerie, could no longer be in charge of monitoring elections in the various CARICOM countries. Apparently, a wife and her husband are politically deemed to be one and the same person, with little independence of thought. (Little did the same Secretary-General know that, later in his tenure, his Chef de Cabinet would be the wife of Guyana's Minister of Finance and that, with a change of Government in 2020, another member of staff would become the wife of the new Prime Minister). It seemed as though, when a Government is in office, the Secretariat does not see its staff as having a conflict of interest; the problem only arises when the interests of the incumbent Government might be threatened by Opposition elements.

A few years prior to the formation of the APNU, what later became the third largest Party in Guyana, the Alliance for Change (AFC) appeared on the political scene, with the founding leaders being Sheila Holder (now ex WPA member), Raphael Trotman (ex PNC member), and Khemraj Ramjattan (ex PPP member). At the 2011 election, the APNU and AFC, combined, managed to secure more votes than the PPP and so a one seat majority in Parliament, given the proportional representation based 'List System'. However, the PPP formed the Government since, according to the constitution, the other two parties would have had to contest the election as a single (coalition) entity and could not form themselves into a coalition after the election. But the APNU-AFC grouping, with a majority of votes, was able to deny the PPP meaningful control over the latter's legislative agenda, even though this was not the case with most aspects of executive authority.

Based on this experience, the APNU and the AFC formally coalesced before the 2015 election and duly formed a Government, with a one seat majority. As a result, the new Government made a number of personnel changes in the leadership of certain institutions and agencies, *inter alia*. I was asked to be Chairman and/or Member of a number of Boards/Committees. But I am getting ahead of myself. Before describing, below, my experiences providing technical support to the 2015 Coalition Government, I need to refer to an interesting regional financial project that occurred a couple of years earlier and for which I was the consultant and Lead author of the resulting Study.

AN INTELLECTUAL INTERLUDE

In early 2012, I was invited by Dr Compton Bourne, the then Chairman of the Caribbean Centre on Money and Finance (CCMF) to be the Consultant assisting the Committee of Central Bank Governors (CCBG) in the preparation of a Report on Caribbean Financial Stability. At this time, the undiversified and primarily tourism oriented economies of the Caribbean, except for Guyana and Suriname, were reeling from the persistently adverse effects of the 2008 originated Global Financial Crisis. The financial sector in the Caribbean was also particularly affected, partly because the degree of regional integration in this sector was much greater than had been realised, with affected commercial banks headquartered in Trinidad and Tobago, and affected Insurance companies headquartered in both Trinidad and Tobago and Barbados, having subsidiaries and affiliates in many of the other Caribbean countries. But the financial conglomerates had invested a considerable portion of their surplus outside of the Caribbean region, particularly in Florida's real estate, and when that sub-prime mortgage market collapsed, it had a devastating effect throughout the Caribbean region.

In the latter period of my employment at the CARICOM Secretariat, a considerable amount of time and effort had been devoted to dealing with the crisis's fallout and diverse repercussions. This, along with my academic experience in the financial sector subject area made me somewhat prepared for undertaking the consultancy task at hand. The next two years featured an iterative process of meetings I had with the Committee of Central Bankers on background financial Studies of mine (on 'National and Regional Statistical Trends and Strengths and Weaknesses', and 'Issues in Regional Financial Stability Assessment') and drafts of the major report. The Caribbean Regional Financial Stability Report, with Maurice Odle as Lead Author, was eventually published by the UWI Press in April. 2016.

But not everything had been plain sailing. I was made aware of a certain underlying tension arising from the fact that two of the Central Bank Governors were not happy with my consultancy appointment, as they had a preferred candidate. This was also evident from a rather mischievous comment that one of them made at a seminar at which the final draft of the holistic Study was being presented. Partisanship is everywhere. This experience partially prepared me for the intrigue that was to follow during the tenure of the 2015-2020 Coalition Government, for which I held certain important technical positions.

TAX REFORM DISAPPOINTS

Within a few weeks of the Coalition Government taking up office in August 2020, the Minister of Finance, Winston Jordan, asked me to be Chairman of a Tax Reform Committee (TRC) that he was in the process of setting up and indicated that the other Committee members would be Godfrey Statia, a former Deputy Commissioner of Inland Revenue; Christopher Ram, a skilled accountant cum lawyer; and Thomas Singh, a Senior University of Guyana lecturer and researcher. In addition, the Minister made available two senior staff members of the Ministry of Finance to logistically and otherwise facilitate the work of the Committee. The Minister was keen to include appropriate tax changes in his budget presentation in late January, 2016 and so the Committee found itself working within a very tight schedule.

The work of the Committee included reviewing the existing tax framework, and identifying the contribution made to direct and indirect revenue by various sectors and household categories. Of critical importance was examination of both the redistributive nature and business incentivised characteristics of the tax system. Accordingly, the Committee's recommendations included measures for making the tax system more broad based, ensuring that the self-employed paid their fair tax share, reducing the rate and incidence of value-added taxes, and improving tax administration and investor facilitation, *inter alia*.

The Committee failed to complete its work before the end of 2015, partly because of the intensive nature of the programme of consultation meetings with various business, labour and civic stakeholders. However, I managed to present the Minister with the Report by the middle of January, 2016.

When the Minister duly presented his budget, its tax measures were subjected to severe criticism by the PPP Opposition Leader and his comrades, who latched onto the fact that a considerable number of new measures were included in the budget and they vastly exaggerated the impact of same, as well as the true number of such measures, repeatedly and falsely claiming, over the next three years, that there had been "over 200 tax measures". It became a public relations disaster for the Coalition Government and might have contributed to the Coalition Government's loss of the 2020 election. The situation resembled what took place in 1962, when the PNC, then the Opposition (supported by a third party, the United Force) demonstrated against the budget of the PPP Government, that led to a series of destabilising events, which resulted in the latter's loss of political power: "Payback time".

As Chairman of the Tax Reform Committee, the distorted reception meted out to its work was a bit disappointing and unsettling. There were a number of lessons to be learnt. *First*, it would have been useful if, at the conclusion of the work of the TRC, the Minister had asked for a de-briefing, which could have informed a meaningful implementation strategy, the independence and prerogative of the Minister notwithstanding. *Second*, timing of implementation and selectivity are important, in that the tax reform measures could have been introduced over a number of annual budgets, rather than mostly in one initial budget. *Third,* the public could have been better prepared if there had been more prior public discussion by the Minister of Finance, himself, on the deficiencies in the national taxation system and the need for reform (thus testing public sentiment) without necessarily indicating what particular tax measures would be contained in any one budget. *Fourth*, it needed to be realised that the typical household taxpayer is psychologically likely to feel adversely impacted by small imposts, like fees, even though these might be simultaneously offset by significant allowances, and other fiscal devices, including reduction of taxes in certain areas and various expenditure relief measures.

NICIL IN TURMOIL

While appreciative of the offer by Minister Jordan in September 2015 to also serve as Chairman of the country's National Industrial and Commercial Investments Ltd (NICIL), there was a feeling of trepidation on my part. This was because NICIL had developed a media driven reputation, during the last few years of the previous Government, of being a 'rogue' governmental entity that facilitated Government corruption, arbitrary behaviour and unaccountability. For example, it had sold exclusively, and at well below market prices, to President Jagdeo and certain other Ministers and senior Government officials, a block of prime (ocean viewing) real estate land ("Pradoville 2") in Beterverwagting, located on the outskirts of the capital, Georgetown. Earlier, President Jagdeo and certain others had benefited from a similar type of arrangement – "Pradoville 1", near the Ogle International Airport, even though the regulations state that no one can benefit more than once from the purchase of subsidised state-owned land. NICIL had also expanded its operations, from being solely responsible for managing government's privatisation activities, to active involvement in arranging certain unorthodox and perverse type public-private partnerships, in which the Government provided the bulk of the capital and bore most of the risk, whereas the bulk of the equity accrued to private investors Moreover, there was little transparency and most major transactions were deemed to be confidential, and information not made available to the public. Critically, the NICIL structure did not make for good governance and accountability, since the Chairman of the Board, under the previous Government, was the Minister of Finance (and one of its Members was the Head of the Presidential Secretariat). These and other defects were elaborated on in a Goolsarran Report that was commissioned by the incoming Coalition Government.

When the Coalition Government assumed office, therefore, the expectation was that the operations of NICIL would be somewhat less controversial. But this was not to be. Immediately, the Board of Directors (which, at this time, controversially included Joseph Harmon, Director-General/Minister, in the Office of the Presidency) had to deal with the issue of whether the Chief Executive Officer, Winston Brassington (originally titled Executive Director) and his Deputy (Marcia Nadir-Sharma) should be replaced. The rather painful matter was not resolved in their favour, and they were relieved of their positions by the Board, as was the wish of the Government.

At the suggestion of Board Member Joe Harmon (who remained a member of the Board for another year) it was decided to ask the Head (Horace James) of NICIL operations in Linden, Region 10, to be interim (Acting) CEO of the NICIL parent company. When the position of CEO was eventually advertised and the adjudged best candidate was offered the post, he declined because the pay and allowances were not sufficiently attractive. But the other candidates were not very attractive alternatives. The Minister of Finance, Winston Jordan, then suggested to the Board that, instead of re-advertising, Horace James be appointed CEO. On reflection, the decision to so appoint was not a very good one. All but one of the senior staff members of NICIL resigned in protest a few months later and, after an uneventful tenure and a protracted illness, the CEO passed away. But not before strenuous efforts were made to deal with companies and individuals that were, for a long time, financially obligated to NICIL. Following the spate of privatisations at the beginning of the 1990s, many who bought or leased previously state-owned property had ceased making regular payments for same. For me, the extent of the practised delinquency of businessmen, with outstanding liabilities to the Government, was an eye opener.

Soon after James' death, I recommended to the Minister of Finance that one Colvin London, based on energetic performance to date, be asked to act as CEO, with effect from October, 2018. The latter had been appointed about a year earlier (August 2017 and contract renewed

February 2018) by the Coalition Government as a consultant to head a Special Purpose Unit (SPU) commissioned to privatise certain failing sugar estates and to rehabilitate the remaining estates of the Guyana Sugar Corporation (GuySuco) whose assets had been a few months earlier vested into NICIL. A G$30 billion syndicated loan was raised on the regional financial market for the rehabilitation. I was to regret making the recommendation, since Colvin London soon began to challenge my authority as Chairman, and later, scandalously sought to destroy my integrity.

The conflict began when Colvin London fired a member of the SPU – Project Officer, Ms Cindy Harbarran. She wrote the Chairman of the NICIL Board asking for his intervention, and claimed that she was being victimised for exposing apparent corruption. The matter was discussed at a regular Meeting of the Board and the Head of its Human Resources Committee was asked to investigate and report back to the Board. In the meantime, a certain amount of tension began to arise between the CEO (ag.) and the Chairman of NICIL, because the former felt that his executive authority was being undermined. The situation worsened when it was revealed that the Junior Minister of Finance (Jaipaul Sharma) had written the President citing complaints he had received about suspect transactions and suggested the instituting of an audit. The CEO (ag.) thereupon wrote the Minister of Finance complaining about his Deputy Minister's supposed unauthorised actions and the latter was soon transferred to another Ministry. Eventually, the Minister of Finance instructed his Central Internal Audit Unit to undertake an 'Investigation of Alleged Fraud, Impropriety and Misappropriation of Funds at National Industrial and Commercial Investments Limited'. (The investigation became excessively protracted and its 'Findings and Recommendations for Management Response' were seemingly never acted upon').

The integrity and cohesion of the NICIL Board also began to be adversely affected, with the CEO (ag.) managing to capture the support of at least half of the Board members through surreptitious means. The

Chairman also had cause to question the apparently conflicting loyalty of the Company Secretary, with respect to her service as Secretary to the Board *vis-à-vis* that of Chief Legal Advisor to her supervisor, the CEO (ag.).

The Chairman thus found himself in an absurd situation and the atmosphere in NICIL soon became very toxic. The CEO (ag.) seemed to even feel that he was accountable to neither the Board nor NICIL itself. For example, when I asked him to send me a copy of his contract (which the Company Secretary said could not be found in NICIL's registry) so as to facilitate completion of the "investigation and audit" (that was mandated by Minister Jordan), his reply on June 2019 was as follows:

> *I respectfully wish to enquire the necessity and relevance for which you require my contract of employment. I have confidentiality obligations to my employer, that is, the Government of Guyana. Accordingly, I cannot disclose my contract to any third parties, but certainly you are welcomed to obtain a copy of my contract from my employer. Furthermore, I have executed Confidentiality Agreement with NICIL.*

Although I solicited the help of Minister Jordan (who, in turn wrote the Director-General of the Ministry of the Presidency, Minister Harmon, to secure same) it was only on 18 September, 2019 that I received the CEO's contract, which had been signed by Minister Harmon as long ago as 15 February, 2018.

Things soon came to a head. At a NICIL Board Meeting, the CEO (ag.) resorted to shouting at the Chairman. A few weeks later, during a period when the Chairman was abroad on vacation leave, there were two scurrilous letters addressed to the media lambasting the Chairman, one by "Concerned Employees" and another by "Troubled Workers". The newspapers declined to publish the ugly fabrication and tissue of lies (that were most probably orchestrated by a certain antagonistic member of the Board who had previously told his friends that he will "skin Odle up").

The Special Board Meeting of NICIL did take place. A major development at that Meeting was a motion that the CEO (ag.) be relieved of that position (and that he reverts exclusively to his contractual position of Head of the Special Projects Unit (SPU) based on the following charges:

1. *By-passing the Board (re approval of land sales and lease transactions)*
2. *Withholding information from the Board*
3. *Misleading the Board*
4. *Seeking questionable round-robin approval of Board members (by deliberately by-passing the Chairman)*
5. *Withholding information from the Chairman*
6. *Disrespectful behaviour at Board Meetings*
7. *Creation of divisions within the Board*
8. *Questionable dealings with politically exposed persons (PEPs)*
9. *Creating unnecessary conflict with the Chairman of GuySuco*
10. *Denigrating the Chairman of NICIL*

There was a quorum and the motion was carried by a majority of Directors present, at what turned out to be a very stressful Meeting. Those in favour were Oswald Barnes, Denise de Souza and the Chairman, Maurice Odle. Those arguing strenuously against were Grantley Walrond and Rawle Lucas. Those Directors that were not present at the Meeting were Keith Cholmondeley and Berkley Wickham. The Minister of Finance, Winston Jordan, was informed of the outcome of the Meeting.

Realising that his position of CEO (ag.) might be rescinded by the Minister, Colvin London sent me the following e-mail on 17 December 2019:

> Dear Chairman,
>
> I greet you well. I am respectfully requesting a one on one meeting with you to discuss various issues concerning NICIL and our working relationship which has deteriorated for whatever reason the latter half of this year 2019. The discussions will include all the on-going issues surrounding NICIL. The entity has made a meaningful contribution this year to the nation as a whole, while revitalising itself placing it on a steady upward trajectory. The Christmas season is upon us and I will be leaving for home latest on December 23, 2019, it's my hope that these discussions could be had so that moving into the vital period of 2020 we could jointly be on a productive course.

I suggested December 20 at 10am for the meeting. However, the meeting did not take place. At 12.24 pm on the appointed day, Colvin London sent me the following e-mail:

> I must apologise profusely. I was not current with my e-mail hence my not attending the planned meeting. This morning also I got consumed with a pressing matter. This in no way was deliberate, noting I requested the meeting. Again, my apologies, it's my hope that we can reschedule.

I was never able to determine whether Colvin London was being genuine or merely 'playing games' and hoping that I would not turn up and he would have the opportunity to tell the Minister, *inter alia*, that I was being uncooperative. The rescheduling of the meeting did not take place, partly because a PPP 'No Confidence Motion' (NCM) against the Coalition Government was passed in Parliament a couple of days later and the whole governmental machinery went into emergency mode. While the Opposition Party now claimed that the Coalition Government was a "caretaker" or lame duck entity (and could not engage in major decision making) according to Westminster Parliamentary Convention, the latter proceeded to engage in a very lengthy legal contestation of the NCM, until the eventual holding of national elections in March, 2020. The election results were also hotly and vigorously contested in the local courts and, later, the Caribbean Court of Justice, where electoral victory was ruled in favour of the PPP, who assumed office in August, 2020.

EMERGING LAND POLICY

Guyana has a lot of unutilised and underutilised land, partly because of its history, considerable size and nature of the terrain. Right up to the actual change of Government, NICIL continued to engage in activity in certain areas that were deemed to be of developmental importance in the emerging oil economy. My view was that the tradition and practice of a 'caretaker' government was that it could not engage in enacting new laws and regulations or initiate major infrastructure projects, but that day to day administrative activities and routine transactions of the governmental bureaucracy would continue. Such an interpretation guided NICIL's administrative actions with respect to dealing with:

(i) land relating to recent closures of certain government owned sugar estates;
(ii) lease, freehold and economically deserving criteria for allocating other state-owned lands for business and residential purposes;
(iii) regularisation of land on which there were squatter settlements;
(iv) pricing of government-owned land; and
(v) acquisition of state-owned land by politically exposed persons (PEPs).

In this regard, it was a rather tortuous process of trying to develop a coherent approach to land acquisition. The establishing by Cabinet on 13 August 2018 of a Property Sale Committee did not help, as it hardly got off the ground. (The Committee had been designed to consist of nominees from the Ministry of Agriculture; Lands and Surveys Commission; Ministry of Finance; and the Ministry dealing with Communities).

A *first* issue was that, of the four sugar estates (Albion, Rose Hall, Skeldon and Wales) of the Guyana Sugar Corporation (GuySuco) which the Coalition Government had closed, pending privatisation; the one at Wales in West Demerara was specially earmarked to facilitate a rice and 'other crop' diversification process away from concentration on sugar. In this regard, a NICIL Board member, Berkley Wickham, recommended that, in the interest of transparency, the CEO (ag.) develops internal guidelines to supplement those in the National Procurement Act. For my part, I instructed, on 9 May 2019, that a written report *"be submitted to the next Board Meeting, and each subsequent Meeting, on each and every transaction, including a matrix showing location; acreage size; persons tendering; valuation; selling price; name of buyer; buyer's organisation; beneficial owner (if information is available) payment institution; etc."*. In addition, there was a carving-out of thirty-six house lots that were originally managers' quarters to be made available to previous sugar workers who had at least ten years of service; this strategy was based on a bauxite company precedent.

A larger issue was one of equitable distribution of land in a Guyana society in which there were considerable disparities. On 14 May 2019, I wrote the following:

> *The email of 9 May from the NICIL Company Secretary (Arianne McLean) concerning the proposed sale of lands at Wales prompts me to address an issue that the Board of Directors might want the Government to take into account: Are there any other socio-economic objectives that should be considered besides the mere maximisation of income from the sale of the 4,800 acres of land contiguous to the GuySuco sugar estates.*
>
> *While it is admitted that income is needed from the sale of such land (along with the proceeds of privatisation of Enmore,*

Skeldon, Rosehall and Wales estates) to service GuySuco debt and also for the financing of the rehabilitation and restructuring of the three remaining estates at Albion, Blairmont and Uitvlugt, there is also need to ensure that there is a wide cross-section of beneficiaries.

However, a policy of selling all the land to the highest bidders is likely to exacerbate the imbalance in wealth ownership in the Guyana society, especially since any one person can conceivably bid for more than one Block of land. In this regard, it may be appropriate to institute a publicly declared policy to 'carve out' (from the traditional procurement process) a clearly demarcated proportion of the lands (say 20%) for equitable apportioning to the most disadvantageous groups in the society at less than market price. Such groups may include fixed income workers like teachers, nurses, policemen, soldiers, civil servants, and sugar workers (earning below, say $100,000 per month) and whose share of national income relative to the rest of the society is likely to become steadily eroded with the rise of a petroleum economy and related rising prices.

There is a certain imperative to such a redistributive approach in light of the housing authorities bewailing the fact that there is currently not enough state-owned land to satisfy the unmet demand for low income housing. Moreover, land ownership is an important criterion for eligibility for mortgage and other commercial loans.

Certain safeguards should be put in place to ensure that the process is a fair one. The workers in the preferred categories who attempt to purchase the newly available lands cannot have benefited from previous Government sales. Also, perhaps the worker should have been in the occupation for a certain minimum number of years and would not be allowed to sell (or lease) the land within, say, ten years without the approval of the housing authorities.

I would welcome any comments on the above proposal.

The Board was divided as to whether it had the authority to enact policy making typically reserved for Ministers/Cabinet and no action was taken on the matter.

Second, NICIL received many investor plans requiring sale of state-owned lands that were historically under sugar cultivation (but had gone out of production in recent decades) in order to establish a business. The focus, was on the Ogle sub-urban area (adjacent to La Bonne Intention-LBI /Goedverwagting) partly because Exxon was in the process of establishing its headquarters there (in proximity to the Ogle International Airport) and international, regional and local investors were accordingly keen to acquire land to set up internationally branded hotels, luxury apartments, entertainment complexes and other commercial establishments in close proximity. In this regard, NICIL's senior executives and Board members engaged in an intensive process of due diligence evaluating international, regional and local (including joint venture) investor business proposals, based on their recent financial statements, sectoral experiences, capitalisation capacities and willingness to adhere to certain performance requirements. At least twenty such project proposals were approved or were in the process of being evaluated, by the time I handed in my resignation as Chairman to the incoming Government. The companies were: Suvam Real Estate; Endeavour Holdings Limited/Trinuyana Inc; Artusanac Project (Eldorado Towers); Debut Guyana Inc; Caribbean Marketing Enterprise Inc; Windsor Estate ECD; CORUM Group; W&T George Inc; Carpen Cardiology Services Inc; Ava Management; Plantation Gulf and Country Club; Elysium Investment; Premium Sales and Services (Consulting Group); Adamantium Holding; Upraising Marketing Inc (Camaria); Residences at Earl's Court; American Marine Services Inc; Pioneer Development Inc; Edge Solutions Ltd; Cellular Planet Inc.(Ogle Heights); Consortium/Oceanside Park Project; and Navigant Builders Inc. (Windsor Estate). A road was constructed from E Field, Sophia to the 'Pradoville 1' section of Ogle (now a two minute journey by motor vehicle) to facilitate business and residential construction activities in what is likely to become a veritable commercial hub. The abovementioned investors were a mix of local, regional and foreign firms.

Third, although another Guyana Government agency, Central Housing and Planning Authority, was primarily responsible for land allocation and related policies, NICIL had been the caretaker of nationalised bauxite property and land lying idle that squatters were occupying in the Mackenzie/Linden area. Post the 2015 change of government there was an intensification in the 'regularisation' of approximately 1300 house lots that were still outstanding. The increased urgency was in keeping with a greater degree of concern for the disadvantaged.

Fourth, the issue of an appropriate price for the sale of state-owned land continues to be a vexatious one in the partly virgin territory of Guyana. How close should it be to the market price for comparable land. In this regard, a distinction might be made between the price of land expected to be paid by real estate developers who take the risk of building finished houses (with related infrastructure, that are then unloaded onto the public) and the real estate builder who only installs basic infrastructure like roads, storm drains, and electric pylons, and then sells plots of land to individual buyers. There is, also, the other situation where the Government owns the land, installs the infrastructure and then sells it to individuals, not by a bidding process but, as in the case of 'Pradoville 2', to fellow Ministers and their friends at a price that is less than a fifth of the comparable market price. At NICIL, with cries of previous Government corruption still ringing, I insisted on near comparable market prices for state-owned land. In this regard, I asked Clive Thomas, the Chairman of the Coalition Government's 'State Assets Recovery Agency' (SARA) for information on the method his agency employed in arriving at a reasonable price for 'Pradoville 2' and similar land that would allow the contrite holders of such land to make the additional payment to SARA. His reply was as follows:

1. Due to the high level of indeterminacy of past land prices in Guyana's regions, we relied on mutual agreements to arrive at a fair price. That is why we term them "settlements". (See background documents enclosed).
2. We collected as many estimates of prices for the land transactions we were interested in, which we could find and noted the date and year. Such prices came from multiple sources: forensic audits, government valuations, private surveyors, government and private architects, real estate agents. We searched these sources thoroughly (as many as we could find).
3. We then calculated the central tendency in these samples: range, mean, mode. We used these to estimate various prices to see what they would yield for our negotiating position.
4. For our negotiations, we established the minimum, maximum and a probable area of agreement. Then we negotiated.
5. If the date of the chosen transaction was not current, we assumed land prices, would double, on average, each decade during the 2000s and used a compound rate of 6% per annum to make current.
6. No serious difficulties were encountered in coming to an agreed price, or settlement.

The Coalition Government lost power in 2020 and the incoming PPP Government immediately had its Director for Public Prosecutions (who herself was a recipient of 'Pradoville 2' property) withdraw all charges against the current President, Irfaan Ali, a past President and current Vice President, Bharrat Jagdeo, and current Minister of Finance (and past Chairman of NICIL) Ashni Singh, *inter alia*, rather than have their case tried in court and possibly win and enjoy vindication. What an interesting situation and rejection of the notion of accountability and incorruptibility.

Fifth, the issue as to whether Ministers of Government should have access to state-owned land while in office, even if at so-called market prices, was never resolved. Such beneficial access by the very persons in charge of decision making could be considered a conflict of interest. In grappling with this issue, I had cause to make the following inquiry on 20 October, 2019:

> *I refer to an Article on page 3 of today's Sunday Stabroek which states that the Official Gazette of October 19 records a NICIL sale of a one-acre plot land to Adams-Yearwood, the Junior Agricultural Minister and that the order was signed by Minister of Finance, Winston Jordan.*
>
> *I shall be grateful to learn whether the report is correct and, if so, how such a transaction was effected without gaining the prior approval of the Board.*

I therefore instructed the NICIL Company Secretary to place the issue of access by politically exposed persons on the Board of Directors' Agenda, but the 'No Confidence Motion' issue raised its ugly head a month or so later and the unsettling and prolonged repercussions, including fiercely contested elections, conspired to prevent a resolution of this matter.

Eventually, NICIL got around to formulating a Land Use Policy Framework oriented towards business development needs of a petroleum economy, with particular reference to the Ogle area, where about 800 acres had been provisionally allocated (with about an additional 600 acres of freehold land and 1000 acres of leasehold land expected to be still available). The statement by Board Member Rawle Lucas on 13 January 2020 suggests that progress had been made within a few months to finalising the Land Policy Framework document:

> *Assuming all things are equal, I think that the policy document can achieve its overarching goal of optimising the use of Guyana's resources for the benefit of the people by addressing seven criteria. The seven criteria are (1) the geographic focus of the policy; (2)*

usage of the land, (3) local content in the context of the wider national interest and the pursuit of equity in the land allocations. The policy must also take account of the territorial and security impact of the decisions on land allocation and the integrity of the financial flows that accompany the investments; (5) required documentation; (6) NICIL's role and (7) the approval process.

The paper already identifies a geographic focus and proposes a usage policy based on size or acreage. The paper also suggests the documentation that would be required and the role that NICIL should play. The proposals with respect to documentation could be strengthened if it contained, in addition to the profile of the investor, the pro forma budget of the project and source of funds. It would also be helpful if the policy paper address the issue of local content, especially as it pertained to economic control in relation to land size and the acquisition option.

However, it can be argued that the land distribution strategy paid too much attention to the wishes of the commercial class and not enough to the needs of the poor and the powerless. Apart from the regularisation of squatter settlements in Linden and sale of land in a certain lower middle income neighbourhood there, no significant sale of state-owned land had taken place in other areas of the country. The one exception (and a small area of Wales) was Ogle and its environs where there were significant approvals involving foreign and local investors, but sale of land in Ogle's residential area in the Development Plan that was reserved for lower middle income households was put on the back burner.

Land is a serious bone of contention in the Guyana polity and society. The NICIL formulated Land Policy Framework would have made a rational contribution to the issue of physically facilitating business but it only tangentially touched on the wider issue of one important section of the society feeling that it was historically and subsequently disadvantaged. The Africans had slaved for nearly two and-a-half centuries for no wages and nothing else but brutality and, on emancipation, received zero reparations but struggled to purchase land to create villages, with their puny savings during the 1834-38 apprenticeship period on the plantations, despite the frequent flooding of their land thereafter by the planter class to force them to go back to work on the plantations. With no source of income except subsistence farming, capital accumulation was not possible. On the other hand, the East Indian indentured labourers, who replaced the Africans on the plantations, were wage earners and given adjoining residential land in lieu of a free passage back to India at the end of their contract period, partly because this ensured that the planter class retained a ready pool of labour. (The native Amerindians, who dwelled mainly in the interior of Guyana, also had a long-standing issue with respect to Land Titling).

Furthermore, the post-colonial development strategy of the PPP's Cheddi Jagan Government focused on opening up, *via* costly drainage and irrigation schemes, vast lands in Mahaica-Mahaicony-Abary; Black Bush Polder; and Canal Polder(s) where East Indians were offered lease land for agricultural purposes. The Africans, on the other hand, found difficulty in retaining "ancestral lands" in the villages where they lived, partly because of deliberate encroachment by others, archaic and complicated land laws, and unsympathetic governmental attitudes.

Ownership of land led to production of agricultural produce, amassing of surplus profits which were used to create more agricultural produce and diversified activities, or the purchase of more land and increasing capital formation. Moreover, land provides collateral for the creation of new economic activities, which can lead to the acquisition of even more land.

The Central Housing and Planning Authority (CHPA) had produced, in November 2017, a Report entitled *'Addressing the Challenges facing the Government Housing Programme: A Position Paper'* in which it was stated that the authors in reviewing the performance of CHPA (to whom there were over 56,000 unsatisfied applications for house lots) recommended the following:

(i)   Improved affordability and financing options;
(ii) A sanitised applicant database that consists of only those who are in genuine need of Government housing;
(iii) Provision of suitable housing on a needs basis;
(iv) Improved occupancy (of allocated lots); and
(v)   Improved capacity of Central and Local Government to deliver the Government's mandate.

Ownership disparities with respect to land are one of the reasons for tension and instability in plural Guyana. The PPP Government that came into office in 2020 prides itself on having an ambitious land distribution policy, but the criteria for ownership are not very clear and there is a 'first come, first serve element' and ad hoc dimensions to the process. There is a certain lack of transparency, as the only publicly available information is about the total number of house lots distributed to date. More disaggregation is required for the purpose of greater accountability (and possible 'Ethnic Impact Assessment').

The time is nigh. Even if the Coalition Government had won the 2020 elections, it is unlikely that I would have wanted to continue as Chairman of NICIL, interesting though the job was. My situation would have been operationally untenable, and my mental health impaired, if Colvin London had remained in the same executive position (although he was never confirmed as CEO, right up to the time of the change of Government). In addition, I was not sure as to whether Minister Jordan was really in a political position to exert effective control over Colvin London who, on more than one occasion, vigorously questioned (in writing) the authority of the Minister.

At a more personal level, the NICIL saga also caused a rift between myself and Clive Thomas, the Chairman of GuySuco, that arose in the first couple of years in the life of the Coalition Government. This occurred because a reporter in one of the daily newspapers, *Kaieteur News*, misrepresenting a comment of mine that had earlier been reported in the media, asked Clive Thomas his views on same and what appeared as the front page headline of the said newspaper mischievously stated that the "Chairperson of GuySuco says NICIL Chair Misleading the Nation". I duly wrote the newspaper indicating that the reporter had misinterpreted what I had said and that the manner of his request, for Clive to comment on same, had elicited a distorted response that was then used to create a mischievous headline. The reporter posted a reply to the effect that, when contacted by telephone, Clive did not wish to change his stance. Clive was also offended when my wife indicated to him that he ought to write the newspaper clarifying the matter, which he never did. I thereupon resigned from my position as an Executive Member of the WPA (which was part of the Coalition Government) since Clive was one of the two co-leaders of that Party.

I did not speak to Clive at all for about two years and we hardly spoke for another three or four years. Those were emotionally very painful years. In fact, mutual family, friends and acquaintances were very surprised at the distancing, since they knew that Clive and I went back a long way. We entered high school (Queen's College) the same year; were members of the same 'gang' of school boys; our student days at London School of Economics overlapped for a couple of years (in fact, it was he and another class mate, Maurice St Pierre, who encouraged me to study Economics); were senior colleagues at UG for a dozen years; and political activists/executive members of WPA for a considerable length of time. Sometimes, politics can be more dividing than uniting, especially at a personal level.

Besides the adverse effect of institutional politics on personal friendships, there can be other consequences, including those of an ex-post bureaucratic nature. Although a new Government had taken up office in August 2020 and I had almost immediately sent in my resignation, there was soon to be a process of reckoning and accountability. Within a couple of months, I received a call from a detective at the Guyana Police Headquarters inviting my presence there in connection with an investigation into certain transactions that had occurred during my tenure as Chairman of NICIL, I told the caller that I was prepared to do so only in the presence of my lawyer and only after I had received a list of the questions that are to be asked of me. (A fellow Board Director, Oswald Barnes, had received a similar call a few days earlier, and he had alerted me). For about a month, I received no further communication from the police. Then I received another call, this time from the Special Operations Crime Unit (SOCU) making the same request as above, to which I gave a similar response. Again, there was no follow-up by the law enforcement authorities. But I could not help remembering the veiled threat, reported in the *Stabroek News* of 9 May, 2018, that Sam Hinds, the previous Prime Minister from 1992 to 2015, was reported to have made:

> *The issue of valuation and all of that ... Maurice Odle, Horace James and Mr Colvin Heath-London should look at this and think if they do fall out with this government what could be their fate. They should think about that fate because they are being asked to do much more controversial things than were done by NICIL in our time.*

However, a few months later, there appeared in the media an announcement that the new PPP Government was charging the previous NICIL CEO (ag.) Colvin London, for collaborating with one James Bond (an APNU Parliamentarian during the 2011-2015 PPP Government) with effecting a secretive and illegal land sale at well below the average selling price of such state-owned property. (The transaction had not been brought before the NICIL Board of Directors for its approval during my tenure!). Soon after, it was announced that Minister of Finance, Winston Jordan, was being charged with affixing his signature to letters vesting ownership of premium land (related to oil sector needs) to investors at prices well below what NICIL Board of Directors had recommended. (Ironically, the PPP, on assuming office in 2020, had dropped similar charges that were the subject of on-going court cases against their current President and Vice President, *inter alia*, for pre-2015 transgressions). Hypocrisy is the dark side of politics.

ENVIRONMENTAL TAX RULING

Early 2017, while employed at NICIL, I also received a telephone call from the Attorney-General, asking me to act as an economic advisor. One of the cases I was asked to deal with, concerned a claim made by a Trinidad and Tobago incorporated firm that, under the CARICOM Treaty of Chaguaramas, the "national treatment " rights of its Guyana based subsidiary were breached from 1 January 2006 (the date the Treaty took effect) to 7 August 2015, when an environmental tax on non-re-usable bottled containers of its beverages was last paid to the Government of Guyana, because locally incorporated beverage companies were not asked to pay the same tax. Guyana, in defence against the claim, alleged that, despite the breach, the claimants were not entitled to reimbursement, since this would amount to "unjust enrichment", as the subsidiary would have passed on the tax to its consumers. Guyana also argued that the claimants were barred by 'laches', given that the subsidiary failed to challenge the collection of the tax at the earliest possible time, eleven years having elapsed. The Caribbean Court of Justice (CCJ) allowed Guyana, besides producing a large number of documents, "to adduce expert evidence and to put before the court a report from two named persons", they being economist, Maurice Odle and lawyer-accountant, Christopher Ram.

The decision of the CCJ was in favour (but not entirely) of the claimants. Because of the considerable time that had elapsed, the Court invoked the doctrine of 'laches' and awarded reimbursement, but for only five of the possible eleven years, this being a rough average of the laches limitation in the laws of CARICOM States. However, the CCJ was anything but ambivalent with respect to the 'unjust enrichment issue', stating that there would have been payment of:

a composite price that covers all the traders' hidden costs, including a tax cost, when the customer freely chose to pay the requested price for those beverages, rather than other beverages *in the market place, taking account of the price and the taste of the bought beverages. Since both parties consented to end this valid transaction, the trader was beneficially entitled, in full, to the proceeds of the sale of its beverages. Guyana could not be allowed to retain, by way of set off, whatever amount of the tax cost that the trader managed to cover despite being subjected to the unlawful tax. To permit this course of action, would be to allow Guyana to be unjustly enriched by exploiting the trader's efforts and by making an illegal profit out of legislation known to be unlawful. In the circumstances of this case, there had been no unjust enrichment on the part of the Claimants through the passing-on of the $10 per beverage container.*

The above legalistic judgment makes no mention of the subtle nature or depth of the "expert evidence" provided by the Guyana Government in the latter's arguing that some amount of passing-on must have taken place and seemed to rely almost entirely on the sanctity of the CARICOM law. The CCJ also admitted that it had relied on precedent in that in 2014 it had ruled in favour of a Suriname Incorporated Company, Rudisa Beverages, that had brought a similar case against the Guyana Government; but in that case, the Government had simply asserted that the environmental tax had been passed on, without providing any argumentation whatsoever. I was to learn that there is a significant difference in conceptual approach between the legal and economics disciplines, as reflected in the following Executive Summary that I had made:

Based on celebrated capitalist paradigm, Guyana Beverages (a subsidiary of S.M. Jaleel of Trinidad and Tobago) would have been expected to make efforts to pass-on the environmental tax on non-returnable containers, in pursuit of profit maximisation, subject to certain constraints. Contestation of the reimbursement claim is therefore warranted. The extent to which passing-on was possible, or absorption by the firm was required, depended on the interstices of demand and supply. However, a coherent body of Guyana Beverages data on quantities sold and related prices is not available for such a definitive determination as to how large a proportion of the tax was passed-on. In the absence of such data, this research exercise resorted to examining other aspects of the firm's behaviour, including: its financial performance; structural and operational factors conducive to, or permissive of, the passing-on of the tax; and the decision of Guyana Beverages to continue using non-returnable containers purchased from its parent firm, instead of seeking out sources that sold re-usable containers.

From the time of entry into the Guyana market in 1997, including the 2007 to 2014 years for which reimbursement is being sought as a result of discriminatory treatment under the Revised Treaty of Chaguaramas, Guyana Beverages enjoyed each year very high gross profit percentages; related very high mark-up percentages (with mark-up percentages varying very significantly among the various beverage products, being probably due to the extent to which the environmental tax can be passed-on); and gross profit and mark-up percentages that were very significantly higher than those of a major competitor, Caribbean International Distributors. One contributor to such a stellar performance on the part of Caribbean Beverages could have been its ability to pass-on the environmental tax, given its not inconsiderable share of the domestic market for non-alcoholic beverages. In this regard, it should be noted that, during the 2007-2014 period, the environmental tax proceeds of the Government of Guyana were less than 60 percent of the amount ascribed to mark-up (over and above costs) by Caribbean Beverages.

From an operational point of view, the proceeds of the environmental tax are small in relation to certain critical categories and this makes it more than likely that the tax was passed on without a very significant adverse impact on quantity sold. The proceeds from the environmental tax are small (percentage wise) in relation to purchases, duty and freight: smaller still in relation to cost of sales, and, as expected, even smaller in relation to sales revenue. All these indices are declining over time, as is the environmental tax in relation to the price of each of the various Guyana Beverages products. Such a decline is as a result of the environmental tax being "specific" or fixed in amount (G$10) rather than ad valorem (percentage) and therefore impactly varying in amount with inflation.

The fact that, on entering the Guyana market and confronted with an environmental tax, Guyana Beverage chose to purchase (and to continue doing same for nearly eighteen years) the non-returnable containers from its parent firm, S.M. Jaleel, rather than seek out an alternative supplier of re-usable containers, suggests either that it found it possible to pass-on the tax or, that, with over invoicing, it would have been able to minimise its tax liability. Either way, a claim to reimbursement would constitute "unjust enrichment".

Based on the above argumentation, the probability is that the bulk of the environmental tax was passed-on to Guyana Beverages' consumers, rather than absorbed by the firm. Guyana Beverages is therefore not eligible to be reimbursed any significant proportion of the environmental tax.

It is unfortunate that the highest Court in the Caribbean Region is less than sympathetic to issues relating to protection of the environment. This judgement should also not detract from the seriousness of the region's environmental fragility, despite the cavalier nature of the current post-2020 government with respect to oil spill risks.

While operating as a Special Adviser to the Attorney-General, I had been made a Member of the Committee evaluating proposals for the establishment of a Law School at UG and, at its very first Meeting,

I had queried why priority should not be given to the creation of a Petroleum and Gas Institute there, as part of the required legislative, regulatory and monitoring framework for the emerging oil economy. (The Committee included such eminent lawyers as Claudette Singh, Duke Pollard, Chris Ram, Harold Lutchman and Rudy James). In any event, the change of Government funds in 2020 did put a halt to the work of the committee.

UNFINISHED BUSINESS

During the 2015-2020 period, I was also a Member of the Bank of Guyana Board, whose duties were mainly the traditional ones of exercising monetary control and price stability, regulating the financial institutions and, to a lesser extent, monitoring economic growth and development. In this regard, the Bank was expected to have a managerial role in overseeing the investment of the financial surpluses accruing to the Government from the exploration and development of the newly discovered oil deposits. I was keen to be given the opportunity to be involved in such an important exercise. My observation was ignored by the Chairman (in the same way that the offer by the Tax Reform Committee, to review then existing petroleum legislation, was ignored by the Minister of Natural Resources, as mentioned above). There tended to be a lack of prioritisation and coordination among Government Ministries and Agencies.

The Ministry of Finance duly took the lead in the formulation of the governance framework of the intended Petroleum Fund and related institutions, but was slow in involving the Board. In the Minutes of the 15 December 2017 Board Meeting, it is therefore stated that *"Dr Odle recalled that he had requested an opportunity for the Board to have an input in crafting of the legislation because of the integral involvement of the Bank of Guyana in the management of the Fund"*. A few months later, at a 27 July 2018 Board Meeting, it is stated in the Minutes that *"Dr Odle observed that there is a paucity of experience in terms of the management of development funds in the region but noted that some experience is reposed in the Caribbean Development Bank (CDB). He suggested that since it is approaching the time when the Bank will be dealing with the Sovereign Wealth Fund, it is important that the experience of the CDB is evaluated, including its investments and rates of return on same;* in addition, *the Directors agreed that there were a few other arrangements which could be examined for guidance including the Dependents' Pension Fund which has a Board that sets policy with its investments being executed by Crown Agents; and the Sovereign Wealth Fund (Heritage and Stabilisation Fund) of Trinidad"*

At this stage, an Inter-Ministerial Technical Committee on Petroleum, co-chaired by the Ministry of Finance and the Department of Energy, was formed and preparations went into full swing. Both the Ministry of Finance and the Bank of Guyana urgently sought advice from International experts and relevant international financial institutions. The Ministry of Finance requested the Commonwealth Secretariat to draft appropriate legislation, which later formed the basis of the Natural Resource Fund (NRF) Act of 2019 and invited the World Bank to assist in capacity building at the Guyana Revenue Authority. The Bank of Guyana, in turn, received assistance: from the Money and Capital Markets Unit of the International Monetary Fund (IMF) on strengthening its existing framework; from the World Bank on coping with the anticipated petroleum expansion impact on the local financial sector and on the virtues of targeting, indexing and benchmarking with respect to foreign asset allocation; and from the Bank for International Settlements (BIS) and the Federal Reserve on choice of external funds manager and placement of surpluses.

In the midst of the above mentioned spate of international assistance, I was requested by the Ministry of Finance on 28 September 2018 to "submit comments" on Dr Wilde's 'Draft of Design of the Natural Resource Fund', since I was not in attendance at the particular Bank of Guyana Board Meeting where he made his presentation. I chose to selectively comment on firstly, his Institutional Framework, and secondly, his Fiscal Rules, as follows:

Institutional Framework

1. Upstream monitoring of revenue sources may be in order and so there is probable need to establish a Revenue Verification Committee. While the current Government may be reluctant to press for re-negotiation of the contract with ExxonMobil, it certainly should endeavour to ensure that every bit of revenue due under the existing contract accrues to the State. This relates to two levels of operation. Firstly, scientific care should be taken to design sophisticated methods of verifying how much oil is actually extracted from the oil wells, particularly since the contract suspiciously stipulates that the Government needs to give the oil companies one week's notice of visits to the well sites. Second, there is accounting need to subject all recovery cost submissions to detailed scrutiny to avoid over-invoicing. Maximising and safeguarding the amount of accrued revenue is nearly as important as maximising the effectiveness of utilisation of available funds. Accordingly, a Verification Committee should probably include representatives from the Department of Energy; Ministry of Natural Resources/Geology and Mines Commission; Guyana Revenue Authority; Auditor General's Office; Environmental Protection Agency; etc.

2. A case could be made for the Macroeconomic Committee to have a larger number of members than the proposed five, so as to accommodate all key stakeholders. For example, representation from the private sector should be counter balanced by the addition of a representative from the labour movement, in the interest of social cohesion.

3. With respect to the management of the Natural Resources Fund (NRF) while the Bank of Guyana's management of same is required to subscribe to the investment mandate of the Sovereign Investment Committee (which reports to the Minister) there is no indication as to whether the Board of

Directors of the Bank of Guyana has any co-supervising role to play with respect to the operations of the Fund.

4. It may be useful to have a representative of the National Insurance Scheme (NIS) on the Sovereign Investment Committee. Like the Fund, the NIS (whose revenue sources could dramatically swell during the oil driven take-off period) is required to adopt an intergenerational strategy and the relationship between the two organisations could be mutually beneficial.

5. Frequently associated with transparency, accountability and good governance is the concept of inclusivity. In this regard, there seems to be no representation from civil society, since proposed composition of the Committees is essentially technocratic. Also, there is no explicit seeking of female Committee members. In this regard, there could be established downstream a sort of multipartite Impact Assessment Committee/Forum to provide feedback on the distribution of benefits among the population from oil production, so as to help to ensure that the integrity of the investment process is consistent with the fairness and equity of the outcomes, and that no socio-economic segments are falling behind.

Fiscal Rules and the Fiscally Sustainable Amount

1. Despite the doomsday scenarios, there is no reason why, in the very early years of oil production, an attempt should not be made to spend more than the proposed two-thirds (say three-quarters instead) of Government take. This is due to both the degree of poverty that exists in Guyana (and present value/time dimension considerations) and the tremendous physical and social infrastructure needs (absorptive capacity notwithstanding) that is required for economic take-off. There should be some notional threshold of annual take (US$1 billion?) when Fund savings as a higher proportion of revenue

should kick-in, which could be partly determined by the expected relatively long life of the petroleum reserves. In addition, rapid growth in the short-term could cause re-migration of many skilled persons, thus enhancing absorptive capacity.
2. There is no consideration in Dr Hyde's design as to how the proposed petroleum driven fiscal rule for determining the fiscally sustainable amount (FSA) mesh with the traditional monetary measures (primarily relating to countering inflation and managing foreign exchange rate movements) available to the Central Bank for effecting financial and economic stability.
3. Questionable, also, is the proposed FSA withdrawal ceiling (in the medium term) of 25% of non-petroleum revenues, purportedly because (as stated in the Paper) "the ceiling ensures that the FSA is not so large when compared to the non-oil economy which would result in a loss of economic competitiveness". This reference to certain levels of withdrawal, per se, from the Fund leading to loss of economic competitiveness is somewhat stylised and unclear, given the wide range of other factors that typically determine competitiveness. Moreover, the ceiling may have pro-cyclical effects. For example, if non-petroleum revenues were to fall, the rational course of action should be to increase withdrawals (in the interest of stability) from the Fund, since maintaining a rigid percentage may exacerbate the downturn. Consequently, there is a need for good judgment and flexibility, rather than hard and fast rules, at the same time bearing in mind the past experiences, positive and negative, of petroleum economies.
4. Fiscal rules and benchmarks should not result in arbitrary or unnecessary restraints on the spending of Government of Guyana petroleum proceeds. Guidelines and targets are indeed necessary, but these should not act as a fetter on pro-active promotion of rapid development and economic transformation.

Strong and vigorous double digit growth in the short and medium term could set the stage and pedestal for true sustainable development.

5. Finally, there is some rational in the statements that, when petroleum production ceases, the Government can continue spending 3% of the balance of the NRF since "this is sustainable as in the long term the real rate of return on the NRF's investments should be equal to (or above) 3 percent". However, one would assume that, if the global economy assumes a sustained higher growth path in the future with higher rates of return on financial assets, a higher level of withdrawal from the NRF may be possible".

Based on the advice received from the various International Financial Institutions (IFIs) and experts, a Green Paper of 8 August, 2018 was presented for Cabinet's attention. One issue related to the extent to which the fund should be engaged in macro-economic maintaining of both financial and real sector stability; how the governance framework should protect the integrity of the process; and what proportion of the Fund should be set aside for future generations. *Second,* whether the depository scope of the Fund should be limited to proceeds from petroleum or whether it should include Government earnings from the mineral sector and any other specified (e.g. privatisation earnings) surplus. (The preference was for a broad-based non-renewable resource fund). *Third,* a risk/reward balance had to be considered with respect to the equity, fixed income and property composition of assets with the long, medium and short duration of the assets partly dependent on the expected life of the natural resource deposits. A decision also had to involve the issue as to whether the asset portfolio, for the purpose of geographical spreading of risks, should include developing and emerging country assets (and, also, any CARICOM or local investments). *Fourth*, there was an issue related to the choice of external fund manager. While the Bank of Guyana would be expected to be the overall manager of the Fund, it would need to select an external entity with the required reputation/integrity and international asset market experience in investing large portfolios. *Fifth*, there was the vexing issue of Governance and the degree to which the institutional framework should reflect elements of governmental, rather than civil society, control, all the while accepting that the Government of the day is the ultimate authority.

Unfortunately, despite the inclusion in the Governance Framework of such institutions as a Macro-Economic Committee, a Sovereign Investment Committee, and a Public Accountability and Oversight Committee, a significant amount of control still resided in the hands of the Minister of Finance in the Coalition Government. Not surprisingly, when the new PPP Government came into office in August 2020, it decided to set up a Board of Directors, a concept that was similar to what I had suggested in my communication to the Ministry of Finance on 30 September, 2018 (see above). The new Government also decided to reduce the size of the Oversight Committee from twenty–two (22) persons to just seven (7) on the grounds that it would be easier for decisions to be made. The formula for withdrawal from the NRF was also made more simple, from an administrative point of view. With the abovementioned changes, the 2019 Act was accordingly repealed and replaced with a 2021 Act.

At the time of writing, petroleum production in Guyana has already reached over 350,000 barrels per day and it is anticipated that, by 2027, the one million barrel per day mark will be surpassed. At the time of reaching this momentous achievement, it might be appropriate for the Guyana Government to create a CARICOM Petroleum Fund, similar to the Petroleum Fund (see Chapter Six) that Trinidad and Tobago operated in the first decade of this century, for the benefit of the fellow Members of CARICOM. This will be a way of returning the favour that Guyana received in the depression years of the 1980s and 1990s and would be in the best traditions of Caribbean solidarity and the lofty tenets of the CARICOM Single Market and Economy (CSME). During the depression years, Guyana was able to draw down funds from a CARICOM

Multilateral Clearance Facility, which were never really repaid to Barbados and Trinidad and Tobago. Guyana, as a CARICOM 'Less Developed Country' at that time, also had preferential access to resources from the Caribbean Development Bank (CDB) and Caribbean Development Fund (CDF), in addition to a significant amount of resources from Trinidad's' Petroleum Fund. In addition, Guyana was able to benefit from Venezuela's PetroCaribe Fund resources. There was a significant grant/loan component in the above, and any initiative on the part of Guyana would need to so determine. (It is a pity that the same degree of effort relating to the formulation of a Natural Resource Fund framework, was not employed in the 2015 contract negotiation and the post 2020 Government dealings, with Exxon and its oil producing partners).

CHAPTER EIGHT

REFLECTIONS

A life remembered has its highs and lows and ups and downs. Its failures and successes pertain to every major area of social, economic and political activity and, also, to events that are played out in specific, national, regional and international arenas and contexts. During an eight-decade period, my consciousness or awareness of developments considerably expanded and deepened. My life has accordingly been a combination of feelings of joy and regrets, hope and despair, and, above everything, I am thankful for living long enough to experience it all. But, I consider myself lucky and, also grateful, for the help that I received at critical points in time. Accordingly, I have tried to "give back" in various ways, including being generous to family members and close friends and making financial contributions to local, regional and foreign academic institutions and various social and political causes. (This is also an opportunity to give thanks to my ex-Administrative Assistant, Cheril Collins, without whose excellent typing skills the recording of this Memoir might not have been possible; and to John Lewis and John Piggott for their technical expertise).

AT THE NATIONAL LEVEL

The social and political situation in Guyana in the early 2020s is as problematic as it has been since the mid-1950s, and the related racial/ethnic divide remains as intractable as ever. The PPP, after the relatively short (five years) occupancy of the PNC-led Coalition Government, was restored to office in August 2020, with a one seat majority, and is once again in a situation in which it has both political and economic power.

The Coalition's loss of power could be attributed to a number of general and specific factors. At the general level, the Coalition (whose main partner, the PNC, had been out of office for twenty-three years, until 2015) lacked experience in running a government. In fact, only two of its Cabinet members, Carl Greenidge of the PNC and Moses Nagamootoo of its main partner, the Alliance for Change (AFC) had previous Cabinet experience.

Second, there was the traditional weakness of a Coalition Government. The AFC, which came onto the political scene in 2006, since then had repeatedly said that, as a minority party, any formal alliance with the ignoble PNC (a Party that previously rigged elections during 1968-1992 in order to keep the PPP out of power), would make it (the AFC) political "dead meat". But the AFC changed its mind and, accordingly, extracted a high price for doing so, following the results of the 2015 Election. It demanded and received forty percent of the Parliamentary seats available to the Coalition (even though it had won less than ten percent of the national vote) and a commensurate amount of the main Ministerial portfolios, including that of Prime Minister (but excluding the Presidency). When the PNC compensatingly tried to create a number of additional Junior Ministerial positions, the AFC demanded its share and I (representing another minority partner, the WPA) along with PNC stalwarts Basil Williams (who later became the Attorney-General) and ex Chief Whip, Lance Carberry, met with AFC representatives Nigel Hughes (their Chairman at the time) David Patterson and Dominique Gaskin to resolve the matter. This scrambling and jostling for positions evoked a certain amount of distrust, to the detriment of the fortunes of the Coalition Government.

Third, the Coalition Government apparently had the sanctimonious belief that, because of the supposedly virtuous and righteous nature of a power sharing type of Government (to hopefully include the PPP later), that it was destined to be in office for a few terms, not realising that the

PPP Government was determined to ensure that it became a one term Government and would not have the opportunity to make effective use of potentially considerable government revenue, based on the recent Exxon oil discoveries, and with which windfall a government could win the favour of the voters for a long time.

There are also some more specific reasons why the Coalition Government lost the 2020 Election. *First*, the AFC Minister (Noel Holder) holding the Agriculture portfolio made the critical error of closing certain non-financially viable sugar estates, instead of privatising same and keeping them open until the purchaser(s) assumed ownership and control. Tactical failure to do so handed the PPP government a cause celebre in which it was claimed that the dismissed seven thousand workers and their related family households had been thrown into abject poverty (even after severance pay had been made!). By the time the mistake had been realised and NICIL, under my Chairmanship, had put privatisation talks in train, a PPP No Confidence Motion (NCM) which AFC renegade Member of Parliament, Charrandas Persaud, supported (illustrating the fragility of coalitions) had been successfully passed in Parliament three years into the Government's term and had scared would-be investors away.

Second, the Coalition Government made the strategic error of failing to immediately embark on an ambitious infrastructure and related development plan that would quickly put money into the pockets of its poverty stricken supporters, even if massive oil revenue would only begin to accrue in a few years, and which therefore required the incurring of a certain amount of debt. I had informed the Minister of Finance that it was necessary to establish a National Council of Economic Advisors, and that I was willing to be a participant, including chairing same, if necessary. The Minister never took me up on the offer. Instead, he concentrated on minimising the budget deficit a la IMF dictates (even though, to be fair to the Minister, he did include, in his budgets, increases in the old age pension and minimum wage, and enhanced income tax allowances, *inter alia*). I had also sent the Minister a copy of my land distribution proposal but, perhaps because of the Minister's preoccupation with day to day challenges, I did not receive either an acknowledgement or substantive feedback, and so I did not pursue the matter. (As I indicated in Chapter 7, there was also push-back from certain members of the NICIL Board of Directors). A good example of a failure to see the woods for the trees.

Third, the style of operations of the Coalition Government made for a public relations disaster. Within a month of their attaining office, they surreptitiously gave themselves (and the Opposition Members) a significant increase in salary (before considering an increase for more deserving segments of the population) and, when the public got wind of this development, there was a huge outcry. The response of the Government was not to apologise for such an insensitive move but, in the words of Joseph Harmon, to exclaim "what do you want us to do, thief like the PPP"? There were also certain acts of corruption, though petty compared with what obtained during the previous PPP regime, which did not seem to have been of much concern to the Coalition Government. This insensitivity continued throughout their term in office, to the extent of the President hardly wanting to hold press conferences (which could have been one of the most effective avenues for marketing the Government and convincing the public of the worthiness of their policies).

Fourth, the Election campaign of the Coalition Government was weak and ineffective, and excessively reliant on making major inroads into the indigenous Amerindian community, that accounted for only eleven percent of the voting population. Moreover, the style of the President was wooden and lacking in charisma. This is reflected in his choice of campaign slogan of "Honesty, Decency and Integrity", rather than a focus on grand designs and projects, jobs, living wages, turnkey homes and house lots, and an end to extreme poverty. It is not surprising that the President failed to take on board the cash transfer proposal of his Economic Advisor, Clive Thomas, virtually dismissing same, by aimlessly repeating the age long adage: "give a man a fish and you satisfy his needs for the day; teach him how to fish and you equip him for life". While morality is always welcomed, politics is not for the faint hearted.

For many, including myself, the electoral loss was a stunning blow to the notion of coalition ideology in a plural society like Guyana, in which there are two large ethnic groups of nearly equal size operating under a predominantly Westminster type political system, whereby "winner takes all" in the sense that the Party that wins an election inherits Executive Power and, also, exercises Legislative Power. In Guyana, the present Government intimidates the Judiciary, overly influences promotions and operations in the Police and Army hierarchy and countenances extra-judicial killings. Analysts speak of a creeping electoral dictatorship. This has evoked renewed calls (which began since the 1960s) by the public for more inclusive government or power sharing. Despite the eloquence of Article 13 of the Constitution on the idealistic goal of inclusive governance, and the pledge of both of the major parties to rule in the interest of all if elected, when in office, effective constitutional reform is put on the back burner.

In truth, the Coalition Government, soon after assuming office in 2015, had invited the PPP Opposition to engage in direct talks on Constitutional Reform, but the latter refused the offer (ostensibly because "the traitor", Prime Minister Moses Nagamootoo, was slated to be chairman of same) even though the agreement that USA ex-President Jimmy Carter had with PNC Desmond Hoyte and PPP Cheddi Jagan in 1992 stressed that the introduction of free and fair elections in plural Guyana was on the explicit condition that inclusive governance would immediately follow same. However, the winner, Cheddi Jagan, when challenged, subsequently argued that his Party's new (but meagre) Civic component was sufficient recognition of the concept of inclusiveness. Fast forward to 2023 and Jagdeo, at a Press Conference, is reported in the newspapers to have said that the PPP is not interested in shared governance with the PNC because of the absence of trust (similar to what he said in 2006) and that the two parties had different values and a different development policy!

The "One Guyana" slogan currently being trumpeted by the Party in power, PPP, is reminiscent of what was proselytised by the PNC during their pre-1992 period in office -"One People, One Nation, One Destiny". A number of countries have a similar motto. They amount to mere 'buzzwords' and political shibboleths. With oil generated revenue being incorporated in Government budgeting for the first time in 2021, there have been accusations of partisanship in both the land distribution cum selection of contractors for infrastructure projects and, even, the distribution of funds to adversely affected and disadvantaged communities. Unfortunately, despite the failings of both the PPP and the PNC over the years, Third Parties such as the UF, WPA and AFC have struggled to retain enough support and vibrancy to weaken the two Party governmental structure, since elections in Guyana tend to be an ethnic census and policies (and the worth thereof) do not induce significant swing voting. (What occurred in 2011 and 2015 was essentially due to a Nagamootoo/Ramjattan 'rump' defection from the PPP and the latter threatens to remain in power for decades – a permanent majority scenario). Inclusivity should be both the watchword and the reality. "Unity in diversity" remains elusive.

While the large oil discoveries will probably help to generate significant government revenue, despite the one-sided nature of the contract(s), in order to ease political tensions, the "Indian Dilemma" and, particularly, the "African Dilemma" need to be addressed. While Indian representation in the police and the military (once so low as to give that Community grave concern for their safety and security) has increased at both the rank and file and leadership level, and representation in the public bureaucracy, and in even certain artisan services, has reached near parity with the Africans, the very low African share in the agricultural, manufacturing and commercial sectors (where Indians dominate) has remained virtually constant and it will take vastly increased entrepreneurial capacity on their part, and greater access to the banking system, for this situation to fundamentally change. Ethnic economic (and political) disparities will continue to destabilise the social fabric of the society. Even the trade union system is split along ethnic lines, with the Trade Union Congress (TUC) consisting of unions with mainly African workers and the Federation of Independent Trade Unions (FITUG) representing unions with mainly Indian workers. An African non-receipt of wages during centuries of enslavement, except for the four year (1834-38) so-called apprenticeship period, and therefore no possibility of asset accumulation and inter-generational transfer of wealth, is a telling legacy that is not mitigated by today's struggle for higher wages in the public sector, partly because of lack of solidarity in the labour movement. The situation in Guyana is so dispiriting and intractable, that I sometimes think that, even If Walter Rodney had removed Forbes Burnham in a popular and genuinely multi-racial uprising, the Guyana society would have slowly and inevitable reverted to inter-tribal strife, a situation in which citizens of more homogeneous countries in the Caribbean find difficult to understand.

The very one-sided nature of the contract with Exxon and its partners, that was signed by the PNC led Coalition Government in 2016, constitutes a real problem. The PPP had severely criticised the contract and, during the campaign leading up to the 2020 Election, emphatically stated that it would "review and re-negotiate" same if it were to successfully form a new Government. However, over the two years (up to the time of writing) in office and under pressure from an irate public, the PPP has been supporting the Exxon defence of "sanctity of contracts" and has even come to the assistance of the Exxon legal team in a court case brought by the publisher of the daily *Kaieteur News* (the newspaper with the largest circulation) concerning the legality of Exxon and its contractors not paying company tax. The concept of a "fair and equitable contract" is just as sacred as "sanctity of contract". The PPP's stance is a good example of the 'hypocrisy of politics'. The only plausible explanation (the Venezuelan territorial claim notwithstanding) is that the PPP is wary of alienating America's interests, remembering that the latter co-orchestrated its ouster in both 1953 and 1964, and was also happy to see it lose office in 2015 (owing to corruption and 'criminalisation of the State'). To the PPP, remaining in office is more important than the effective maximisation of benefits accruing to the people of Guyana. A true Faustian bargain.

All of the above have been very engrossing and, throughout my adult life, it has been a personal struggle to maintain the correct balance between professional cum political activism and the requirements of private life. In this regard, my first wife, Margaret, (serene and even tempered) had given me free rein to cope in whatever way seemed fit, right up to her untimely death in 1980, and my second wife, Brenda, who I married in 1984, being a political activist herself, understood fully the situation.

However, my marriage in Georgetown in late 1994 to Valerie (who at the time was working in the CARICOM Secretariat) made for a totally different situation in my life. When she gained 'no-pay leave' and joined me in Geneva, Switzerland, (by this time I was a part of the UNCTAD bureaucracy) she immediately began re-arranging my home, with energy that only rivals that when she is in a department store shopping; declaring that I was living a boring workaholic's life ("all work and no play"). She also set about establishing social links with my UN colleagues and other expatriate friends. Valerie is the consummate social animal and loved entertaining guests or being invited to the home of others. She was also unhappy that I spent so many Saturdays in the office and persuaded me to spend a bit more time exploring Switzerland and cross-border territories, as either yours truly in tow or with various friends. She was also keen to be in Atlanta, USA, in 1996 and in London in 2012 for the Olympics and enjoyed herself thoroughly during that fortnight. When I retired from the UN and returned to Guyana to take up a job at the same CARICOM Secretariat, Valerie and I continued to find time for relaxation and embarked on various boat cruises, including in the Northern Caribbean; the Mediterranean; Alaska; and the Baltics. But the last attempt to go on a cruise, through the Middle East in 2019, was a disaster, since we were denied boarding on the appointed departure day in Dubai, as Valerie did not have a visa for the scheduled stop in Sri Lanka. It was a huge disappointment, bordering on the traumatic and we lost our US$7,000 deposit fee. We also subsequently learnt, from two close friends who were on the same cruise, that a few other passengers, all white and without the required visa, had been permitted on board; an unwanted addition to one's lifelong experience of discrimination. We are unlikely to go on another cruise.

But despite her ever present smile, life was not all fun and there is a very serious side to her persona. Valerie supported me fully in what turned out to be quite a rewarding latter period of my professional career at UNCTAD and the CARICOM Secretariat. At this time, she was still at the stage of building her diplomatic type career in the Directorate of Foreign and Community Relations (and had interrupted same for a few years to be with me in Geneva). It meant that when I retired from UNCTAD and took up a job of Technical Adviser to the RNM, we saw a lot of each other during the course of most days, including sometimes attending the same conference abroad, although there were at least two occasions when, interestingly, I was in the departure lounge at the international airport in Guyana waiting to board a plane that had just arrived and saw her descending the stairway. I resigned from the Secretariat with effect from April 2011 and Valerie, now Advisor to the Secretary-General, is planning to do the same in 2023. In the meantime, Valerie remains her hard driving, multi-tasking self, and is eagerly and excitably looking forward to having more time for her next home remodelling project.

Valerie loves to chat with her colleagues, friends and family members. While I am more of a leftist persuasion than Valerie, our conversations are sufficiently amicable, even though it is sometimes difficult to get Valerie, given her fighting instincts, to change her mind, once she has adopted a certain position on a political, social or economic issue. Valerie's warm and loving nature is reflected in her frequent and interminably long conversations with her sisters, and with her daughter, Malika, and son-in-law, Joel Persico.

Father Time is taking its toll. Only three of the core Odle family, Stanley, Norma and Maurice, are still alive at the time of writing and, in

An inter-generational gathering of some members of the Odle and Brewster families

Left: Maurice and Valerie Odle on a successful cruise

Malika and Joel Persico with baby Zara

Left: With Ronnie and Akanni Odle at latter's MBA graduation

these premium years, there are increasing efforts to generate more intra-family gatherings and telephone contact with nephews, nieces and grandchildren, such that there is an Odle's WhatsApp Chat Group that includes Valerie, Akanni, Jacqueline Ofokansi, Wendy and Rod Brewster, Abenna and Bobby Satcher, and Marvin and Michelle Williams, *inter alia*. I regret not giving enough time to this family oriented aspect of my life. I also regret an earlier estrangement with my older son, Ronnie, that lasted several years.

AT THE REGIONAL LEVEL

Over the last sixty years or so, the former colonial territories in the Caribbean have tried to forge themselves into a more coherent whole and, while the degree of success is not very great, some experiences are memorable, both as an academic doing teaching and research in the Region and as an Advisor in the CARICOM Secretariat, I have had the opportunity and privilege to visit almost every Caribbean territory and to reflect on the problems and challenges.

When I was interviewed for entry into the London School of Economics (LSE) in 1961, a question that was asked of me was why was the West Indian Federation about to collapse. I am not sure that I gave an acceptable response at the interview, but, in Chapter Two of this memoir, I did offer certain traditional explanations and, in Chapter Five, gave a critical review of the CARICOM integration experience, which I will not repeat here. However, I will still make a few random observations:

First, the large oil discoveries in Guyana could give the economic integration process another spurt by way of facilitating increased food security, through Guyana Government revenue and land resources, complementing Trinidad and Tobago private financing, and the resulting joint venture could significantly reduce the near US $5 billion food import bill in the CARICOM region. But the Region is still wary of production integration. For example, the current Guyana Government has apparently taken a decision to establish an oil refinery on its own soil (Crab Island, Berbice Region) rather than utilising the virtually idle refinery plant in Trinidad and Tobago. The "light" and "sweet" nature (generally a good thing) of Guyana's crude oil might be incompatible with the technology employed at the Point Lisas oil refinery in Trinidad, but the Guyana Government has not provided an explanation. In addition, I mentioned earlier the need for oil producing Guyana to eventually establish a Petroleum Fund, a la Trinidad and Tobago of a decade and-a-half ago, to assist the less Developed CARICOM countries. In particular, Guyana also needs to review its recently promulgated legislation relating to 'local content' which, in relation to CARICOM's 'national treatment' precepts, should really be replaced by the more appropriate concept of 'regional content' (*vis-à-vis* Exxon and other 'international content').

Second, in the new Cold War atmosphere, outside interference and pressure on the part of the USA is threatening to make consensual foreign policy-making even more difficult. It brings back memories of the fierce split that occurred among CARICOM Member States in 1983, when the USA invaded Grenada, following the assassination of Prime Minister Maurice Bishop, whom I knew as a comrade dedicated to the struggle on behalf of the poor and the powerless and whose death I found nearly as traumatic as that of Walter Rodney.

Equally traumatic was what occurred in 1976 involving a neighbour of mine who lived in Prashad Nagar, Georgetown, Guyana. A Cubana Airways plane was scheduled to fly from Guyana to Trinidad, Barbados, Jamaica and then on to Havana, Cuba. Nine minutes out of Barbados, and at 18,000 feet, an explosion occurred. The captain did not make it back to Barbados and crashed eight kilometres short of Seawell Airport. All 48 passengers and 25 crew members perished – 57 Cubans, 11 Guyanese and 5 North Koreans. Two Venezuelan nationals, Ricardo Lozano and Freddy Lugo Ricardo, confessed to working for Louis Posada Carriles and receiving $25,000. Both were sentenced to 20-year prison terms. Carriles fled Venezuela where he had been held for eight years awaiting sentence and lived thereafter as a free man in the USA. Another conspirator, Orlando Bosch, was acquitted and moved to Miami where he lived until his death on 27 April 2011. One of the Guyanese students going to Cuba was one Jacqueline Williams, a daughter of George Williams, former Permanent Secretary of the Ministry of Works and Hydraulics (when I was a consultant to the Ministry) and Bursar of the University of Guyana (at a time that I was also there as a Professor). This was probably the first act of terrorism involving an aircraft and was commonly believed to have been orchestrated by the CIA. For me, it was a learning experience of the unexpected consequences of being in America's backyard. It is also an example of the confluence and conflicting aspects of national, regional and international (American) relations.

Third, the CARICOM approach to helping a failing Member State, Haiti, is as tepid as that which was demonstrated towards Guyana in the latter's economic decline during the 1970s and 1980s. Haiti is treated as a pariah State and its citizens are almost invariably not accorded the rights of "free movement" within CARICOM. Instead of a relaxation of restrictions in the interest of fleeing refugees, the situation has become worse since the assassination of President Moise and the descent into gang rule. The Caribbean countries being militarily weak and financially strapped, have not done enough lobbying of the UN and powerful countries to take effective action to assist credible local forces in rectifying the current situation in Haiti. France has been strangely silent on the matter, even though the desperate situation in Haiti partly stems from as far back as 1822, when France imposed huge reparations on that newly liberated country (with which it was burdened for over one hundred years) for the planters' loss of slave property; and when popularly elected President Aristide raised the matter in 2006 and asked for reparations to be paid by France to the ancestors of the previously enslaved, he was ousted from power by the USA on behalf of its French ally, with no discernible protest by CARICOM Member States. Equally pathetic was the material response of CARICOM to the plight of Haiti when the latter suffered that devastating earthquake in 2009. (In this regard, I had proposed, as a lasting monument to integration, that each Member State contributes, in addition to emergency assistance, an agreed at least two bedroom pre-fab houses to the construction of a city to be called 'CARICOM', with the streets and avenues given the names of the contributing countries and capitals. The proposal got nowhere).

Fourth, violent crime is rapidly increasing and is much more prevalent and vicious than it was a few decades ago, such that the classless housing structure I referred to in Chapter 1 is giving way to clear social stratification, with the well to do retreating to gated communities. This crime factor, detrimental to the viability of a vibrant tourism industry, is partly related to the drugs trade. It is also a product of the ease with which guns can be easily and illegally secured from the USA, as a result of the latter's constitutional right to arms policy (facilitating stockpiling) and Hollywood's unwitting glamourising of their usage. The Caribbean needs to demand a USA contribution to a Security Fund. Greater inter-country cooperation among CARICOM's security forces is also required to reduce transmission of dangerous weapons and other adverse cross-border effects.

Fifth, ethnic diversity might prove to be both a strength and a weakness. While the majority of CARICOM citizens are descendants from Africa, a very significant minority (citizens of primarily Guyana, Suriname and Trinidad and Tobago) are from the Indian sub-continent, who take pride in their culture and are weary of being "creolised" (which probably helps to explain Guyana's absence from the earlier attempt at West Indian Federation and Guyana's reluctance to be part of the UWI tertiary education system, despite the past efforts, to the contrary, of Eric Williams, Arthur Lewis and Shridath Ramphal). The East Indians are also conflicted as to who to support when a touring cricket test team from the sub-continent (India, Pakistan, Bangladesh or Sri Lanka) visits the Region, as I have myself observed years ago in Guyana and Trinidad and Tobago. The apparent reluctance in Guyana to ascribe a name of a legendary cricketer to the national cricket stadium, in the same way that

Sir Clive Lloyd at the Honorary Doctorate Award occasion with UG Chancellor, Dr Eddie Greene in December 2022

there is a name attached to the national airport, and also names to the various stands, is probably related to the ethnic dilemma. Lasting honour is due to players like my lookalike Sir Clive Lloyd, Rohan Kanhai, Lance Gibbs, Basil Butcher, Joe Solomon, Robert Christiani, Alvin Kalicharran, Roy Fredericks, Colin Croft, Roger Harper, Shiv Chanderpaul and Ramnaresh Sarwan, *inter alia.*

Sixth, increasing economic disparities, within and among countries, is a concern for each nation, region, hemisphere and internationally. It is an intractable problem, given the way the capitalist economy articulates itself, but governmental authorities and international institutions need to address the problem more frontally. In this regard, one of the last presentations I made, as a regional bureaucrat, was on the theme *'Time for Equality, Closing Gaps, Opening Trails'* at the Thirty-Third Session of the UNECLAC in Brasilia, Brazil, 30 May – 1 June, 2010.

AT THE INTERNATIONAL LEVEL

My whole life existence has been against a background involving the playing out of intense rivalry among the great powers and challenges thereto, and I acquired a keen interest in such developments, as one of the university courses I took at LSE was 'International Relations'. I later spent seventeen years as an official in the United Nations system, dealing with economic aspects of international relations and the struggle for equitable trade, investment, financial and technology relations, which intersect inextricably with the political. My observations of what is memorable are therefore two-fold. One is the struggle for true and democratic multilateralism in global economic governance, and the second is the struggle for geopolitical security and stability.

Global Economic Governance: As a senior official at both UNCTC and UNCTAD, this is a subject that has interested me greatly. My first really serious observation on the global economic system was reflected in the following comments, dated 29 May 1991 (two years before UNCTC was merged with UNCTAD) that I wrote to Havelock Brewster, an UNCTAD Director stationed in Geneva, when I was based at UNCTC in New York, on his headlined subject of 'Strengthening Multilateral Cooperation in International Economic Affairs':

Dear Havelock,

I enjoyed very much reading your paper. I think it is an excellent analysis of some of the weaknesses within the United Nations economic system, and the sort of issues that will have to be taken into account in any restructuring of this system, both from a functional and institutional point of view. I will only make a few comments on your paper where I think perhaps you might have omitted a significant point or the thrust of the analysis could have been modified to some extent.

First, I feel that the present day economic context and the issues which preoccupy it do not make for easy restructuring in order to take into account the needs of the developing countries. I refer to the new preoccupation with what is happening in Eastern Europe and the fear that resources will be diverted to the needs of those countries, as is already evidenced by the setting up of the European Development Bank and the significant loans earmarked by the IMF and bilateral entities, like the US and other Western Governments.

A second related factor is the pre-occupation with environmental issues which I feel are tending to cloud the focal need for more rapid development in the developing countries. Concern for the environment should, as far as the developing countries are concerned, be subordinate to the need to accelerate the process of economic development. Moreover, the major destruction in the environment is being caused by the developed countries.

The third factor is the new wave of enthusiasm for market mechanisms as a panacea for all the problems of the developing countries. I feel that this emphasis on market mechanisms is being made in an attempt to say that all the developmental problems of the third world can be solved by more effective use of market forces. Market mechanism is merely an instrument for development, and this, like everything else, has limitations in terms of its effectiveness for the transformation of developing countries. I feel that some comment should be made about this development.

A fourth comment relates to your analysis of the overriding importance of the Bretton Woods institutions and the extent to which they have monopolised policy making at the economic level. I feel that your point is very valid and can be made even more valid by reference to the fact that debt flows are now subject to an IMF clean bill of health.

Another significant factor relating to the monopoly of the Bretton Woods institutions with respect to economic policy making is that UNDP, an institution which has offices in virtually every developing country, is now hitching its policy to that of the World Bank. UNDP no longer has an independent position in terms of satisfying the development objectives of the developing countries. UNDP in a sense is beginning to set conditionalities for its assistance and, in that respect, UNDP is working in tandem with the World Bank, and policy options for the developing countries have now narrowed. The remote control aspect (your para 45) is being reduced but in a rather perverted sense. Still on the subject of the Bretton Woods institutions, I have attached a critique by the late Sidney Dell which attacks not only the socially unacceptable results of the policies of those institutions but, also, the internal logic of the theory underlying same.

Fifth, while I agree with your critique of the principle of clustering and linkage (para 27) I do not agree with all your proposals for grouping of various economic organisations. I would accept the rationalisation behind the proposed merger of DIESA, ODG, and UNCTAD Secretariat and some of the sectoral reorganisations mentioned in para 29. However, I feel that an International Technology Centre encompassing the science and technology activities of UNCTAD, DTCD and CSTD do not constitute the sum total of the United Nations work in this area. For example, the UNCTC deals with foreign investment which is the major source of technology transfer. Given the organic link between foreign investment and transfer of technology, I would be wary of hiving off the latter from the former in an institutional sense.

Finally, on the subject of democratisation versus concentration, the ending of the Cold War and the lessening of Security Council paralysis may result in a reduction in the power/influence of the General Assembly. The Security Council may arrogate to itself more of an economic role, not because of any peace dividend, but under the pretext that economic matters will be the main new cause of world instability.

Just over ten years later, the issues tended to be the same. In a Paper entitled '*Global Governance in the Context of Globalisation: The*

Imperative of Economic Change' (later published in UWI by editors Denis Benn and Kenneth Hall) that I presented at the 2002 Mona Academic Conference that was held in Jamaica during 30 August – 1 September, I began by saying the following:

> *Global governance has tended to become more arbitrary than accommodating to the interests of the disadvantaged; that corporate capital has assumed a more concentrated, corrupt and co-opting form; that financial crises are now more systemic than serendipitous and the solutions more perverse and pauperising; and that there is less coherence and more contradiction in tackling the phenomenon of underdevelopment... there is an imperative for global governance to be better structured and more cognisant of differences in levels of development, to be more flexible with greater scope for safeguarding adjustment to adverse economic changes and for policy-makers in developing countries to be placed less in a straight-jacket.*

I then selected eight issues for analysis with respect to the impact on developing countries, particularly the Caribbean, under the following headings: (1) Imbalances in Global Rules and Asymmetry in Compliance/Enforcement; (2) Warped Mandates and Skewed Implementation; (3) Crushing and Escalating Conditionalities in Accessing Multilateral Capital; (4) Extra-Judicial Decrees and Unilateral Impositions; (5) Perverse Application of Special and Differential Treatment; (6) Failure of Global Corporate Governance; (7) Bankruptcy Governing Approach to Financial Crises; and (8) Limitations of Process of Promoting Development by Global Conference Declarations and Exhortations. I then concluded as follows:

> *The management of the global economic system is quite undemocratic in the sense that its major pillars or institutions are essentially in the hands of the developed countries, and*

organised and operated to serve the interests of the latter. (The imminent takeover by a Thai of the reins of the WTO will constitute a first). The United Nations has been emptied of any meaningful economic decision making function and relegated to the role of providing humanitarian and peacekeeping services. Although the Monterrey ('Financing for Development') Conference encouraged the UN, the World Bank, the IMF and the WTO to address issues of coherence, coordination and cooperation as a follow up to the conference and ascribed a focal point role to the UN General Assembly (and its Economic and Social Council arm) with respect to overseeing implementation of the results of the conference, this is likely to turn out to be a grand public relations exercise since the developed countries have in the past (the latest evidence being the decision not to make the new WTO a part of the UN system) studiously avoided bestowing economic power on the UN.

There is no separation of economic powers. The global concentration of economic power is enormous, since there is an alliance of capital surplus countries (even if economic disputes between them may arise from time to time) and an alliance of international economic institutions all working in tandem with each other (under a Supreme Commander of Allied Economic Forces). These forces are not afraid to employ cross retaliatory measures to protect their interests when dealing with developing countries and are in full control of the legislative, executive and rather expensive judicial/dispute settlement agenda.

The system is also non-accountable in nature, in the sense that if, for example, a misguided IMF programme succeeds in causing social disruption and increasing pauperisation, or the World Bank denies a country a loan for essentially political reasons, or unconscionable conditionalities are made a requirement for financial access, there is no recourse to a higher body for redress or a constituency that can be effectively mobilised.

The result is that global rules are enacted which do not always serve the interest of the disempowered and disadvantaged. Distortions and discrepancies abound. At the same time there is increasing global economic integration, there is growing global policy disconnect. The economic gaps are ever widening but the system seems unwilling or incapable of devising measures to effectively deal with the imbalances between countries and between groups within countries.

Developing countries are in something of a straitjacket. Unlike the South-East Asian countries who managed to achieve their economic miracle partly by being able to exercise various economic policy options, late comers now find themselves boxed in by various mandatory and pseudo mandatory rules in the area of trade, finance, investment and technology. There is little room for manoeuvre in the egregious free market system. There is also a "one size fits all" approach that makes little allowance for the most disadvantaged and their very limited supply capacity.

A sceptic could very well describe this era of rapid international economic integration as being characterised by global mis-governance, rather than global governance. There is need for fundamental economic change.

Selected List of Pathologies of Incoherence in the Global Developmental Process

1. Over-riding emphasis and clarity with respect to domestic policy reform without comparable messianic zeal and vision concerning the parameters of an enabling global environment. (Moreover, the policy reform, especially its structural adjustment aspects, sometimes conflicts with the goal of poverty reduction).
2. Specification of trade as an engine of growth without sufficient concern for the pre-requisite of effective market access. A lack of fair trade increases the reliance on Official Development Assistance (ODA) and exacerbates the debt burden.

3. Protection by developed countries of certain industries (e.g. agriculture and textiles) which are precisely the ones in which developing countries are able to exercise some degree of competitiveness.
4. An emphasis on foreign direct investment as a supposedly adequate source of long-term capital for developing countries when the bulk of it goes to a mere handful of countries.
5. Persistent, nay chronic, reductions in ODA at a time when competitiveness in the increasingly globalising environment requires massive expansion of human and infrastructural capital, especially in the disadvantaged least developed and small economies that are recipients of negligible flows of foreign investment.
6. An avalanche of unpredictable and speculative short-term private international bank and portfolio capital in the face of the developmental need for crisis free and stable flows of long-term capital.
7. A financial architectural system in which reaction to its increasing volatility and complexity, paradoxically takes the form of demands for more liberalisation and deregulation, including elimination of capital controls.
8. A market-driven system in which the increasingly mandatory rules and obligations placed on governments are not matched by the imposition of comparable strict accounting, legal and other responsibilities on corporate behaviour.
9. While extolling competition, there is increasing oligopoly as a result of mega mergers, alliances, and other cross border arrangements, and increasing global reach.
10. A system of global governance in which decisions are taken by the powerful in non-democratic economic fora, that claim to represent the interest of the powerless and adopt a guise of conferring "ownership". The Washington Consensus has now become the Washington-New York-Geneva Consensus.
11. A labour market in which developed countries actively recruit from developing countries skilled workers (IT specialists, teachers, nurses, etc.) that could contribute positive economic benefits while vigorously deporting those who are said to represent negative social benefits. There is no compensatory mechanism.

> A fundamental and over-arching disconnect between the lofty goals trumpeted at various United Nations and other global fora and the financial and other resources the developed countries are willing to provide, in a situation which amounts to a genuine crisis of development and ever-widening economic gaps.

Source: Maurice Odle, 'Global Governance...', Sept., 2002

Twenty years later, the message of the effects of global financial instability on developing countries remains more or less the same, as reflected in the following extract from the November 2022 Trade and Development Report of UNCTAD:

> *At a time of falling real wages, fiscal tightening, financial turbulence and insufficient multilateral support and coordination, excessive monetary tightening could usher in a period of stagnation and economic instability for many developing countries and some developed ones. This year's interest rate hikes in the United States are set to cut an estimated $360 billion of future income for developing countries (excluding China) and signal even more trouble ahead.*

Finally, as is my want, I wish to refer to an interesting, but disturbing, behind the scenes happening which is illustrative of the unequal nature of global economic power and governance. At the abovementioned Monterrey Conference, that took place in Mexico during 18-22 March 2002, a couple of hours before Fidel Castro was due to speak word began to spread that he was being asked by the host Chairman, (President Vincente Fox of Mexico) not to take any further part in the International Conference proceedings after he had made his speech, since President George W. Bush had indicated that he would not share the same space with Fidel Castro, who would then leave the country that very evening. I was a member of the Caribbean delegation at the Conference and the news of

Castro's imminent eviction must have triggered memories of my unhappy experience at the hands of a school boy bully. I therefore told my Caribbean colleagues that, when Castro enters the hall to speak, we should stand up and applaud the regional brother (an honour that had not been accorded the previous speakers). To my surprise, the Caribbean delegation duly rose and began to applaud when Castro entered the hall and the thousand and more participants joined us in giving Fidel a thunderous welcoming ovation, which must have helped to soothe the pain.

Global Security Developments: The developments can be considered within the following historical framework:

1. *A Cold-War standoff between the Union of Soviet Socialist Republics (USSR) and the West (USA and Western Europe) that occurred parallel with the de-colonisation process*
2. *Collapse of the USSR resulting in an unrestricted global hegemonic quest of the USA.*
3. *NATO proxy war against Russia, trade tightening and semi-conductor technology blockade against emergent China, and a New Cold War.*

The post-World War II formation of the USSR was motivated by both an ideological drive (communism) and a defensive factor (with Eastern Europe a physical buffer against any future invading Germany, in defeating whom Russia had lost about twenty million of its population, not to mention the memory of loss from invading Napoleonic soldiers a century and-a-half earlier). However, Winston Churchill saw the USSR in aggressive "iron curtain" terms and the West formed the North Atlantic Treaty Organisation (NATO); the USSR countered with formation of its own military alliance, the Warsaw Pact. My first awareness of this tense state of international affairs arose with USSR's shooting down in 1960 of the Gary Powers spy plane, that originated from Turkey, a member of NATO, over its territory and whose real mission the USA for a long time denied. Less sensational news relating to the then described two superpowers, but more insidious in its involvement of third parties, and which at the time I did not quite understand (even with knowledge of the 1953 intervention in my native Guyana) was the USA participation in the 1950s, fuelled by "McCarthyism", in a civil war in Korea and CIA inspired coups against elected Governments in Iran and Guatemala, *inter alia*. Then came the Cuban revolution, the failed USA-sponsored invasion, the threat of nuclear war unless Russia removed missiles stationed in Cuba (solved by the reciprocal removal of missiles in Turkey and Cuba by the respective super powers, and a promise by the USA not to ever invade Cuba) and the perennial economic blockade against that country. Just as startling was the USA involvement in the civil war in Vietnam (a country that a few years earlier had liberated itself from France) in which chemical warfare was employed by the USA, who lost 53 thousand and Vietnam three million. The stakes at large seemed to be worth all costs in men and materials and the USA's strategic goal appeared to be to eliminate, by any means necessary, leftist regimes world-wide that were potential allies of the USSR.

The Cold War struggle was also taking place in other theatres in the 1960s (with my being able to put the intervention in Guyana in better perspective) and beyond. Foreign inspired coups occurred in Argentina and Brazil, with disastrous social and human rights consequences and the CIA-organised coup in Chile (which indirectly resulted in my later becoming a United Nations official) was described by Secretary of State Kissinger as the USA "saving Chile from itself". In Africa, Algeria paid a terrible price for its liberation war against France, given the latter's population targeting and scorched earth policies; and a CIA inspired coup occurred in Ghana in 1966, the same year as one in Indonesia, S.E. Asia. In Southern Africa, the indigenous black population was waging a brave and relentless guerrilla struggle (with arms from the USSR and, for a very limited period, troops from Cuba for liberation in the 1970s and 1980s, against the white settler governments in Southern Rhodesia (Zimbabwe), South Africa, South-West Africa (Namibia) Angola and Mozambique, with little support from the developed Western countries, and with Margaret Thatcher exhibiting contempt for the freedom fighters and Ronald Regan referring to Mandela as a "terrorist". (In Chapter 3, I also made reference to my very limited role as a United Nations official in monitoring the impact of the economic boycott campaign that Non-Governmental Organisations (NGOs) and world conscience had forced Western Governments to support, even if very reluctantly). And in the liberated vast mineral rich territory of the Congo, Belgium returned in neo-colonial fashion (with the help of the CIA) to assassinate leader Patrice Lumumba and install Mobutu, and resulting instability reigns to this day. But although a certain amount of territorial liberation constituted some gains for the Third World, no New International Economic Order (NIEO) emerged and the latter was enmeshed in such huge borrowing from Western banks to finance fiscal deficits associated with higher oil prices (that began with the 1973 Arab oil embargo) and to compensate for declining terms of trade, as to find themselves in a Debt Crisis and IMF structural adjustment, thus making the 1980s for them a Lost Decade and ushering a trend of increasing inequality between developed and underdeveloped countries. (For the USA, Reagan's 'voodoo economics' of corporate tax reduction and trickle-down effect also ushered-in increasing domestic inequality).

The other super power was also exercising a right to a sphere of influence, this time close to home, rather than globally as the USA wanted to do. Uprisings in Czechoslovakia and Hungary were put down, but resistance in Poland simmered into the late 1980s. But it was the costly response to the request of the Afghanistan Government for military assistance that was to contribute to the ultimate unravelling of the USSR. The USA opposed the presence of USSR troops in Afghanistan and provided shoulder held anti-aircraft and other lethal weapons to Mujahedeen forces based in neighbouring Pakistan, one of whose leaders was Osama Bin Laden. The fierce guerrilla resistance drained the resources of the USSR who withdrew after a decade of battle. With the economy performing badly, the USSR leader, Gorbachev, felt it necessary to introduce economic reform (Perestroika) and, unexpectedly, also decided to pursue a path of political reform (Glasnost). That proved his undoing and East Germany and the other Eastern European States, that yearned for the higher standard of living that obtained in the West, decided to seize the opportunity to re-assert the nationalism that existed before the formation of the USSR. The leftist Parties in Guyana, and I dare say in most other countries, were in dismay at how an ideology, and the centre of its physical manifestation, could dissolve so easily. Capitalism had triumphed.

The USSR dissolution process, including the conversion from a state-owned to a mainly private/market based economy, was a messy one and the consequences, particularly international governance issues, would prove to be enormous. The over-riding context in which international relations would henceforth take place, according to the State Department, was that the USA was the sole super power, and President George H Bush endorsed and ominously amplified same by stating that the USA will forever be the sole super power.

An immediate issue was the fate of the respective alliances. Boris Yeltsin, the emerging new Russian leader, was of the view that both the Warsaw Pact and NATO should be dissolved. When only the Warsaw Pact was dissolved, he was adamant that NATO should not move another inch towards the Russian border and claimed that he had gotten assurances to that effect, but apparently no formal agreement was signed. Because nothing seems to have been put into writing, the encircling of Russia a couple of years later resumed, with a number of Eastern European countries and Baltic States, that were formerly part of the USSR, joining NATO. Russia had even expressed an interest in joining NATO, but the then USA President, Bill Clinton, had stated that Russia was too physically large to be absorbed into NATO.

The USA and its NATO partners would soon take other actions that would be of concern to Russia. NATO presided over the bombing and dissolution in 1999 of Yugoslavia's several republics during which Serbia, with strong ethnic ties to the people of Russia, being humiliated and its Kosovo province effectively weaned away. Very importantly, NATO had shown its intention to be operationally a global alliance, rather than one restricted to only containing Russia. Particularly significant, and very threatening to Russia, as reported by Tricontinental's Institute for Social Research, was the action that the USA was to later take involving the unilateral withdrawal from three treaties that had been the bedrock of military stability between the USA and the former USSR: They were a Missile Defence Treaty (which says that erecting a system to defend against missiles is itself aggressive and endangering to the other Party, who would therefore find it necessary to increase its arsenal of attack missiles); Intermediate Range Missile Treaty (whose repudiation and consequent installation of missiles on the border of Russia would give the latter very little time to react to an attack, whereas there are no possible missile sites very near to the USA's border); and the Open Skies Agreement (which facilitated aerial observation of any aggressive plans by the other party). A weak Russia could do nothing but protest but the stage was being set for an explosion.

Eventually, in 2014, Russia was forced to respond. The President of Ukraine, in the process of negotiating a comprehensive trade agreement with Russia, was ousted in a coup which the West seemed to support. In retaliation, Russia seized Crimea, a territory it had ruled for centuries but which its leader in 1954 (Khrushchev, being himself a Ukrainian) had administratively transferred to Ukraine because of its contiguity with that territory. In retaliation, Russia also supported certain separatist forces in the Donbass region of Ukraine, who wanted to be aligned with Russia because of ethnicity and family ties. The West (primarily the USA) imposed sanctions on Russia and began to arm and train the Ukrainians in their fight against the separatists, in which over 8,000 died, even before the start of the February 2020 Russian invasion. Tensions were long simmering.

In other parts of the globe, the lone super power was operating without any need for restraint, and its actions were frequently adding to instability. The indiscriminate bombing of Afghanistan arose in reaction to the 11th September 2001 aerial hijacking and Kamikaze demolition of important symbolic targets in the USA by Al Qaeda which, in turn, was as a result of leader Osama Bin Laden (flush with military skills gained earlier on behalf of the USA) demonstrating his disapproval of Israel occupation of parts of Palestine and Syria and cultural objection to USA military bases in Saudi Arabia and other parts of the Middle East. (The USA was only able to extricate itself from that country twenty years later). Despite the failure of the 'Arab Spring' to produce the regime change that it supported, the USA also unilaterally invaded previously stable Iraq without finding any evidence of weapons of destruction. In the devastating process, the USA disbanded the Sunni army (that Hussein had used to control the Shiite majority in Iraq) soldiers from which later formed the Caliphate along with disaffected Sunni militants that were against the Shiite rule of Assad, in a country that was also in chaos and whose insurrection USA President Obama militarily supported with the regime change cry of "Assad must Go". The Caliphate was eventually defeated but Assad, with the help of Russia (which has a military base there) is still in power in a physically destroyed and partly dismembered state, similar to that in Iraq.

But regime change was probably at its most destructive in Libya. Citizens in the province of Benghazi were in a state of rebellion and Gaddafi had assembled his troops outside the city demanding a halt to the resistance, when the UN Security Council passed a seemingly innocent resolution permitting intervention to prevent a possible "massacre". The West, always unhappy with Gaddafi, cleverly seized the opportunity to have France and Britain, with aerial refuelling support from the USA, bomb Gaddafi's forces unmercifully until he himself was killed by local ground forces, a deception which Russia said showed how untrustworthy the West was and vowed it will never again allow itself to be a victim of such UN Security Council related deception. With Gaddafi gone, succession wars have made Libya a "Failed State" of warlords and the aftermath has had disastrous consequences also for the Sahel region of Africa (affecting Burkina Faso, Mali, Mauritania,

Niger, and Northern Nigeria) where illegally acquired guns from Libya are being used by Al Qaeda and other Muslim elements to create such chaos, that even invading French troops do not seem able to quell. Al Shabab also operates in Somalia, East Africa.

But it is the China investment presence in Africa that has really gained the attention of the West, with the latter promising to promote more of their foreign investment capital there, as a counter to the Chinese influence. At the military level, the US Africa Command (AFRICOM) has spearheaded the rapid increase in the number of bases on the continent and this was intensified with the recent rise in hostility towards Russia. As with the Latin American "backyard" concept of the USA, NATO now considers Africa as its "Southern Neighbourhood".

In Iran, an agreement had been reached with the West, under the threat of sanctions, to limit its nuclear research programme below the stage where a bomb could be produced, even though a blind eye was turned on Israel producing and stockpiling of same; and, later, Israel was a recipient of the West's unconditional support. Moreover, Iran was mindful that the leaders of Iraq and Libya (Hussein and Gaddafi) that had been pressured by the West to give up a nuclear research programme, and had been killed after doing so. (Iran eventually reached agreement with the West to limit production of fissionable material, but the succeeding USA Government unilaterally withdrew from the deal).

More recently, in Latin America, where the existence of leftist governments, and regional organisations such as ALBA, CELAC and PetroCaribe (of which Guyana was a member) were a perennial concern, the West unsuccessfully maneuvered to remove Maduro, the President of Venezuela, a coup against whose predecessor (Chavez) they had supported in the 1990s, and continue to impose economy shattering sanctions against that country. But, closer to home, there is no guarantee that the USA and the West would continue to support Guyana against the territorial claim of Venezuela. In fact, it was the USA that had prodded Venezuela to begin the claim in 1964, so as to give that country, then its South American darling, an opportunity to invade and overthrow the leftist Cheddi Jagan Government. Though Jagan lost office in late1964, the Venezuelans never relinquished the claim.

Such was the dangerous state of the world when President Trump won the USA election in November, 2016.and began to confront China. The West always had a fear of China which, before their 18th century (to early 19th century) industrial revolution, was probably just as materially advanced as they were. In fact, when Britain colonised India, it tried to make Tibet a buffer territory (and also Afghanistan) between its colony and the hording millions in the rest of China. Later, it carved out Hong Kong from mainland China, following the Opium Wars; and in the south-west, the Portuguese seized Macao. In 1886, the United States Government enacted a Chinese Exclusion Act and, in the 1930s, the Japanese began their occupation of certain regions of China. This wariness of China increased after World War II, with the USA taking the side of Chiang Kai-shek during the civil war, when the latter retreated to the island of Taiwan from the advancing Maoist communist forces.

At the United Nations, the West engineered the absurd situation of Taiwan representing the whole of China and this situation only changed when the USA decided to try to wean China away from its close relationship with Russia, with the Henry Kissinger visit in 1971. (A year earlier, Barbados, Guyana, Jamaica and Trinidad and Tobago became some of the first countries in Latin America [and the world] to recognise the Government of mainland China). The China visit led to the promulgation of a "One China" policy and the United Nations decreed the formulation of the term 'Taiwan Province of China' to describe the less than sovereign status of Taiwan.

China's real emergence began with the decision of Deng Xiaoping to experiment with the introduction of capitalist methods in certain rural areas and the success rapidly led to countrywide application. The country began to rapidly develop and foreign investors became interested because of the large market and plentiful low wage labour. When China was admitted to the General Agreement on Trade in Services/World Trade Organisation (GATS/WTO) system, the real boom began, since foreign investors were able to lobby for their 'Made in China' manufactured products to be admitted duty free into their home country. (In Chapter 4, I made mention of UNCTC's role in China's opening up, regarding which I was to lead three missions to that country). Sustained double digit growth over a three decade period took place and China became the manufacturing capital of the world, during which time it accumulated trillions of dollars of balance of trade surpluses, particularly with the USA. The dollar surplus was used to purchase bonds issued by the USA to offset the latter's fiscal deficits.

It is when China, using its surplus dollars, began to invest overseas to secure vital minerals and other raw materials for its explosive development and, later, embarked on its Belt and Road Initiative that financed infrastructure development in Asia and Africa, in particular, that the USA began to really see that country as a challenge to its global supremacy. This gave rise to President Obama's "Pivot to Asia", designed ostensibly to ensure that the South China seas remain open to international transit, but really intended to counter China's influence in that part of the world (and also reinforce its containment of nuclear armed North Korea). The USA later began to increasingly voice its concerns about "human rights" and "freedoms" in Xinjiang Province, Tibet, Hong Kong and Taiwan Province, but which were really part of a policy to destabilise, dismember and weaken China. Then, President Trump, at the height of the covid pandemic's effect on the world economy, issued a series of tariff measures against Chinese imports and restriction against use of Huawei G5 technology for ostensibly national privacy/security reasons, while at the same time blaming China for "stealing" American technology. Geopolitics was now joined by Geoeconomics. He then sent his Secretary of State Pompeo around the world pressuring countries to stop accepting Chinese investment lest it leads to a "debt trap". This was followed by his successor, President Biden, militantly announcing that China's influence and economic size exceeding that of America "will not happen under my watch". Instead of congratulations for lifting over 600 million people out of poverty,

China was to be punished for daring to be successful. If India, with its so-called "teeming hordes" were to similarly economically and technologically 'take off', comparable treatment would be meted out to it. There is no need to ask why. As the American pundit James Carville would want to say, 'it's the imperative of imperialism, stupid'!

Not surprisingly, the USA then launched a policy of technology embargo against China, denying it access to the latest and most advanced American technology and threatening with sanctions any country or foreign firm, that allows, directly or indirectly, American technology to fall into Chinese hands. In fact, the USA is encouraging Apple and other American electronic firms operating in China to switch production to other countries, like India and Vietnam, for "geopolitical and other supply risks" reasons. The USA, in October 2022, also clearly said for the first time that it would come to the defence of Taiwan against any Chinese attack. All the while, the USA has been creating and strengthening encircling alliances and partnerships in the Asian-Pacific region to counter Chinese influence, such as the 'Quad' (a grouping of Australia, India, Japan and the USA); AUSNUS (made up of Australia, New Zealand and the USA); a USA/New Zealand-Fiji Agreement; and a Friendship Association of eighteen Pacific territories.

It was at this time that relations between the USA-led West and Russia reached rock bottom, when the former, at a NATO Summit Meeting in 2021, announced that a decision had been made to admit neighbouring Ukraine as a Member, sometime in the future. While no specific date had been announced, for Russia this was the last straw and it was not prepared to wait for the inevitable final tightening of the Western encirclement screws. It immediately began to mobilise troops along the long Ukraine border and issued an ultimatum for that country to renounce any intention to join NATO. That was not forthcoming and France and Germany visited Moscow to discuss a way out of the dangerous situation, including a proposal for "Finlandisation" or neutrality status for Ukraine. However, no agreement was reached, since it seems that USA had persuaded Ukraine to stand firm and arrogantly dismissed the peace-making efforts of its junior European partners, a subservient situation that Charles De Gaule, Willie Brandt and Olof Palme (advocates of a less USA dependent policy space) would not have approved. Russian troops eventually invaded and headed for the Ukraine capital, Kyiv, expecting a quick capitulation, but found surprisingly stiff resistance and therefore scaled down their plans to merely seizing control of the southern Donbas region. But massive supply of advanced weaponry (including howitzers, multiple rocket launchers, Stinger air defence missiles and Javelin anti-tank guided missiles, along with live intelligence) from the USA and, as Tri-Continental's Institute for Social Research has pointed out, other Western countries, has allowed Ukraine to stall Russian advances, even within the Donbas region (as this is being written) nearly a year later. Russia has unexpectedly found itself in a proxy war against NATO and the USA's Defense Secretary, Anthony Austin, has stated that the intention is to, accordingly, permanently "weaken Russia".

I have taken some time and effort to recap international relations since World War II (with a view that is not normally voiced in the West) to indicate that nothing has fundamentally changed, except the ranking and style of the players. We have been witnessing what can be described as the 'New Imperialism', and the context in which everyone is caught up, including my own Guyana. It seems to me that there are certain critical features of the power of the New Imperialism.

First, the New Imperialism is not built on the possession of exploitative colonies, but on the access or command over territorial space and strategic location that allows for easy intervention and control. In this regard, the USA has over 200 (army/naval/air) bases (more than one in certain countries) worldwide, 11 roving/floating territories called aircraft carriers, a military budget of around $750 billion (that was increased to $830 billion for 2023) and a CIA budget of $60 billion.

Second, the USA, an Empire founded on 13 colonised continent located territories that aggressively and expansively grew into 50 States (plus a number of off-shore island territories in the Caribbean and the

Pacific) is driven by creed and ideology. Whereas the old imperialists justified their action of "civilising the savages" as one of bearing the "white man's burden", the new are guided by a marauding and rampaging concept of "manifest destiny"; the extension of the 200-year-old Munroe Doctrine to include the whole world; the invoking of God's will at times of crisis with the ringing call of "God Bless America" (and, presumably, damn the rest of the world! Similar to "God save the King/Queen" when Britain ruled the waves). Thus, the dangerous combination of Guns and God. It was widely reported at the time that President George W. Bush, on realising that there were no weapons of mass destruction in Iraq, ventured a supposed justification to the effect that God had told him to invade Iraq.

Third, the New Imperialism is underpinned and enforced by both hard and soft power and includes military power, economic and financial power, diplomatic power and information/communications/propaganda power. When the West feels that it is not appropriate to exercise military power, or trade measures are not effective, it uses denial of access to loans in the international banking system and the IFIs and, when this in turn does not work, it resorts to weaponisation of the dollar and denial of access to the Swift international clearance and settlement system for financial transactions. The denial of Venezuela's Maduro Government of access to its considerable ($1 billion) gold reserves in the Bank of England and the denial of Russia's use of its $650 billion dollar reserves in the Western banking system, are glaring examples. It is also interesting to note that, in 2021, when speculation was rife that Russia or China may be contemplating establishing a military base in Venezuela, in order to dissuade the West from physically imposing Juan Guaidò as President, the reported reaction of Jake Sullivan, the USA National Security Advisor, was that such an attempt to set up a base would be met with "swift and decisive action", despite the existence of USA bases all over the world. Over thirty countries (including certain of their citizens) are currently under USA sanctions. Most alarmingly, if a country dares trade with a country against whom the USA has imposed sanctions, that country is also subjected to sanctions, a clear negation of sovereignty. The Western rhetoric and narrative are in strong support of this position.

Fourth, the West (which now seems to include Australia and New Zealand) self-righteously uses precepts such as freedom, democracy and human rights as a justification for intervention in other countries and ignores the United Nations principle of "non- interference in the internal affairs of other States". These precepts can be considered at times a fig leaf, as they are used in a rather selective manner: for example, a legitimate Hamas electoral victory in Palestine was not recognised and undemocratic oil producing sheikdoms and sultans and emirs are never punished. When every other excuse fails, the furthering of USA's national interests is invoked. The USA is unchallenged and there is also miniaturising of the authority of the United Nations, from whose Agencies and multilateral agreements (for example, the Convention on Biological Weapons) the USA withdrew when the situation supposedly warranted it to do so. The USA also, in exceptionalism fashion, refuses to be a member of the International Criminal Court (ICC), even though it participates in determining who should appear before the Court.

Fifth, the mainstream media (and the international distribution outlets, such as Reuters and Associated Press) in the West, act not as a watch-dog, but as a veritable lap-dog. This is particularly the case in the USA, where there are no debates aired relating to USA foreign policy and, when a crisis or important development abroad occurs, the speakers invited to comment are invariably military, national security and other establishment figures, and academic and NGO figures are rarely ever invited. This is reinforced by the nature of the two-party system, in which there is a surprising degree of similarity of views with respect to foreign policy, USA's aggressive stance abroad, and the expenditure choice issue of "guns *vs* butter". The USA's military budget is more than that of the rest of the world, combined.

Sixth, the New Imperialism is a Western collective which is overwhelmingly led by the United States. In that regard, it practices unilateralism, rather than the multilateralism or "balance of power" ethic of the old imperialism of competing European blocs. Whereas when the USSR existed, there was a "balance of terror", with its collapse the US has sought to perpetuate a unipolar world and an American rules-based order, with only the new capitalist China as a serious rival. Global nationalism of the New Cold War matter, rather than the market ideology differences of the Old Cold War. "White Supremacy" was now prepared to confront any challenge from the yellow, brown or black peoples of the world. It has its own imperatives and its own dynamics. According to the New York Times of 6 June 2022, the Biden Foreign Policy elite team believes that "maintaining the United States' global dominance is essential to ensuring American safety and international peace" ("Pax Americana").

The dominant and monopolistic position that the USA and its Western partners have enjoyed since the collapse of the USSR, and the absence of a countervailing force, or alternative support, have engendered a lack of empathy for the developmental efforts of developing countries. These consequences for the Caribbean include the following:

- less grants and loans from Governments in Western countries and less willingness on the part of commercial banks in those countries to restructure existing loans;
- less willingness of Western Governments to provide assistance in emergency situations, such as with respect to hurricanes and, more recently, access to vaccines for pandemic relief;
- continued 'non-preferential treatment' at IFIs, with per capita income the sole criterion with respect to borrowing conditions and no concern for vulnerability and lack of resilience;
- less empathy to grant small underdeveloped economies 'special and differential treatment', as in the case of the EU Partnership Agreement;
- relatively more stringent implementation required of OECD tax haven regulations;
- requiring unnecessarily harsh implementation of money laundering and anti-financing of terrorism laws;

- undue pressure with respect to reducing carbon emissions, despite the miniscule environmental impact of such countries (and lack of financial assistance for mitigation and adaptation and to erect renewable energy infrastructure);
- threats of sanctions unless investment and other links with China are reduced;
- actual sanctions, including triviality of denial of visas to the important denial of IFI loans; and

lack of concern that the sharp anti-money laundering regulations have resulted in the withdrawal of correspondent bank facilities.

This Memoir ends, as it effectively began, amidst swirling paradigmatic issues of immense economic importance. We are now in the second quarter of 2023, with a profit-maximising transnational, ExxonMobil, enlisting full diplomatic support from the West, in its resistance to the efforts of the Guyanese people to derive greater benefits from its national oil resources. It is similar to sugar producer, Booker Bros in 1953, fearful of perceived threats to its Guyana investments, enlisting Anglo-American support that (adding to cold war pressures) contributed to the Suspension of the Constitution and the unravelling of whatever ethnic unity existed in Guyana. The only difference is that, at this time, the incumbent government (PPP in both instances) seems to be on the side of the transnational corporation and has joined forces with ExxonMobil against the wishes of the population, in appealing the decision of a judge in favour of Guyana having full guarantee against liability for any oil spill damage. Astonishingly, the Vice President, Bharrat Jagdeo, at a press conference, emphatically stated that, "Our economic nationalism will not hold water in the new dispensation". There remains a situation of massive Private Profits (for ExxonMobil) and significant risk/threat of calamitous Social Costs (on Guyana). The struggle continues.

INDEX

A Partnership for National Unity (APNU), 201-2, 223
Abeng Group, 62
Abrams, Bertrand, 51
Adams-Yearwood, Valerie, 218
Adelphi University, 81
Afghanistan, 261, 263, 266
Africa Connect, 99, 107, **111**, 174
Africa, Caribbean Pacific Grouping (ACP), 123, 137, 142-3, 148
Africa, West, 32, 81, 170, 260
Agard, Carl, 22
Agard, Squeaky, 22
Alan, Rory, 92
Alexander, Arthur, 55, 64
Ali, Asgar, 74
Ali, Irfaan, 217
Ali, Jack, 25
Allen, Leslie, 22
Allende, Salvador, 84
Alliance for Change (AFC), 202, 237-8, 241
Allied Insurance Institute of the Caribbean (AIIC), 125
Andaiye, 73
Angola, 260
Antigua and Barbuda, 61, 102, 129, 172, 197
Apatha, Kwame, 66
Applewhaite, Lolita, **126**, **165**, 176
Argentina, 123-4, 260
Arjune, Prem, 57
Armstrong, Aubrey, 55
Arthur, Joan, 57
Arthur, Owen, 75, 128, 175, 187, **188**, 197
Asante, Sam, 90
Asian Miracle Economies, 152
Assad, Bashar al-, 264
Association of Caribbean States (ACS), 43, 138
Association of Cultural Relations with Independent Africa (ASCRIA), 68
Association of South-East Asian Nations (ASEAN), 91, 96, **97-8**, 101, 106
Atkinson Field, 16

Augustin, Donald, 38
AUSNUS, 268
Austin, Anthony, 269
Australia, 268, 271

Bacchus, Zinul, 55
Bahamas, 88, 173, 189, 195-6
Balance of Power/Terror, 41, 271-2
Bangladesh, 249
Bank for International Settlements, 229
Bank of Guyana, 52, 228-31, 233
Barbados, 21, 24, 61, 75, 117, 128, 135, 155, 162, 173-4, 187, 192-3, 195, 197, 203, 235, 247, 266
Barcellos, John, 25
Bardouille, Nan, 75
Barnes, Oswald, 210, 223
Barnett, Carla, 181
Barrow, Errol, 39, 61, **189**, 197
BBC (Bush House), 43
Beckford, George, 62
Beckles, Hilary, 21
Bedford Methodist School, 12, 15
Belgium, 261
Belize, 88, 172, 195
Benn, Brindley, 68
Benn, Denis, 149, 185, 254
Bent, Cherita, 44
Bernal, Richard, 185
Bernard, Desiree, 64
Bernasconi-Osterwalder, 162
Best, Lloyd, 62
Bhagwan, Moses, 68, 70
Bickerton, Derek, 55
Biden, Joe, 267, 272
Bilateral Investment Treaty (BIT), 109
Bin Laden, Osama, 261, 264
Bird, Vere, 61, 197
Bissember, Enid, 175
Bissessar, Kamla Persad, 172, 193
Black Power, 60
Blake, Byron, 69, 126, 130-1, 133-4, 183

275

Bolivarian Alliance of the Peoples of the Americas (ALBA), 195, 265
Bolivia, 123
Bone, Bonita, 66
Booker Bros, 23-4, 28, 273
Bosch, Orlando, 248
Bourne, Compton, 55, **89**, 125, 132, 158, 184, 203
Brandt, Willie, 269
Brassington, Winston, 207
Brazil, 56, 85, 118, 123-4, 250, 260
Brewster (Satcher) Abenna, 246
Brewster, Erwin, 26, 38
Brewster, Havelock, 22, 26, 62, 113, 141, 190, 251
Brewster, Rod, 246
Brewster, Wendy, 246
British Guiana, 9, 12, 25
Brockleman, Hans, 52
Brosan, George, 50
Brown, Adlith, 88
Brown, Roland, 103
Burkina Faso, 264
Burnham, Forbes, 20, 39, 43, 50-2, 54, 57-9, 61, 63, 65, 67-72, 80, 83, **189**, 197, 242
Burnham, Viola, 64
Bush, George, H, 262
Bustamante, Alexander, 61
Butcher, Basil, 44, 250

Campbell, Jock, 56
Carberry, Lance, 237
Cardoso, Fernando, 85
Caretaker Government, 211-2
Caribbean
    Integration, 62, 101, 116, 118, 122, 124, 126, 138-40, 146-8, 151, 170, 172, 175-7, 179, 181-2, 185-94, 196-9, 203, 246, 249, 256
    Publications, 74, 175-85
    Research activities, 57-8, 63
    Single currency, 164, 193, 196
    USA possessions, 269-70
Caribbean Association of Investment Promotion Agencies (CAIPA), 162, 171
Caribbean Catastrophe Risk Insurance Facility (CCRIF), 194
Caribbean Centre on Money and Finance (CCMF), 203
Caribbean Community (CARICOM), 69, 106, 113-5, **115**, 116-20, 124-6, 128, 131-3, 136, 138-41, 144, 146-8, 152-3, 155, 160-7, **165**, 169-82, 184-90, 193, 195-8, 200-3, 224-5, 233-5, 243-4, 246-9

Caribbean Connect, 174
Caribbean Court of Justice (CCJ), 163, 195, 212, 224-5
Caribbean Development Bank (CDB), 148, 171-2, 176, 184, 229, 235
Caribbean Development Fund (CDF), 164, 171-2, 235
Caribbean Examination Council (CXC), 194
Caribbean Free Trade Area, 61
Caribbean Regional Financial Stability Report, 203
Caribbean Trade and Investment Report (CTIR), 175-7, 180-4
CARICOM,
CARICOM Financial Services Agreement (CFSA), 136, 146, 163-4, 193
CARICOM Investment Code (CIC), 146, 160-4, 174, 193
CARICOM Multilateral Clearance Facility, 169, 235
CARICOM Single Market and Economy (CSME), 139-40, 144, 146, 148, 185-7, 189, 234
CARICOM Strategic Plan for Regional Development, 172, 174, 197
Cariforum States, 137, 139-40, 145
Carmichael, Stokely, 60
Carmichael, Trevor, 125, 132, 158
Carr, Bill, 55
Carrington, Edwin, **126**, 134, 138, 147, **165**, 175, 184
Carter, Margaret, 44
Castro, Fidel, 87, 258-9
Catholic Standard newspaper, 67
Central Intelligence Agency (CIA), 43, 72, 84, 248, 260-1, 269
Chavez, Hugo, 265
Chiang Kai-shek, 266
Chile, 84, 260
China, 7, 102, 104-5, 110, 195, 258-9, 265-8, 270, 272-3
Cholmondeley, Keith, 210
Chung, Geoffrey, 23
Churchill, Winston, 22, 259
CL Financial Group (CLICO), 173, 191
Clark, Ramsey, 200
Clarke, Lawrence, 125, 132, 158
Clinton, Bill, 262
Coalition Government (Guyana), 202, 204-8, 211, 213, 217, 221-2, 234, 236-40, 242
Code of Conduct on TNCs, 90, 106, 108
Cold War, 22, 108, 148, 247, 253, 259-60, 272-3

INDEX

Collins, Bertrand, 55
Collins, Cheril, 236
Colombia, 102, 123
Coltress, Courtney, 17, 22
Columbia University, 81, 88
Commissiong, Bert, 43
Committee of Central Bank Governors (CCBG), 164, 171, 203
Commonwealth Heads of Government Conference, 50, 57
Conference of Heads of Government, 138, 160, 162, 164, 171
Congo, 261
Consultative Group on Smaller Economies, 124
Corbin, Robert, 201
Council for Finance and Planning (COFAP), 132, 135, 160-1, 164, 174
Council for Foreign and Community Relations (COFCOR), 177, 244
Council for Human and Social Development (COHSOD), 177
Council for Trade and Economic Development (COTED), 130-1, 133, 135, 139, 177
CTC Reporter, 86
Cuba, 62, 87, 115, 247-8, 260
Cunningham, Head Prefect, 19, 21
Czechoslovakia, 261

D'Aguiar, Peter, 59
Darke, Father, 66-7
David, Wilfred, 55, 73
Day, Allan, 41
De Castro, Steve, 62
De Cuellar, Perez, 85
De Gaspar, Diego, 85
De Gaule, Charles, 269
De Peana, George, 58
De Souza, Denise, 210
De Souza, Karen, 66
De Vera, Jacinto, 91
Demas, William, 175
Deng Xiaoping, 266
Denmark, 84, 168
Dependency Economics, 61
Do Harris, Brenda (see also Odle spouses), 80-3, 92, 112, 243
Dominica, 172
Dominican Republic, 123, 137, 139-40, 197
Drayton, Harry, 55
Dublin, Edward, 69
Dunning, John, 85

Ealing Technical College, 48
Economic Commission for Latin America and the Caribbean (ECLAC), 116, 124, 180, 250
Economic Partnership Agreement (with EU), 124, 144, 198, 272
Economist Bookshop, 37
Edwards, Adolf, 43-4
Egypt, 102
Eisenhower, Dwight, 22
Ellis, Clarence, 113
Elmina Castle, Ghana, 96
EMPRETEC Training Programme, 90
Enfield College of Technology (see Middlesex University), 49
England (Britain),
  Culture, 33-4
  Employment at Board of Trade, 36
  Examinations for University entry, 36-7
  Return from London, 35, 50, 83
  Teddy boys, 34
Ethiopia, 102
European Commission (EC), 138-41, 143-5, 176
European Union (EU), 117, 123-5, 136-8, 140-2, 145, 148, 166-9, 185, 191, 196, 272
Exxon, 92, 215, 235, 238, 242, 247, 273

Federal Reserve, 229
Fiji, 268
Finland, 84
Finlandisation, 268
Forde, Jacqueline, 181, 183
Fortune, Vernon, 22
France, 32, 248, 260, 264, 268
Francis, Alfred, 62
Fraser, Leon, 22
Free Trade Area of the Americas (FTAA), 115-20, 123-4, 136, 148-9, 161
French, Stanley, 44

Gaddafi, Muammar, 264-5
Gara, John, 92, 98
Garraway, "Tear-away", 25
Gaskin, Dominique, 237
Geopolitics / Geoeconomics, 267-8
German submarines, 16
Germany, 108, 259, 262, 268
Ghana, 41, 90, 98, 102, 260
Gibbs, Lance, 31, 44, 250
Girvan, Norman, 42, 44, 62, 86, 88, 138-9
Gittens, Theo, 176
Global Financial Crisis, 156-7, 174, 203
Global Governance, 149, 253-4, 256-8
Gonsalves, Ralph, 164, **165**

277

Goolsarran, Anand (Report), 206
Gorbachev, Mikhail, 261
Goring, Ian, 17
Goshers, school 'gang', 22-4, 27, 33, 35, 49
Governance Framework for Natural Resource Fund (Guyana), 228, 233
Granger, David, 201
Grant, Cedric, 26
Great Fire, 16
Green, Hamilton, 57, 64
Greene, Eddie, 62, **126**, **165**, 183, **250**
Greenidge, Carl, 201, 237
Grenada, 172, 189, 247
Guaidò, Juan, 270
Guyana (see also British Guiana), 9, 11-2, 20-3, 25-8, 30-6, 38, 42, 50-8, 60-1, 63, 65, 69-70, 72, 74-6, 78-80, 83, 91, 99, 102, 112-7, 127, 137, 141, 153-5, 157, 172-3, 187, 191-2, 195, 197, 200-4, 208-9, 212-22, 224-36, 240-4, 246-9, 260, 262, 265-6, 269, 273
   Advisory mission, 101
   Conditions, 11
   Desire to return, 30, 35, 38, 42, 50, 80, 83, 114-5
   Ethnicity, 10-2, 20-1, 501-2, 54-5, 58-60, 219-21, 236, 239-42, 249-50, 273
   Politics, 43, 63-5, 67-72, 113-4, 200-2, 204-8, 211-2, 216-7, 221-3, 227-8, 234-43, 246-7, 273
   Regional Integration, 116, 118, 122, 124, 147-8, 176-7, 181, 185-6, 191, 198, 203
   Suspension of the Constitution, 273

Haiti, 172-3, 193, 196, 248
Hall, Kenneth, 149, 185, 254
Hamas (Palestine), 271
Hansen, Peter, 84
Harbarran, Cindy, 208
Harmon, Joseph, 207, 209, 239
Hemispheric Cooperation Programme of Technical Assistance, 124
Holder, Noel, 238
Holder, Sheila, 200, 202
Homer, Peter, 13
Howard University, 83
Hoyte, Desmond, 201, 240
Huddleston, Trevor, 33
Hughes, Nigel, 237
Hungary, 261
Hussein, Saddam, 264-5
Hutson, Margaret, (see also Odle spouses), 28, **30**, 31, 37-8, 44, 47, 53, 71, 79, 81, 116, 243

Imperialism, 268-72
India, 75, 93, 220, 249, 266, 268
Indian Revolutionary People's Association (IRPA), 68
Indonesia, 102, 260
Institute of Development Studies (at UG), 65, 74, 147
Institute of Social and Economic Research (at UWI), 65, 73
Inter-American Development Bank (IDB), 113, 128, 141, 176
International Criminal Court (ICC), 271
International Development Research Centre (IDRC), 75, 81
International Financial Institutions (IFIs), 87, 173, 229, 233, 270, 272
International Institute for Sustainable Development (IISD), 162
International Labour Organisation (ILO), 109
International Monetary Fund (IMF), 56, 72-3, 156, 159, 229, 238, 252, 255, 261
International Standards on Accounting and Reporting (ISAR), 109
Intra-CARICOM Negotiating Dynamics, 160
Investment Promotion Agencies (IPAs), 98-9, 106-7, 162, 171
Iraq, 264-5, 270
Irvine, Denis, 65
Isaacs, Michael, 22, 33
Ivory Coast, 94, 102

Jackson, Patsy, 26
Jagan, Cheddi, 21-2, 43, 52, 54, 59, 71, 91, 113, 200, 220, 240, 266
Jagan, Janet, 22, 200
Jagan, Sirpaul, 22
Jagdeo, Bharrat, 200-1, 206, 217, 240, 273
Jagger, Mick, 41
Jamaica, 42-3, 59, 61-2, 72-3, 88, 102, 112, 114, 125, 127, 129, 133, 153-7, 164, 172-3, 175, 194, 247, 254, 266
James, CLR, 44, 188
James, Horace, 207, 223
James, Rudy, 55, 228
Jefferson, Owen, 62
Jeffrey, Henry, 75
Johnson, Barney, 10
Johnson, Oscar, 64
Joint Cariforum-EU Council, 137
Jones, Edwin, 62
Jordan, Winston, 204, 206-7, 209-10, 218, 221, 223
Joseph, Cedric, 77

INDEX

Kawamura, 85
Kennedy, John, 39, 45
Kenya, 22, 94, 102, **102**
Kenyatta, Jomo, 22
King Jr, Martin Luther, 43
King, Colin, 22
King, Eric, 13
King, Sydney, 52
Kirton, Claremonte, 114
Kissinger, Henry, 84, 260, 266
Koama, Ohene, 69
Korean War, 27
Kwayana, Eusi (see Sydney King), 52, 68, 70

Land Use Policy Framework, 218
LaRocque, Irwin, 201
Lee, Alan, 11
Lee, Bud, 11
Less Developed Countries (LDCs), 164, 172
Lewis, Arthur, 39, 249
Lewis, John, 236
Lewis, Laurie, 72
Lewis, Vaughn, 62
LIAT Airline Authority, 172
LIAT, 194
Libya, 264-5
Lindsay, Louis, 62
Lipsey, R.G, 39
Liverpool, Hartley, 12
Lloyd, Clive, 44, 250, **250**
London County Council, 37
London School of Economics (LSE), 32, 37-9, 41-50, 73-4, 222, 246, 251
London, Colvin, 207-8, 210-1, 221, 223
Look-Lai, Walton, 44
Lord, David, 175, 183
Lord's Cricket Ground, 44, 48
Louis, Joe, 25
Lozano, Ricardo, 247
Lucas, Rawle, 210, 218
Lugo, Freddy, 247
Lumumba, Patrice, 261
Luncheon, Roger, 113
Lutchman, Harold, 55, 228

Mackenzie (aka Linden), 28, 57, 216
Mackenzie, Herman, 42
Maduro, Nicholas, 265, 270
Makeba, Miriam, 60
Malan, Pedro, 85
Malaysia, 102, 155
Malcolm X, 43
Mali, 264

Malik, Mahnaz, 162
Mandela, Nelson, 102-3, **104**, 105, 261
Manley, Michael, 39, 61, 72-3, **189**
Manley, Norman, 61
Mann, Lawrence (Bonnie), 22, 24, 28, 42, 59
Manning, Patrick, 172, 193
Manservisi, Stephano, 138
Mars, Perry, 55, 64
Marx, Karl, 50
Mauritania, 264
Maxwell, John, 43-4
Mc Andrew, Wordsworth, 26
McCarthyism, 260
McIntyre, Alister, 62, 73, 125, 127-8, 130-1, 133-4
McIntyre, Arnold, 127, 129, 133
McTurk, Dianne, 56
Mexico, 116, 123, 258
Middlesex County Council, 38, 42
Middlesex University (formerly Enfield College of Technology), 49-50, 52
Millette, James, 62
Millington, Tom, 36
Miro, Alfredo, 25
Misir, Prem, 75
Moise, Jean, 248
Monetary Studies Programme, 73, 88, **89**, 125
Montserrat, 172
Moore, Bobby, 63
Moore, Clairmonte, 22, 26, 28
More Developed Countries (MDCs), 164
Morrison, Father, 67
Mottley, Mia, 39, 162
Movement Against Oppression (MAO), 60, 68
Movement of Skilled Nationals, 192
Mozambique, 260
Mugabe, Robert, 77
Multilateral Agreement on Investment (MAI), 109
Multilateralism *vs* Unilateralism, 271
Munroe Doctrine, 270
Munroe, George, 22
Munroe, Trevor, 62
Murray (teacher), 15

Nadir-Sharma, Marcia, 207
Nagamootoo, Moses, 237, 240-1
Namibia (South-West Africa), 102, 260
National Council of Economic Advisors (proposed), 238
National Industrial and Commercial Investments Ltd. (NICIL), Guyana, 206-13, 215-19, 221-4, 238-9

279

Natural Resource Fund (NRF), 229-30, 233-5
New International Economic Order (NIEO), 76, 261
New York University, 81, 88
New Zealand, 268, 271
Nichols, Shelton, 164
nickname (Maurice Odle's), 19
Niger, 265
Nigeria, 39, 94, 265
Nkomo, Joshua, 77
No Confidence Motion (NCM), Guyana, 211-2, 218, 238
Nobbs, Captain, 17
Non-Governmental Organisations (NGOs), 100, 142, 261
North American Free Trade Agreement (NAFTA), 115, 119, 123-4
North Atlantic Treaty Organisation (NATO), 259, 262-3, 265, 268-9

Obama, Barack, 264, 267
Odle, Dr Maurice – Academic
  Achievements
    Lecturer, Middlesex University, 49-50
    Lecturer, Senior Lecturer, Professor, 74, 81, 110
    Professional Fellow, University of the West Indies, 74
    University of Guyana, 52-6, 58, 64, 74
  Author – Books, articles, papers, monographs, reports, 41, 56-7, 73-6, 84-6, 88, 91-2, 96, 107, 116-7, 119, 122, 124-5, 132-3, 136, 147, 150, 152, 160-2, 165, 175, 181, 184, 188-99, 203, 224-5, 229, 253-4, 258
Odle, Dr Maurice – CARICOM Secretariat, 113-5, **115**, 119, 124-7, 152, 158, 160, **165**, 171, 174-8, 181, 203, 243-4, 246
  Conference/Council papers, presentations and speeches, 73, 83, 87-8, **89**, 92-6, 98-101, 107, **111**, 117, 119, 124-5, 147-52, 160-2, 164-71, 173-4, 177-8, 201, 205, 244, 250, 254-9
  Special Economic Advisor, SG and CSME, 113, **126**, 147, **165**, 187, 224, 238
  Investment Code, 146, 160-1, 174, 193
  Financial Services Agreement, 136, 146, 163, 193
  Regional Financial Architecture, 170
  Policy Framework, 146, 151, 218-9
  Policy Advice, 109
  Technical Advisor, RNM, 115, 125, 128, 130, 132, 244

Odle, Dr Maurice – Coalition Government
  Advisor, 224, 227
  Board Director, 83, 106, 223, 228-35
  Chairman (to Boards and Committees), 202, 204-5
  Chairman, NICIL, 206, 208-11, 215, 221-2
  Land Acquisition Policy, 212-23
  Natural Resources Fund (NRF), 229-30, 233-4
  Privatisation and Investment, 86, 88, 105, 110, 206-7, 213, 233, 238
  Special Environmental Tax, 224-7
  Tax Reform, 204-5, 228
Odle, Dr Maurice – Offspring
  Akanni, 79-83, **245**, 246
  Malika, 244, **245**
  Ronnie, 47, 54, 79-82, 116, **245**, 246
Odle, Dr Maurice – Other roles
  Member of selected International Committees:
    Member of UNESCO Expert Group on Higher Education (1984), 87
    Member of UNIDO Expert Group on Alliance for Africa's Industrialisation (1996), 87
    Member of UNDP (TCDC) Expert Group on South-South Cooperation, Investment and Finance (1996), 87
    Member of various National and Regional Boards; Task Forces and Working Groups, 64, 106-7, 125, 127, 131, 164, 171, 202, 208-9, 228
Odle, Dr Maurice – Parents
  Isidora, 9-10, **11**, 13-6, 18, 22-4, 28, 35
  James, 9, **11**, 17-9, 21, 24-5, 28-9, 38
Odle, Dr Maurice – Siblings
  Bridget (Evelyn), 9, **11**, 25, 28, 30, **34**, 35, 38, 53
  Jeanne, 9, **11**, 19-20, 25, 30, 38-9, 44
  Marva, 9, **11**, 13, 15-6, 25, 29-31, **34**, 38, 50, 82, 112
  Norma, 9, **11**, 25, 30-1, **34**, 38-9, 53, 71, 79, 244
  Patrick, 9, **11**, 13, 31, 53
  Pearl, 9, **11**, 25-6, 30, 38
  Stanley, 9, **11**, 15, 31, 35, 53, 60, 67, 79, 244
Odle, Dr Maurice – Spouses
  Brenda, 80-3, 92, 112, 243
  Margaret, 28, **30**, 31, 37-8, 44, 47, 53, 71, 79, 81, 116, 243
  Valerie, 7, 80, 83, 96, 111-4, 116, 183, 201-2, 243-4, **245**, 246

INDEX

Odle, Dr Maurice – United Nations, 47, 77, 79, 83-8, 91-2, 96, 98, 101-2, 110, 113, 200, 243-4, 251, 260-1
   Education – BSc; MSc; PhD, (LSE, London University), 37, 39-41, 48-50, 74
   Code of Conduct on TNCs, 90, 106, 108-9
   Policy Advice on TNCs, 85, 88, 91-2, 96, 98-9, 101-2, 104-5
   Policy Research on TNCs, 76, 84-7
   Senior Official, UNCTC; UNCTAD, 77, 79, 83-4, 86-7, 90, 92, 96, 98-9, 101-3, **111**, 113, 243-4, 251
   Training Officials re TNCs, 90, 92, 96, 98
Ofokansi, Jacqueline, 246
Omawale (Walter Green), 58, 65-6
Organisation for Economic Cooperation and Development (OECD), 109, 272
Organisation of American States (OAS), 117, 176
Organisation of Eastern Caribbean States (OECS), 133, 155, 164, 167, 172, 198
Oval Cricket Ground, 44

Pakistan, 34, 249, 261
Palme, Olof, 269
Pan Caribbean Partnership (PANCAP), 194
Parris, Haslyn, 42, 64
Patterson, David, 237
Patterson, Orlando, 43-4
Patterson, P.J., 39, 42, 125, 197
People's National Congress (PNC), 51, 58-60, 63-5, 67-9, 113, 201-2, 205, 236-7, 240-2
People's Progressive Party (PPP), 21-2, 51-2, 63, 71, 75, 113, 200-2, 205, 211-2, 217, 220-1, 223, 234, 236-43, 273
Persaud, Charrandas, 238
Persaud, Rabindranauth, 22
Persico, Joel, 244, **245**
Persico, Malika, 244, **245**
Persistently Uneven Playing Surface (PUPS), 149, 160
Peston, Maurice, 74
Peters, Amos, 183
Peters, Patsy, 11
Petro-Caribe, 195
Petroleum Fund, 172, 193, 228, 234-5, 247
Philippines, **97**, **98**, 102, 106-7
Piggott, John, 236
Pilgrim, Bogus, 21
Poland, 106, 261
Politically Exposed Persons (PEPs), 210, 212, 218
Pollard, Duke, 127, 183, 228

Pollard, Frank, 26
Pollydore, Joseph, 56
Poshyananda, Kovit, 91
Power Sharing, 51, 201, 237, 240
Powers, Gary, 259
Prebisch, Raoul, 87
Prest, A.R., 74
Privy Council (UK), 195
Programme of Nationalisation, Guyana, 63

QUAD, 268
Queen's College, 11, 15-23, 25, 30-1, 54, 79, 222

Rahman (race horse owner), 20
Rainford, Joan, 44
Ram, Christopher, 204, 224, 228
Ramjattan, Khemraj, 202, 241
Ramphal, Shridath, 59, 125, 130, 133-4, 249
Ramsahoye, Jimmy, 20
Ramsahoye, Lyttleton, 52, 55
Ramcommy, Josh, 60, 68
Rastafarian community in Jamaica, 62
Ratoon, 60, 68
Reagan, Ronald, 261
Regent Street Polytechnic, 36-7
Regional Investment Promotion Associations, 98
Regional Negotiation Machinery (RNM), 115-6, 124-6, 128-32, 134-5, 144, 147, 149, 162, 178, 185, 244
Regional Stabilisation Fund, 171, 193
Regional Trade in Agriculture and Manufactured Goods, 192
Rhodesia, Southern (see also Zimbabwe), 46-7, 78, 92, 260
   Cold War involvement, 260
   Labour Party (UK), 46-7
   The Guardian and *Daily Worker* newspapers, 47
   Unilateral Declaration of Independence, 46, 92
   Workers Party (UK), 47
Richards, Vivian, 44
Richmond, Angus, 17
Ricupero, Rebens, 99
Robinson, Patricia, 42, 74
Rock, Victor, 21
Rodney, Patricia, 65
Rodney, Walter, 44, 51, 62-6, **67**, 68-72, 83, 200-1, 242, 247
Rodrigues, Malcolm, 55
Rome, Italy, 78

Roopnarine, Rupert, 65-6, 68
Russell, Bertrand (Lord), 45
Russia (and USSR), 259-66, 268-70, 272

Saghren, Klaus, 84-5
Saint Kitts and Nevis, 88, 102, 172
Saint Lucia, 39, 125, 172
Sampson, Geoffrey, 18
Samuelson, Paul, 39
Sandys, Duncan, 43
Sankar, Kayman, 113
Saudi Arabia, 43, 264
Sauvant, Karl, 86
Sayers, Reginald, 41
School of Oriental and African Studies, 63
Scott, Hazel, 79
Seaga, Edward, 61, 73
Sharma, Jaipaul, 208
Shearer, Hugh, 61
Simmons, David, 43-4
Simon, Joerg, 111
Singapore, 42
Singh, Ashni, 217
Singh, Chandra, 42
Singh, Paul, 55
Singh, Ricky, 59
Singh, Thomas, 204
Slusher, Alan, 184
Small, Richard, 44
Smith, Gregory, 70-1
Smith, Ian, 46, 78, 92
Sobers, Garfield, 44
Socialist Vanguard Party (SVP), 68
South Africa, 28, 33, 37, 60, 98-9, 102, 104-5, **111**, 174, 260
South and Central America (and Latin America), 93, 107, 123, 125, 148, 265-6
Sovereign Wealth Fund (see Natural Resource Fund), 229
Spain, 32, 125
Special and Differential Treatment, 120, 161, 254, 272
Special Operations Crime Unit (SOCU), 223
Sri Lanka, 243, 249
St Pierre, Maurice, 22, 35-7, **38**, 47, 51, 222
St Vincent and the Grenadines, 43, 164, 172
State Assets Recovery Agency (SARA), 216
Statia, Godfrey, 204
Stoby, Kenneth, 55
Stoll, Wilfred, 25
Stone, Carl, 62
Strategic Plan for Regional Development, 172, 174, 197

Sullivan, Jake, 270
Suriname, 12, 203, 225, 249
 invasion of Guyana by, 12
Surrong, Junior, 22
Switzerland, 83, 111, 243
Syria, 264

Taiwan (Province of China), 195, 266-8
Tanzania, 63
Tax Reform Committee (TRC), Guyana, 204-5, 228
Thailand, 102
Thatcher, Margaret, 261
Thomas, Clive, 22, 24, 35-6, **38**, 55, 59, 62-3, 68-9, 190, 198, 216, 221, 239
Tiewul, Sylvanus, 76-7, 79
Too Chung, Cyril, 25
Transnational Corporations (TNCs), 76, 79, 84-8, 90, 93-5, 98-9, 102, 105-8, 110-1, 124
Treaty of Chaguaramas, Revised, 146, 188-9, **189**, 196, 224, 226
Trembley, Bill, 55
TRIMS, 108, 117, 149, 198
Trinidad and Tobago, 23, 28, **29**, 32, 61, 69, 74, 80, 117, 125, 127, 153-5, 157, 162, 165-6, 172-3, 189, 191-3, 195-7, 203, 224-5, 229, 234-5, 246-7, 249, 266
TRIPS, 108, 149
Trotman, Desmond, 200
Trotman, Raphael, 202
Trotz, Marilyn, 116
Tudor, Cameron, 21
Turkey, 259-60

Ukraine, 263, 268-9
United Force (UF), 59, 205, 241
United Nations Centre on Transnational Corporations (UNCTC), 76-7, 79-80, 83-7, 90-2, 93, 98, 102-11, 113, 251, 253, 267
United Nations Conference on Trade and Development (UNCTAD), 83-4, 87, 92, 96, 98-9, 101, 106-7, 109, **111**, 111, 113, 141, 157, 170, 243-4, 251, 253, 258
United Nations Development Programme (UNDP), 79, 87, 176, 252-3
United Nations Educational, Scientific and Cultural Organisation (UNESCO), 87
United Nations Industrial and Development Organisation (UNIDO), 87, 101, 107
United Nations, 26, 47, 76-7, 79, 83-4, 90, 93-5, 101, 107, 109-10, 113-4, 152, 176, 195, 200, 251, 253, 255, 258, 260-1, 266, 271

INDEX

United States of America (USA), 7, 16, 21-2, 25, 27, 36, 39-40, 43, 45, 60, 65, 82-4, 113, 115-8, 123-4, 157, 159, 166, 173, 176, 191, 193, 215, 240, 242-3, 247-9, 259-73
University of Dar-es-Salaam, 63
University of Guyana (UG), 26, 52, 54, 58-9, 62-5, 73-5, 88, 114, 147, 204, 222, 227, 248, **250**
University of Pennsylvania, 83
University of the West Indies (UWI), 21, 54, 59, 61-2, 64-5, 73-5, 88, 112, 114, 125, 127-8, 133, 152, **173**, 187, 194, 203, 249, 254
Uzbekistan, 78, 102

Venezuela, 25, 123, 195, 235, 242, 247, 265-6, 270
Verwoerd, Hendrik, 33
Vietnam, 28, 45, 260, 268
Von Eden, Horace, 18

Walcott, Clyde, 23
Walrond, Grantley, 210
Warsaw Pact, 259, 262
Washington Consensus, 86, 98, 109, 257
Washington, Rabbi, 66
Wayne, Evelyn, 175
Weaponisation of the dollar, 270
Weekes, George, 69
Wessendorp, Paul, 98
West Indian Student Centre, 44
West Indian Student Society, 42, 51
West Indies Federation, 54
White Supremacy, 272
Wickham, Berkley, 210, 213
Wilde, Daniel, 229
Williams, Basil, 237
Williams, Donald, **34**, 38
Williams, Eric, 61, 96, **189**, 197, 249
Williams, George, 57, 248
Williams, Jacqueline, 248
Wilson, Harold, 46
Working People's Alliance (WPA), 65-6, 68-72, 200-2, 222, 237, 241
World Association of Investment Promotion Agencies (WAIPA) 98-9, 101, 104-7
World Bank, 42, 101, 107, 110, 145, 150, 229, 252-3, 255
World Economic Forum, 150
World Investment Report (WIR), 86
World Trade Center, 81

Yeltsin, Boris, 262

Zaitzev, Nikolai, 112
Zambia, 69, 77
Zimbabwe (see also Southern Rhodesia), 47, 92-3, 95-6, 102, 260